Niakhar, Senegal

Uzuakoli, Nigeria

Ayos, Cameroon

Kisumu, Kenya

Amani, Tanzania

Traces of the Future

An Archaeology of Medical Science in Africa

Traces
of the
Future

An Archaeology of Medical Science in Africa

Edited by

Paul Wenzel Geissler, Guillaume Lachenal,
John Manton and Noémi Tousignant

With special contributions by

Evgenia Arbugaeva and Mariele Neudecker

Contents

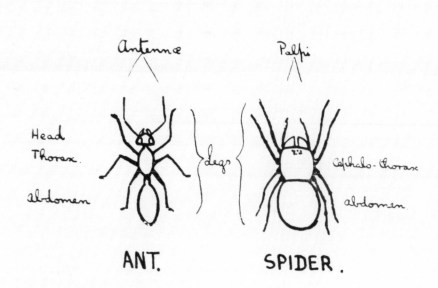

IMAGINARY CASE OF MAMMALIAN MIMICRY.
Drawn by Dr. H. Eltringham.

Illustration by H.Eltringham; in Carpenter, G.D. (1920) A Naturalist on Lake Victoria, London: Fisher Unwin, p.228,
from Amani Hill Station library

Nancy Rose Hunt

Being with pasts: a preface

My wondering and experimenting with "colonial debris" began in a once medicalised field, and long before I began attending to daydreams found and sensed for another Congolese history, this one about violence, nervousness, and reverie. Both concepts – debris and reverie – also became sensibilities and writerly techniques, enabling idiosyncratic ethnographic histories of medicine and health in Africa.[1]

I have hardly been alone. Many historians and anthropologists have moved toward the material and affective, deepening the postcolonial with leftovers, ruins, "the residual and the emergent" in relation to "structures of feeling,"[2] practices, and moods. While the archival has produced a contagious, unquenchable fever across the humanities and social sciences,[3] time, temporalities, and past futures have become a second, dense, crisscrossed stream. Both kinds of practice look back, wittingly or not, to Walter Benjamin's frenzied collecting procedures and antihistoricist words (those against "homogeneous empty time"). If concrete debris and imaginary reverie opened novel ways of practice, they also served to unsettle ethnographic modalities and *history as form*.[4]

This impressive book does something similar but utterly fresh. It demonstrates how remains in scientific fields may generate affective encounters about pasts and futures. Assembled by a talented, committed collective of engaged research scholars, it combines minor – almost parodic – didactic timelines with elastic, fluid shapes of time. Having journeyed in five African countries to "be with the past" in and near scientific landscapes, these anthropologists and historians sought out the orderly, the disorderly, and bafflement. Their results are unfamiliar, disconcerting, pointed, and new. Working

intimately in and across several fieldsites, making the most of collaboration and counterpoint, they document with camera work, memory production, layout, and powerful texts.

As teams, they travelled to several modern scientific spaces and appreciated when stumbling upon the awkward or voids. Their traces embrace interview segments, photographs, ruminations, echoes of malfeasance, commemorative excess, and remains of early 20th century sleeping sickness graves. They found papers dissolved and gaping, eaten through by termites. Medical ruins *anticipated* turned into searing regret in one instance, when erasure and a new-fangled hospital stung as theft. Whether through archival or ethnographic encounters, dreams and past daydreaming surfaced. Sometimes fieldwork process or sound added the "rhapsodic" to medical remains.

All their angles mine the history of science and medicine in Africa and also teach about novel ways of "being with the past,"[5] a philosophic stance that turns up and beautifully so, again and again.

Five sites
A constellation of modern scientific sites, some first built before World War One, are the subject of this collection. These five workspaces facilitated admirable, innovative parasitological, epidemiological, pharmaceutical, and demographic research in colonial and postcolonial times. They transformed lives and generations, forging mediating subaltern health workers and expert researchers, and conveying new skills, publications, and prestige, with fame and uniforms sometimes achieved.[6]

Most laboratories, hospitals, and their experimental and clinical practices prospered during a seemingly utopian epoch in African history, a time of investments in development plus early biocapital that many historians would date from 1940, lasting some fifty years. These modernist workrooms combined science with research, health care, and promises of advancement. They flourished during relatively flush and confident years, a plastic time when many Africans, their nations, as well as expatriate (often colonial) masters, experts, and guides looked toward science to spawn favourable presents and plentiful futures. By sharing their encounters in Nigeria, Cameroon, Tanzania, Senegal, and Kenya, these assembled findings suggest complex layers to scientific practice in and across former German, British, French Africa, as well as Cold War Africa and since. Global health zones in today's Senegal and Kenya receive important attention, too.

Uzuakoli Leprosy Centre, founded by the Methodist Church in 1930s Nigeria, is remembered less for medical work perhaps than for its "acoustic register"[7] of choral singing. Ayos, a hyper-commemorated site set down in France's former empire, first emerged as a German sleeping sickness camp before morphing into a leading biopolitical enterprise. It tackled "the colonial disease" and produced proud African staff from 1926. Amani, a spa-like research site, suggested a "dream capsule."[8] Perched on a Tanzanian mountain, its German remains, British-era dreams, and a Soviet scientific method became some of the excavated layers, alongside iconic figures of decolonisation and Africanisation. Also embraced in this volume's fold is Niakhar, a postcolonial Senegalese space whose research goals have flickered with intensity since 1962 among demographic surveillance, pilot studies, and medical research. Lastly, a global HIV city, Kisumu in western Kenya, tells of successive layers of scientific enterprise involving major international collaborations, enclosures, and exclusions. A place of waiting amid vanity and daydreaming, it discloses Cold War memories of both American and Russian experiments and their past horizons.

Less, vanishing, not

Each fieldsite startles. The authors trace contours and lineaments, exhuming tender objects and vivid perceptions. Ethnographic tales, archival remains, and recollections spill out amid futures once mused.

Persistence in time, the chapters suggest, may be coupled with debris, the "failure of paper," scattering, and ironic decay or veins. Few sites suggest colonial relics, deserted though "still occupied." Words once ubiquitous in scholarly publications are relatively rare: melancholia, nostalgia, even ruins. It is worth wondering why.

The mood suggested is rarely forlorn or despondent. The language at play rarely evokes any of several recent, raging historiographic themes – memory studies, heritage, or silence and forgetting. Notions of survival and recovery have moored many a history of Africa, shored up with naïve, distilled recollections. While Africa's ethnographic historians have jettisoned more positivist versions of oral history, exposing tenuous, mutable pasts via memory work, this book does something original in seeking less remembrances than material pictures, dreams, reveries, and the clatter and colorations of satisfaction.[9]

Subverting the commemorative, these scholars not only amplify archival sensibilities but extend new material methods that hasten toward the affective. Evanescence, more than the decomposed or shrunken, is lurking. Their keen questions linger less around what remained or stayed than about what may have vanished. Still, the impulse to locate "the edge of order, that which persists by chance"[10] suggests a new line for historians and anthropologists of all hues.

Tracing lines

While ruins and vestiges are sometimes smuggled in as alternative objects or terms, ruination and violence remain pale, even absent.[11] The important anchoring word here is not debris but *trace*. They underline it as verb, process, and method: as *tracing*. Their research often proceeded as contemporary archaeology: through modes of excavation, unearthing, *tracing* the arcs and dreams of futures.

They grapple with crisscrossing lines and timescales in their once thriving scientific sites. Material *unlayering* sometimes discloses past narratives, with some interrupting contemporary stories. Time remains plastic, anti-historicist,[12] met and disclosed first as pasts, presents, and past futures. The assembled findings suggest strata of scientific remainders and past, unvanished dreams that once motivated idle daydreams and futures.

The affective

Tonalities, resonances, and the affective are ever the intention. They seek not only to trace but also to ignite the affective. Circumventing emotion-reason and feeling-thought polarities, they steer clear of any narrow emotional "turn" in historical practice. They excavate temporal registers, sensations, perceived times, and often as *aftertime*. Their sensing techniques go beyond the forensics of microhistorical sensibilities, of historians eager for clues. At a time when new passions for African futures prepare to rip through the academy,[13] we should avoid branding terms – like the reductive "affective history" – for this inventive, groundbreaking work. They succeed not through convention but through ambling, ingenuity, and surprise.

They clarify the affective as *not* emotions and feelings, *as* sensations rather, ones that may erupt from temporal junctions. In this, they build striking philosophical and procedural lines for others to follow. They show that at such intersections – a past meeting a future, say – the affective may surface and also swell or erupt, as a rush or "surges."

Innovation lies in letting process sometimes turn performative and transgressive, with a site remade through special meetings with time, ones that pit "anachronicity" against "desires in time." Such fictional, theatrical techniques for opening and reanimating a past time enable traces to emerge – material, involuntary, or some inadvertent. Such methodological play highlights the volume's rejection of the historicist: the empirical, positivist, and sequential. When former lives or doubles come to life, so may past wondering about or hankering after futures. Enabling daydreaming by rousing a partial *once upon the time* may also disclose scientific tools as still lively props.

Upheaval

What ultimately should we make of this upheaval that moves away from memory gathering toward tracing pasts and futures?

One achievement lies in the ways this book disturbs prevailing images about today's "global health," providing strong pasts with these modernist antecedents. The range of sites exposes labour, attachments, and fancy. Systematic comparison is not the ambition; though these counterpoints show why comparative colonial histories of scientific infrastructures, careers, and practices across Africa's empires and blocs deserve further investigation. Conducting their explorations during millennial years, these teams sometimes found pasts withered though rarely bleak. The lingering ebullient tones are remarkable. These architectural forms and land-scapes had once been busy places for making knowledge, engineering progress, and witnessing daily improvements. With living standards rising as part of development goals, dreaming seemed lively, buoyant, even if semiotically contrived. Some aspirations surely lapsed when privatization, structural adjustment, and flagging postcolonial states hollowed out capabilities and futures from the late 1980s on. Yet this book suggests circum-spection before assuming a singular, 1989-rupture point, a neoliberal trigger that plunged all Africa and its sites of scientific experimentality into austerity, precarity, and bare life. In Senegal and Kenya, for example, Niakhar and Kisumu persisted, even thrived. Africa's histories of science, readers will learn, were never linear or uniform.

In turning to recent approaches in contemporary archaeology, this book will make an important mark too. It also joins the best, enduring instincts of Africa's ethnographic histories, an intimate genre long unique that crosses – "blurs" – disciplinary sensibilities with hermeneutics and wondering.[14] This intensely *sutured assemblage* of a book is another feat. I first grappled with *history as form* when stumbling upon anachrony as a concept and technique.[15] Such a device felicitously meddles with narrative sequencing to complicate time, (as Gérard Genette showed in his canonical reading of knotted fiction – Proust's! – with skewed, involuntary, and erupting temporalities). My point is this: anachrony disorders and complicates senses of time. Refractory *and* pleasurable, its mayhem reminds how strongly history, as a discipline and craft, remains a realist genre wedded to chronicle and serialization. Anachrony led me toward a more accessible concept with surgical, filmic, and psychiatric senses: authorship and joining as suturing. Canny "spectator positioning' may mean stitching in ragged, unsettling bits to jar readers.

This book-like package *sutures*.[16] It seeks to elicit recognition and wonder. These tracings entailed journeys, digging, insightful reflection, but also a mischievous approach to curatorial matters: of *layout*. The book's arresting design approaches an interactive exhibit for wide publics – less in a didactic natural history museum than in a contemporary art space. By curating as they do, they steer readerly senses. Collage and bricolage heighten senses and an appreciation of their ambulatory methods. Some collaborated with artists, enhancing seeing in fields. Later team-work led to patchwork-like formats with stitching in of jagged bits – images, timelines, diary entries, analysis, epiphanies. A spectrum in potential audiences is suggested by the wide mix of the accessible and knotty. May its readers or viewers embrace scholars and experts, those still living in and near these African sites, and the many students of global health in the South and North.

Ajar

Although subtly, imperceptibly, this handsome, marvellously quirky tome is a powerful engage-ment with STS scholarship. It will be generative in decisive, elastic ways, and well beyond this academic domain. One finds lightness and mischief but also urgency about Africa. This extraordinarily diverse continent with rich and undue pasts is often disparaged still, conjured as singular, as sheer negativity in popular and scientific imaginations alike. This same continent deserves new imaginative histories regarding its relatively affluent past with scientific, develop-ment fantasies as well as their implications for contemporary medical and experimental practice.

Here, we find a sense of being afloat amid musings traced, alongside a resoluteness: that Africa's scientific, medical sites merit excavation and peripatetic soundings.[17] So it is worth admiring the many ways this volume's creators seek not coherence or recuperation, but perplexity. Beside their handy, almost sardonic timelines, their layouts and ruminations call for plastic, liquid lines: time kept ajar.

1   Nancy Rose Hunt, *A Colonial Lexicon: Of Birth Ritual, Medicalization, and Mobility in the Congo* (Durham: Duke University Press, 1999); and Nancy Rose Hunt, *A Nervous State: Violence, Remedies, and Reverie in Colonial Congo* (Durham: Duke University Press, 2016). I worked out writerly dimensions in Nancy Rose Hunt, "Between Fiction and History: Modes of Writing Abortion in Africa," *Cahiers d'Etudes Africaines* 47, no. 186 (2007): 277-312; Nancy Rose Hunt, *Suturing New Medical Histories of Africa,* Carl Schlettwein Lecture, no. 7 (Berlin: Lit Verlag, 2013).

2   This language began with Raymond Williams; see his *Marxism and Literature* (Oxford: Oxford University Press, 1978).

3   A fever still gaining momentum in interesting ways, as they show, one merging with new histories of aesthetics and empire in Parisian circles; see *ARTchives,* special dossier of *Gradhiva,* forthcoming. For a marvellous demonstration of a wandering archival, material imagination, seeking ordinary "dreams of history" in objects, practices, places, and traces, see Philippe Artières, *Rêves d'histoire. Pour une histoire de l'ordinaire* (Paris: Les Prairies Ordinaires, 2006, 2014).

4   Simmel's essays on time, form, and history are a precious, strange, and still neglected way to enter this vast problematic; see Georg Simmel, *La forme de l'histoire et autres essais* (Paris: Gallimard, 2004).

5   On "being with the past" and also "rhapsodic," see Introduction and Uzuakoli, this volume.

6   On "middle figure" semiotics, and subject aspirations, see Hunt, *A Colonial Lexicon.*

7   See Nancy R. Hunt, "An Acoustic Register: Rape and Repetition in Congo," in *Imperial Debris: On Ruins and Ruination,* ed. Ann Laura Stoler (Durham: Duke University Press, 2013): 39-66.

8   On "dream capsule," see Amani, this volume. On trypanosomiasis as "the" colonial disease, see Maryinez Lyons, *The Colonial Disease: A Social History of Sleeping Sickness in Northern Zaire, 1900-1940* (Cambridge: Cambridge University Press, 1992).

9   The emphasis on dreaming and wonder is in keeping with Bachelard's material, poetic imagination; see Gaston Bachelard, *La Poétique de la rêverie* (Paris: Presses Universitaires de France, 1960), which enables locating daydreamed futures (as in Hunt, *A Nervous State*). Coloration is one of Simmel's words.

10   See Archives, this volume.

11   On ruination, "imperial debris," or often ecological, rotting durations, see Ann Laura Stoler, "Introduction. 'The Rot Remains:' From Ruins to Ruination," in *Imperial Debris,* 1-35.

12   While historicist routines often sequence events, breaks, and ruptures within a continuous flow or chronicle of time, Deleuze showed the value of thinking otherwise – with and through lines; see, for example, his *Deux régimes de fous : textes et entretiens 1975-1995* (Paris: Editions de Minuit, 2003), where he writes variously about multiple lines, including as "veritable becomings" (in the English translation, 310).

13   See Brian Goldstone and Juan Obarrio, eds. *African Futures: Essays on Crisis, Emergence, and Possibility* (Chicago: University of Chicago Press, 2016, in press). On futures, horizons of possibility, and temporalities, see too Guillaume Lachenal and Aïssatou Mbodj-Pouye, eds. "Politiques de la nostalgie," special issue, *Politique Africaine,* no. 135 (2014): 5-21; and Hunt, *A Nervous State.*

14   For hermeneutics, see Thomas Conrad McCaskie, *Asante Identities: History and Modernity in an African Village 1850-1950* (Edinburgh: Edinburgh University Press, 2000). For a poetic ethnographic history, Landeg White, *Magomero: Portrait of an African Village* (Cambridge: Cambridge University Press, 1987). On genres, refiguration, and blurring, see the classic Clifford Geertz essay: "Blurred Genres: The Refiguration of Social Thought," *The American Scholar* 49, no.2 (1980): 165-79.

15   Hunt, "Between Fiction and History."

16   Hunt, *Suturing New Medical Histories of Africa. Suturing* travels and transfigures; for a fascinating mutation, see Filip De Boeck and Sammy Baloji, *Suturing the City: Living Together in Congo's Urban Worlds* (London: Autograph, 2016).

17   The accent placed on dreams and wonder is in keeping with Bachelard's material, poetic imagination; see Bachelard, *La Poétique de la rêverie*; and Hunt, *A Nervous State.*

Pour penser la trace, il faut à la fois la penser comme effet présent et comme signe de sa cause absente. Or dans la trace, il n'y a pas d'altérité, pas d'absence. Tout en elle est positivité et présence.

Paul Ricœur, La nature et la règle, 1998

La trace authentique, par contre, dérange l'ordre du monde. Elle vient "en surimpression."

Emmanuel Levinas, Humanisme de l'autre homme, 1972

Seules les traces font rêver.

Rene Char, La parole en archipel, 1962

Zòg ekële eligi metin.
L'éléphant s'en va laissant l'empreinte de ses pattes.

Beti Proverb, Cameroon

The Utopian idea… keeps alive the possibility of a world qualitatively distinct from this one and takes the form of a stubborn negation of all that is.

Fredric Jameson, Archaeologies of the Future, 2005

P. Wenzel Geissler and Guillaume Lachenal

Brief instructions for archaeologists of African futures

"This time of African existence is neither a linear time nor a simple sequence in which each moment effaces, annuls, and replaces those that preceded it, to the point where a single age exists within society. This time is not a series but an interlocking of presents, pasts and futures, each age bearing, altering, and maintaining the previous ones"

Achille Mbembe[1]

Archaeologists are, irrespective of the depth of the strata they excavate, archaeologists of the present.[2] They do not "discover the past," wrote Lewis Binford in 1983. "*The archaeological record is here with us in the present*. It is out there, under the ground, quite likely to be hit by someone building a new road; it is very much part of our contemporary world and the observations we make about it are in the here and now, contemporary with ourselves. They are not direct observations that remain from the past."[3] Archaeologists are concerned with "the entanglement of the material remains, which constitute the heterogeneous mass of our present."[4] They study things (living or not), arranged in landscapes, assembled in vestiges, or scattered as mere debris and traces, in the multiple senses of the term – objects that remain, marks of passage, residual amounts, vanishing inscriptions.

Conversely, while archaeological artefacts are not just from the past, the present faced by the anthropologist is also always the presence of multiple pasts. What exists is a remainder, carrying traces of past actions, thoughts, or relations. Hence, ethnographic fieldwork is always a labour of synchronisation,[5] of making and sharing, disentangling and interweaving discreet and sometimes contradicting temporalities, rather than a synchronic undertaking premised upon

"coevalness" in a shared present,[6] or a nostalgic quest for authentic others. Synchronisation allows social actors to move – momentarily or through sustained periods – as if in the same time. Modernisation theory offered a powerful engine of synchronisation. It operated through colonial fantasies of separate development, with their consensual "denial of coevalness," as well as in progressive illusions of a shared commitment to modernity – as in the Rhodes Livingstone Institute's anthropologists' stated aim to "study the life of modern man, white and black."[7] In the aftertime of this imperial *pax temporalis*, it is incumbent to anthropology to collect the pieces. Anthropology becomes a science of traces (more and more explicitly reflected upon as part of the contemporary "material turn" of the discipline).[8]

Traces are what remain of past action. They may be objects, leftovers, marks left by something that passed, architectural ruins, and defunct apparatus. Or they can be less distinct imprints of past process that may never have had a delimited form and function: records of past labours, archives of expired movements. Traces can be touched, outlined or followed, ignored or rejected, eliciting affect, provoking responses. Like Proust's Venetian paving stones or madeleines, they may conjure up illusions of what was, engender an essence of what might have been, condensing previously unknown sweetness or bitterness, open pathways not just to the past, but to the futures it once promised. Traces are always traces of others; the recognition of traces both relates and marks difference. Traces may be overlooked or discovered, intimately relished and forgotten, turned into tokens of sociality, or made banners of conflict. Traces are surprising, unexpected, rarely intentional, and sometimes scandalous in the original sense of the word: stumbling stones. Traces always point to the absence of their cause, but are at the same time positively present. They may, of course, be constructed as signs, and read as indices, by hunters, detectives, archaeologists, or historians – who turn traces into documents as they ask their questions.[9] But they are a specific, destabilizing set of signs: as Emmanuel Levinas wrote about the human face as trace of the other, they "signify beyond any intention of giving a sign and beyond every project for which it may have been the intended object."[10] As Paul Ricoeur, quoting Levinas' meditation on traces, expressed it: "the trace is distinguished from all the signs that get organized into systems, because it disarranges some 'order.' The trace is 'this disarrangement expressing itself' (p.63). The trace left by a wild animal disarranges the vegetation of the forest: 'the relationship between signified and signification, in the trace, is not one of correlation but one of unrightness' (p.59)."[11] Traces are puzzling. Traces (and perhaps, as the poet Char had it, traces alone) engender wonder. Their significance has to be established and re-established in material engagements. They remain as inchoate matter, irregular detritus, until momentarily recognised and re-established as form, by someone who happens upon them – sometimes wilfully researching the historical past, sometimes carefully tracking signs of passage, more often unintentionally, while doing something else.

In this book, we are interested in these gestures: discerning traces, excavating-as-remembrance. We are intrigued by the ways in which traces disarrange and reshuffle our disciplinary conceptions of anthropological and historical research (in Africa) through "tethering the past to the present;"[12] and by breaking open the linear and serial temporality of history – piercing holes through the seeming solidity and positivity of the present. In this book, we attend to remnants that not only manifest what once was and trace the contours of debt and loss, but that also actualize possibilities and expectations carried from the past. Traces are always remains of something alive: reminding us that "life is also the heritage of living potentialities."[13] They are traces of the future.

Our curiosity is directed at the journeys and explorations needed to reach towards the past, at the forms of politeness and civility that attending to traces requires, at the relationships and at the projections that it inspires, at the quickening discomfort that stirring up remains, disturbing their guardians, provokes. Beyond rethinking our disciplines' engagements with the past, we wish to shed light on a vital dimension of lives in Africa today: being with the futures of the past is entangled with the search for movement towards the near future. Archaeology is part of such future making.[14]

Lust for traces in Africa

A "crisis of time"[15] – mounting doubts about a progressive, modernist temporality – marks our age, following political-economic destructions, the vitiation of the welfare state, and disillusionment of failed political projects. After a period of erasure and amnesia, this crisis stimulates a near-global lust for traces. Just when archaeology discovers the remnants of modernity, it is losing its monopoly over remains and ruins. Social scientists, political activists, contemporary artists, photographers, and countercultural youth are mining and recycling the remains of English industrial landscapes, East German consumer goods, crumbling Soviet monuments, and 1980s UK labour and environmental struggle sites into new configurations. The results range from retro-fashion, steam punk, synthetic nostalgia, and reactionary politics, to new forms of radical critique and playful assemblages that trade old certainties for future potentials.[16]

The contemporary hunger for traces might seem an occidental fantasy, a befitting pastime for the aftertime of modern, imperialist privilege. Madeleines in Africa call to mind Marie Antoinette. Yet few other regions of the world have experienced the ravages of twentieth century temporality more acutely than Africa, a continent that went from being described as a living fossil of mankind or a continent without history to being pressed into forced-march modernization, eventually to find itself waiting in an inescapable present. Indeed, the intrigue of the ruin and the pleasure of the trace as sensuous sign, as suture between past and future, are not unfamiliar to the African 21st century either. Zarina Bhimji's stagings of postcolonial East African Asian archives, Sammy Baloji's careful yet pitiless historical inquiry, Mestre Paulo Kapela's ironic meditations on post-socialism, Jacob Dlamini's South African "Native Nostalgia," the "Nigerian Nostalgia Project," Chimamanda Adichie's melancholic returns to Lagos and to post-independence Nigerian academe, Guy Tillim's avenues of broken dreams,[17] along with the burgeoning genre of African science fiction that reappropriate the aesthetics of the modernist past for appealingly counterintuitive alternative futures – all these bear witness to the creative and critical nostalgia that is also part of a contemporary African search for different futures.[18]

The pleasure of tracing is a historically specific desire, characteristic of an "aftertime"[19] – a period of heightened awareness of pastness, over-determined by what no longer is. It responds to the global "post-socialist" realisation that what "was forever is no more,"[20] that European industrialisation and welfarism have faded,[21] or that the African post-colonial project of sovereignty, development, and citizenship has become the stuff of commemorations.[22] Sensitivity for the trace is particularly acute, and potentially more painful, where there is nothing new, where remains saturate a landscape unbroken by

reclaiming, rebuilding, renovation, or redevelopment – destruction without distraction, as in abandoned northern English factories, disused Cold War military testing grounds, depopulated socialist frontier cities.[23]

Traces thus rise to prominence across Africa, where the wastelands of the aftertime are interspersed only by few urban spaces of exception such as gated housing and sheltered malls, Dubai-style architectural antitheses of the trace,[24] built to obscure their conditions of production, and repelling the traces of future contradictions – pretending instead to inscribe timeless architectures onto *terra nullius*.[25] Except for the momentary tracelessness of these enclaves of pure present – soon (to be) defaced by cracking concrete and broken escalators – Africa's landscapes are saturated by traces,[26] ranging from majestic infrastructural ruins[27] to the perpetually reused remnants of industrial consumer goods.[28] Remains that are continuously re-appropriated and recycled, but neither neatly erased, nor built over and buried.

The stranded spaceships of modern science

Among such landscapes, we have chosen a set of older enclosures. These are just as out-of-the-ordinary as today's African neoliberal "enclaves:" gated communities, shopping malls, export production zones, or mining concessions.[29] Yet, they differ on account of their old-fashioned progressive, expansive, colonising spatial logic: sites of twentieth century medical and biological science. These are not millennial mirages in the aftertime of modernity, but solidly modern places, marked not by amnesia and infertile presentism but saturated with temporality, whose vestiges are as futuristic as they are proud of their past. Our choice is unlikely and obvious. *Unlikely*: when it comes to the production of scientific knowledge, Africa is often seen as failure and absence, as a "hole in the map,"[30] to quote

Jean-Paul Sartre, whose relationship to modernity's attributes (science, democracy, or industry) was one of lack or even parody. *Obvious*: according to another familiar trope, Africa was once a "laboratory" for modern science.[31] Even if such description reiterates a colonial genre and takes planners for demiurges,[32] the quintessentially modern Africa built around the middle of the twentieth century – notably after political "independence" – was to be founded on enlightenment, development, and eventually nationhood. It looked to science for its future.

The continent is littered with ageing (not all ruined) architecture and landscapes of knowledge making: scientific institutions, field stations, hospitals, universities, study villages, surveillance areas – sites of investigation and experimentation, of hope and failure, and of benevolence and cruelty. These places capture the power and ambivalent beauty of science, its utopian and dystopian potentials. They evoke contradictory political projects: imperial subjugation, colonial welfare, national independence, socialist internationalism, and economic liberation.[33] They remind of (imperial) violence and loss, but also of hopes for different futures, shared and contested across inequalities of race, class, and gender,[34] which are instantiated in buildings and tools, archives and collections, and inscribed on the bodies of research workers, medical personnel, and participants.[35] Past practices of science also persist in the aspirations and convictions of the communities living in their vicinity, and are a fundamental part of their experience of place. These sites materialise the past futures of African science. Some are rebuilt, reused, thriving, vacated, or otherwise appropriated. Few are as yet totally transformed or destroyed. They are loci of memory and forgetting, of encounters and confrontations among the changing visions, values, and possibilities of science. Like defunct vehicles of time-travel from another age, they provide shelter, tools, or raw materials, and

evoke distant memories of the future.[36]

Laboratories (as in Helen Tilley's inclusive understanding) are peculiar places when it comes to traces. Tim Edensor suggested, following Benjamin's reflections on modernist urban form, that sites produced by *modern* practices (notably capitalist commodity production) are particularly rich in "spectral, interstitial residue,"[37] set free by material decay – precisely because their fiction of perpetual novelty is premised upon the denial and burial of their pasts, i.e. their conditions of production. They contrast with, e.g., domestic spaces where the present absence of those who departed is given a place, rather than suppressed, in dusty photo albums or vacated rooms, or with ancestral mud-huts of older African ethnography – generative dwellings where decaying remains are permeated by overlapping, generative processes of life, past, and future.[38] Such (commodity) fetishized sites "haunt" occasional visitors as well as returning inhabitants or workers, with the double violence of establishing the appearance of permanence, and subsequently abandoning it.[39]

Laboratories, harbouring scientific production, demographic surveillance, or medical diagnosis, are quintessentially modern, innovative places. Like Edensor's (and Benjamin's)[40] commodity-sites – factories, shopping malls – laboratories seek to defy the deposition of traces, exclude ubiquitous processes of deterioration, and resent contamination by uncontrolled life-forms. They do this, however, for practical Pasteurian, mythological, and aesthetic reasons that might point beyond commodity fetishism. Defined as controlled, static, and clean, laboratories are envisaged not only as "placeless,"[41] but also as traceless spaces, untouched by time. The things left in/of scientific workplaces, from bench-tops and glassware to patient files and demographic survey forms, were once instruments of purification – the quintessentially modern quest to chase out hybridity, separate subjectivity from the material world, society from nature – by isolating and aggregating, cleaning out the signal from the noise, and standing guard over the enclosures of experimental control. Pushed into hiding, hybrids return, when control falters or ceases, with a vengeance;[42] not unlike the "ghosts" visitors to ruined factories like Edensor feel "haunted" by. With decay, reagents that are now stains, files and forms now riddled with termite bites, broken glassware and moth-eaten lab coats, lab walls and roofs open to rain and rodents, have lost their power to purify. They may rupture the polished surfaces of the laboratory's incontestable present-for-the-future, corrode or dissolve once-ordered boundaries, and amplify the leakiness of experimental control and historical period-ization alike: they are re-vivified as traces.

Yet, if our labours of re-vivification often mimic, even reenact, sometimes parodically, past practices of science, our goal is not to mock their acts of separation and enclosure. True, we do not, as scientists in these places once did, approach material traces (much less the past) as positivists. Nor is our interest in repetition concerned with replication, that is, with testing reproducibility as a condition of validity. Yet we are sympathetic towards, and in some way try to learn from, scientists' efforts to foster the audibility of the material – that is, to create conditions, in laboratories as well as in clinics and field-sites, under which things might "talk back," so that they might answer, but also object, to their interrogation.[43] In other words, we, as they did, at times *like* they did, fumble for ways of letting things be things. We recognise that things cannot speak, obediently or "for themselves" – whether as representatives of nature or as historical sources – and yet that we may listen for them, as vibrant, unpredictable, affecting, and transformative. As remains, scientific spaces and instruments have double lives: as tools for counting trees and births and infections, for discerning patterns in organisms and populations,

for seeing through vectors and viruses, then as unruly traces that keep these pasts audible yet not "spoken for," expose all pasts, even of exper-imental replication, as un-replicable, and all presents as accretive, uncontained, decomposed, and contaminated. They make for a particularly rich terrain for archaeologists of African futures.

A guided tour to the modern we have never been

Studying this particular dimension of Africa's rich heritage may be suspected of a peculiar exoticism, an inverted orientalism that delights in the most alien form of ourselves – an ultimate ("last") abuse of class and race-based privilege. The familiar critiques of "ruin porn" could well be transposed to our project, as it might seem to take part in the recent scramble for African modernist ruins and dreams – siphoned off from Brazzaville to Basel, ending in glossy catalogues and rapacious galleries, like Jean Prouvé's tropical houses.[44] Our impulse runs counter to this scramble. It is not aroused by the titillating appeal of alien futures, nor voyeuristic curiosity about loss. Instead, we search these sites as the remains of a shared past, in the hope of discern-ing patterns of a common future.

"We," "us," "our:" the archaeologists of African science are an interdisciplinary collective that embraces the anthropological tenet of making oneself the key instrument of knowledge gener-ation, and shares a fascination with a world that immediately preceded us, post-independence, pre-millennial. The historical futures materialized in African scientific remains – diverse in their political points of departure, yet united by their progressive direction – will not return in a simple, linear beauty. It is through a collective excavation and reanimation of these sites through shared, if differential, inhabitation that their return – and beauty – can be materialised. Through our motions and entanglements we trace the remains of African science, and expand our collective by including others – ageing scientists, nurses, local youths, fieldworkers, drivers – and by negotiating the tensions inherent to our different statuses and positioning.[45] Yet, the first person plural also makes a broader claim: irrespective of (though not untouched by) geographical origins and geopolitical homes, the past futures of twentieth century science are ours – on account of differentially shared postcolonial entanglements, but also on account of an older universal hope, vested in science, for knowledge and transformation, for the human faculty to engender change.

We chose a set of key African clinical and laboratory sites that shaped twentieth century medical science and international public health, including some iconic sites of African medical research. We could have chosen different places. This volume does not purport to be a guide to Africa's scientific geography, but an index of our collective curiosity. Some sites are century-old, others created a generation ago; most are rural, some urban, they are all colonial and postcolonial. Their science confronted a variety of diseases and drew on diverse technical tools; it produced knowledge for public health or drug development, and exhibited national styles and imperial histories. All materialize diverse and divergent temporalities.

In Kisumu, Prince, Madiega and Geissler – the latter initially working as scientist – became intrigued by early post-independence government disease control and public health. The remains of the latter coexist in this "global health city" with large transnational trial sites, creating stark contrasts but also uneasy encounters between amnesia and commemoration.[46] In Nigeria, at the leprosarium of Uzuakoli, Manton – seeking archival evidence of colonial clinical experimentation – became witness to an on-going, organic transformation and destruction of

archival materials.[47] In Cameroon, at the former colonial sleeping sickness camp of Ayos, Lachenal, Owona Ntsama, and Manton confronted haunting memories of imperial heroes, coercive public health, and mass death.[48] In Niakhar, Senegal, Tousignant, Mbodj-Pouye, Ouvrier, and Desclaux describe how accumulated data and encounters become scientific memory and technologies of anticipation, but also release unruly traces of gratitude, obligation, filiation, resentment, and ambivalence.[49] And, in the research station of Amani – first German, then British, now Tanzanian – Mangesho, Gerrets, Kelly and Geissler encountered pleasures and anxieties, promises and regrets of 1960s "Africanisation,"[50] and attended to the everyday life of a suspended science-site: a station in stasis.[51]

The diversity of our destinations took us to different pasts and kinds of traces. The deep layers of pre-colonial habitation and traces of early colonial occupation featured in the landscape of most sites. Yet our attention gravitated towards the present and its immediate antecedent, from World War Two to the 1980s, the long middle of the 20th century and a short era of African modernity, the time of welfare and development, scientific progress and collaboration, and, crucially, political decolonisation and the "Africanisation" of science.[52] Our interest in this segment of time derives from its relation to ourselves, to today's present and its futures, in Africa and well beyond.

This African present, variously described by scholars with reference to its "neoliberal" economy, its politics of "exception" and "emergency,"[53] and its "global health" paradigm,[54] is often explicitly contrasted to the preceding "high modern" and "developmentalist" era.[55] To qualify fictions of rupture and regime change (without resorting to revisionist arguments of historical/historicist "continuity"), we attune our sensitivities to points of contact between presents and pasts: fleeting brushes with the past, which make up the present, where affective surges, contradictions, and motions arise, and that make us what we are, engendering subjectivities, forging relations, assembling collectives, triggering action. This affective making of the present, upon the materials of the past, is what this book is about.

Modes of excavation

"True, for successful excavations a plan is needed. Yet no less indispensable is the cautious probing of the spade in the dark loam, and it is to cheat oneself of the richest prize to preserve as a record merely the inventory of one's discoveries, and not this dark joy of the place of the finding, as well. Fruitless searching is as much a part of this as succeeding"

Walter Benjamin, 1932 – the translator's addition of "dark joy" gratefully acknowledged.[56]

This does not mean our book is about memory. Or rather, our concern is not with memory as "instrument for the exploration of the past," as the explicit and interested fashioning of the past from the present, which defines commemoration (and to a larger extent historiography).[57] Our sites are not to be understood as "lieux de mémoire" as elaborated by Pierre Nora, strategic places that serve a top-down, nation-state-centred narrative about the past.[58] We begin from, but eventually subvert, the ethnography of commemoration and monuments:[59] firstly, because we literally take part in commemorations, staging them, organizing them, funding them, applauding them, laughing at them, and (as is perhaps the essence of commemorations) being bored by them. Secondly, our interest lies in implicit and unexpected manifestations of the past unearthed through excavation, literally and metaphorically (including commemorative events as forms of excavation, among other, more ordinary and happenstance digs). To follow one of Walter

Benjamin's fragmentary interventions on the theme of archaeology, we take memory as the "medium of that which is experienced,"[60] in which to dig and unearth traces and images.

This is also not about writing history "without written records" – a trope used in both Africanist history and antiquarian archaeology. In all five sites, we were confronted with major lacunae in historical documents. In all five, our approaches combines ethnography, oral interviews, and explorations of material traces and landscapes. But our aim was never to triangulate (incomplete) written sources, (biased) oral accounts, and (enigmatic) material evidence to allow the reconstitution of an accurate, stable, and enriched image of the past. Our approach is not "evidential" ("indiciaire").[61] Nor do we seek to build an "alternative" archive, not even "our own archive."[62] Rather, we look at archives ethnographically (treating them as subjects and forms, not merely as sources),[63] and see them archaeologically, by acknowledging them as artefacts and as our contemporaries. Thus they "do not in themselves inform us about the past at all,"[64] but are only informative if we are attentive to their transformations in time and to processes that brought them to us (or not). In a word, we attend to their "being in time."

Failed, absent, disordered archives take on another dimension: not as obstacles to historical writing, but as complements to it. We try, following Luise White, "to see messy archives for what they are, fragmented records of shambolic events, of false starts and donor-driven policies and impossible development schemes and missed opportunities."[65] More generally, we were not driven by an antiquarian pulse ticking for old remains or relics of imperial science. It is precisely their contemporariness that matters to us – a status from which no object of the past, however well preserved, may escape, as Sarah Farmer told us in her work on Oradour sur Glane.[66]

If our work is not about memory as history, neither is it about the "ethnography of memory," interrogating how shared narratives about the past produce present social life, or about a "historical anthropology" that applies ethnographic sensitivities to historical sources or studies history's impact on sociality.[67] Insofar as our work is about "the past and the present," it is so in a circumscribed and material way, working on time through matter. This became, then, about using "debris as method," to follow Nancy Rose Hunt's exploration of Congolese medical history through old bicycles and cherished birth certificates.[68] It is about irruptions of traces in the present, and the advent of the past (and the futures it contains) that such presence enables. It is about acknowledging (a crucial move) that our knowledge of the past is fundamentally *relational*, and that "the place of the past is not the past itself, but really the present and the present only."[69] This does not mean that the past has not taken place, or that the past *itself* does not matter. Quite the contrary, acknowledging its very existence (without taking it for granted as armchair story-tellers) requires that we trace its material mediations and modes of being: what is at stake, following Bruno Latour, is again to account for the *traceability* of the world: to identify and follow connections across another binary "great divide" (*grand partage*) and reassemble past and present.[70]

Being with the past

Starting from the present and only the present, our research had a plan: to journey together as anthropologists, historians, nurses, fieldworkers, doctors, researchers, wanderers, gardeners and security guards, sometimes with colleagues from neighbouring disciplines such as architecture, geography, STS, and the visual arts. This volume is the record of these collective, repeated encounters. This record does not propose a refined form of reflexivity, as an individual meditation on our

positioning in the field or towards history, nor does it suggest a "good practice" of participatory, collaborative anthropology. We propose a methodology that takes inspiration from some virtues of naturalist observation – though resisting its classificatory urge – to merge and move beyond both historicist reconstruction and ethnographic empiricism, by way of an account of our "being" in the place. For "genuine memory," wrote Benjamin, must "yield an image of the person who remembers."[71]

Such a project draws from the so-called "affective turn" in history and anthropology, and its "post-subjective" rendering, mediated by readings of Deleuze. Affect is understood here not as "emotion" but as intensities emanating from objects and space – or, in Navarro-Yashin's critically eclectic usage, intertwining subjectivity and exterior materiality, subject and object.[72] Contemporary sensitivities, expressed across a wide spectrum of cultural production and social thought, have turned to affect in this sense, for example in the artistic and curatorial work of Patrick Keiller's Robinson Institute, in Teju Cole's postcolonial Sebalderies, or in Lauren Berlant's and Kathleen Stewart's examinations of "cruel optimism" and "ordinary affect" in the late capitalist Euro-American present.[73] Affect, as everyday encounters with the materials through which one moves, engages the world as an accumulation of traces, each giving rise to momentary "intensities," pulsating, disappearing, or lingering, adding up to presence within a larger, albeit diffuse, "shared historical sense."[74] Such encounters with the jumbled, though not coincidental, landscape of remains, is often described in terms of ephemerality and momentariness – surges, intensities, flashes, brushes – "illuminations" in Benjamin's vocabulary.[75] Sensual, contingent contact with traces accumulates but does not cohere. The resulting account is not a representation of a past or present condition, but a diary of encounters.[76]

Material encounters in everyday movements may produce sharp, punctual affective responses. Yet the resulting picture often remains spectral and imprecise, as Proust's reminiscence, or "involuntary memory."[77] It arises from contingent contacts and expands laterally through the associations of a wandering mind. Affect triggered by remains and traces of decay is particularly inarticulate and fragmentary, owing to the lack of discreteness of the material itself and the progressive unbounding and dissolution of matter that, over time, returns into an undifferentiated substrate.[78] If remains, and our affective contacts with them, are contingent, fragmented, and ephemeral, tied together only by everyday life motion (usually determined by different intentions than a search for traces), this makes for a peculiar methodological stance. Tim Edensor speaks of "porousness," opening "surfaces to other surfaces"[79] or "empathetic recouping,"[80] allowing for "epistemic and ontological insecurity."[81] In the practice of the archaeologist of the future, this means unfixing the gaze, allowing ambiguity by relinquishing focus: the researcher's absent-mindedness as epistemic stance. Following Levinas' terminology, this "non-intentionality" may be thought of as "radical passivity," receiving by way of bodily and performative engagement,[82] "being possessed"[83] by the trace. In practice, this does not imply a "vain" *flâneur* – as in disinterested observer – but a researcher in motion, tiptoeing, porous, distributed, pervaded by smells and textures, fingers upon the surface of the real, open to contingency and entanglement. Fieldwork, then, is less pursuit than exposure that allows one to pick up histories that "can begin and end anywhere"[84] – *Wahr-nehmung* (literally "reception of truth") instead of *Begreifen* ("grasping"). In other words, the non-intentionality of the trace's production might require an equivalent "passive" or non-intentional stance of enquiry.

How does one plan his/her own passivity, porousness, and availability? Not by suspending action, nor by cultivating idleness, as the romantic cliché of the islander-ethnographer had it, nor by replacing focused, systematic modes of enquiry, such as conventional archival work, observations, and interviews. Rather, it is by comprehending these *also* as movements in the (material) world, which facilitate affect, even in the absence of effect. Undirected strolling and contemplative staring, attention to the other, recognition of the face[85] may be possible, not only *in spite of* repetitive occupation – survey data collection, serial interviews, repetitive oral histories, archive inventories, even just photocopying files – but also because of it. Here repetition is a condition of possibility of reverie and other affective encounters. There can be, in other words, a pursuit of exposure. Traces come to us even if/ especially when we merely occupy ourselves with redundant research tasks; even if we were to invent "systematic" modes of enquiry without a definite purpose. This has been the case for us in Uzuakoli, Ayos, or Amani: despairing at being a historian of drug development in Nigeria, and finding the organic life of a destroyed medical archive; listening for hours to repetitions of well-rehearsed, commemorative biographies of a French-Cameroonian colonial researcher – meanwhile, observing the small children named after him; or photographing diligently all the facades and interiors of a scientific settlement, documenting colonial architecture – yet confronting inhabitants' postcolonial waiting and anger.

Applying this way of being-in-research to scientific field stations revealed an unexpected parallel with the natural sciences: the absent-minded, receptive, and passive stance of ethnographic porousness was mirrored by the naturalists' attitude to the field, as described in autobiographies and conversations, and witnessed during our shared field work. Working together with natural scientists in the field, we commenced from an assumption of mutual epistemic incompatibility, only to be surprised by our shared passion for the material, for unexpected empirical pleasures. Sometimes the scientists' "passive" stance seemed entirely open-ended, e.g. finding new species or phenomena by *not* looking for anything in particular, but even where (and perhaps especially where) scientific field activities followed rigorous protocol (aiming to confirm preconceived hypotheses), naturalist scientists readily acknowledged the contribution, to their own knowledge and role, of the field coming to them.

Being in and moving around sites was central, then, not in the conventional sense of participant observation, but in this rather playful way. Edensor once observed that ruined spaces "give no rules for movement"[86] and thus allow for "childish movement," play, or aimless wandering. Heeding this incitement, our *déambulations* went beyond directed, task-oriented use of movement – as in oral history walks, participatory mappings or reconstructive reenactment. We rather imagined movements guided by arbitrary, invented rules: walking transects, creating inventories, re-performances, some of them analogous to proper excavations. This paradoxical (at times parodic) use of scientific work routines (repetitive and repeatable by definition) as instruments of wide-angled perception is one of our specific methodological propositions.

Disarranging the "global health" moment: tracing alternatives

What have we brought back from this journey? On a basic level, our peregrinations and experiments shed new light on various dimensions of African pasts and presents, on science, medicine, and society. Engaging with relatively marginal actors (patients, cleaners, neighbours), with humble objects (bottles and bricks, inventory catalogues and abandoned specimens, grass cutters, and office furniture), and peripheral spaces (stores and workshops, servants' houses and experimental

animal colonies, disused psychiatric wards, and leprosy camps), we unearthed obscure histories, destabilizing conventional imaginaries of colonialism and decolonisation. Allowing ourselves to be drawn by the force of material traces and led by their human bearers and guardians, we attended to (and became entangled in) hitherto invisible links among places, people, and objects. We established unexpected genealogies and provocative kinship ties, while documenting how historical lineages continue to shape the present. Four or five things came of all this.

Firstly, we navigated a landscape that had just been remade by a recent industry and industriousness: global health. The "new present" of medical sciences in Africa is one of unprecedented global attention and financial investments, epitomized by "vertical" programs, public-private partnerships, or philanthropic initiatives aiming at solving Africa's health problems, one after another. Now is a time of boom and promises, virus hunters, and TED talkers.[87] At least in some narrowly bounded spaces, the ruins of modernity, which marked African cities in the years following structural adjustment, are relegated to the past. Post-independence dreams of modernisation seem an even more distant memory when they are juxtaposed to the custom-built Level 3 laboratories and open-floor academic office landscapes of transnational collaborative science. In our sites, global health operations manifested themselves as bulldozers clearing rubble for new projects, as empty, brand-new buildings that appeared as ruinous as the derelict infrastructure they replaced. The booms driven by philanthropic foundations and development banks seemed suspect – *booms* always destroy as they build, always extract as they give, always indebt as they distribute. They erase and forget, just as they urge to remember and commemorate.[88] From Amani to Ayos, memories of colonialism provided ready-made theories of value to interpret and contest the arrogant realizations and millennial pronouncements of global health. In this prom-issory present, many African scientists sense that the promise is a mirage, the hyperactivity futile, that the past is a critical resource: a reservoir of alternatives, a library of futures. The nostalgia that we found is then not so much a reaction to abandonment and decay or a diagnosis of abjec-tion. It is rather a sceptical, sometimes amused, sometimes angry, reverie on the grotesque, the obscene, and the absurd of global health's billionaires, who parachute their free gifts, cheap hopes and platitudes across the continent.

Secondly, our visits in Africa's medical landscape led us to qualify post-Foucauldian representations of African biosciences as part of wider projects of discipline and surveillance. Our attention shifted to the force and persistence of civic ideas, the motivating power of and longing for duty, commitment, and service, compounded by lasting attachments to state and nation.[89] "Biopolitics, including national medical government, calls here forth not threat and loathing, but nostalgia and desire"[90] for its subjects as much as for its technical experts – and for their archaeologists. In turn, the collapse of purpose and meaning in the decaying African science sites of the present provides a glimpse onto the necessary "stabilising networks,"[91] within which the purpose, commit-ment, and seriousness of scientific work once were construed.

Thirdly, our stories are not all rosy. Collapsing structures reveal the skeletons of underlying power relations and lay bare past forces, past violations that had been necessary to maintain structures, and circulations, and to keep decay and disintegration at bay.[92] For example, in Amani, the Constablesque beauty of the English lawnscapes research station, was once maintained by two "hedge-men," fourteen "grass-cutters" and no fewer than twenty-three so-called "Lantanas" – named after the thorny shrub whose uprooting was their only task. Archived regulations

prescribing the annual whitewashing of houses, prohibiting domestic gardening or trading, invoicing power, water and subsidised milk, and documenting attendant litigations and punishments for breaking such rules, slack work discipline, or minor misappropriations, witness to the amount of labour and surveillance that facilitated the functioning and beauty of scientific sites in the field.

Read amongst overgrown meadows, crumbling habitation, dried up taps, and dysfunctional power plugs, they evidence the double violence of their imposition and of the subsequent withdrawal of the stability they once underwrote. Tracing violence seeping from past into present and continuously being exerted by contemporary ruins – now places of valueless labour, deprived habitation, and hopeless waiting – led our atten-tion to the violence of mimesis. The destructive force exerted by imposed dreams – of particular visions of societal progress, attendant lifestyles, habitus, subjectivity and longings imported wholesale with the project of colonial medical science – produced what Sartre, a propos Franz Fanon, referred to (in slightly anachronistic terms) as "possession with Western culture," "wreaking havoc on the oppressed themselves."[93] This was a possession by visions of progress that were obstructed and paternalistically ridiculed almost as soon as they had been imposed and bequeathed upon the African heirs of imperial science. Other forms of violence and subjection, of anger, paternalism, mockery, death, and disappointment were also turned up in our excavations of Ayos, Kisumu, Uzuakoli, and Niakhar. For example, uncomfortable questions, about the end of independence in Ayos, or the end of research in Niakhar, about the return of projects or of scientists, accusingly pointed to the flimsiness of promises made, to the absurdity of claims of compliance, conviviality, and duty, and to the endurance of debts incurred, in blood, labour, and hospitality.

Fourthly, the radical polytemporality of the present became evident as we peeled apart, sometimes literally, layers of past that provided material for the present: past futures and failures, futile departures and open ends, far-fetched hopes and long waits, haunting nightmares and pipe dreams of futures, nostalgias for pasts and futures, are only some of the times and tempos which, upon closer examination, dissolved into a seemingly stable present.[94] Against the backdrop of such a multiplicity of times, monolithic practices of commemoration – monuments or anniversaries – became recognisable as exotic events, idiosyncratic attempts at closure, outcomes of struggles between interested parties, and the confluence between forces of forgetting and remembering. And private habits of remembrance, rehearsed memories reeled off in particular situations for visitors (like us), became legible as situated social practices, shaped as much by past as present concerns.

Being with others, not just on site but also in time, joining into movements and circulations, affinities and repulsions, made us aware of the necessary labour of synchronisation, the continuous effort and struggle required to achieve occasional, momentary attendance in one temporality, as construed from a substrate of radical polytemporality. Time does not come in cultural or political-economic regimes or historical periods, as anthropologists and historians have often proposed, and it rarely converges in events and ruptures, but as an entangled multiplicity that calls for continuous, imaginative, and relational labour. And like all labour, this entails objective contradictions, as witnessed by regimes of scholarly value that unfairly distribute remuneration and credit, by the stark contrast between the effortless mobility of our archaeological expeditions among interlocutors who felt "stuck" in abandoned locales, or the mundane fact that many of those who joined our excavations either were paid (at so-called "local rates")

or joined in the hope that the labour of excavation and of synchronization would generate some form of opportunity.

Lastly, co-inhabiting sites opened our senses to invisible worlds: the alternative versions layered across the smooth surface of a seemingly impermeable reality. In addition to merely being "haunted" by what Edensor refers to as the "ghost" of previous inhabitants,[95] this is a matter of opening momentary vistas, brief moments of transformative recognition, onto other worlds that are not only possible but also co-present with more obtrusive reality. Wandering in and out of these interpenetrating realms affects – transforms – the observer. It is not just a matter of being able to see, or of being "possessed" by past others, but of being differently, imagining subjectivities, performing roles. This process, once set in motion, extends through dreams and a wandering mind.[96] Surprising, untoward connections arise. Immersion in others' times, however shallow and temporary, will always produce excess.[97]

Enacting time

Our joint work is about the entanglement of materiality and temporality, in general, but also more specifically about the performative quality of time. Our explorations of material traces can be described as a continuum of enactments. Purposive reenactments – in commemorations and contrived theatrical stagings of past experiments and other re-performances of anachronistic practice – in which we wilfully infringed the boundaries of time, were highlights of our search. Yet, such returns, in which a shadow of the past comes to life, also commonly occur in everyday moments: as more or less involuntary and inadvertent engagements between past and present (and with past and present futures), in gestures of dwelling, eating, conversing, traversing, that touch upon past materials, trigger affect, release emotions, shape subjectivities, and provoke motion.

This ordinary, affective entanglement with the past is key to how the past continues to work in the present, how history shapes subjectivities and engenders action, draws together collectives or stirs antagonisms. Importantly, the results of one's everyday brushings with the past are open-ended, and surprising, inchoate and ephemeral, though never random, caught as they are within the wider force fields of political economy and suspicion. They need not be harnessed into coherent historical narratives, coherent regimes, or periods. This book is an attempt to resist our own recuperative urge as scholars, to "slow the quick jump to representational thinking and evaluative critique,"[98] and instead to capture a glimpse of the opening, the rabbit-hole in the existing and obvious, that traces can afford.

The result is fragmentary and idiosyncratic, sometimes surprising and often contradictory, mundane, and emotionally charged: rhapsodic, to use Benjamin's term, from the Greek *rhaptein*, to "to stitch, sew, weave." Our writing is an attempt at "suturing," and as Nancy Hunt suggests our journeys should not add up to one picture, one reconstruction.[99] The openness of this trajectory is constituted/underlined through this book's structure. Yet, neither our collaboration with artists, nor the unusual format of this photographic, textual collage can provide a definite solution to the challenges of archaeological fieldwork, or can tame jarring traces into stable objects of knowledge and discussion. We offer this assemblage, trusting that it will not only give the reader insights into past lives, but also, unsettled and unsettling as it is, trigger new affective responses, provoke moments of recognition and refusal, and thus invite further conversation, opening new futures rather than turning another page on the past.

1   Achille Mbembe, *On the Postcolony* (Berkeley: University of California Press, 2001), 16.

2   Cornelius Holtorf and Angela Piccini, *Contemporary Archaeologies: Excavating Now* (Frankfurt am Main: Peter Lang, 2011).

3   Lewis Binford, *In Pursuit of the Past. Decoding the Archeological Record* (London and New York: Thames & Hudson, 1983), 19.

4   Laurent Olivier, *Le sombre abîme du temps: Mémoire et archéologie* (Paris: Seuil, 2008), 87.

5   Helge Jordheim, "Against Periodization: Koselleck's Theory of Multiple Temporalities," *History and Theory* 51, no. 2 (2012): 151-71; Jordheim, "1. Introduction: Multiple Times and the Work of Synchronization," *History and Theory* 53, no. 4 (2014): 498-518; Reinhart Koselleck, "On the Need for Theory in the Discipline of History," in *The Practice of Conceptual History: Timing History, Spacing Concepts*, ed. Reinhart Koselleck (Stanford: Stanford University Press, 2002): 1-19; Steffen Dalsgaard and Morten Nielsen, "Introduction: Time and the Field," *Social Analysis* 57, no. 1 (2013): 1-19.

6   Johannes Fabian, *Time and the Other. How Anthropology Makes Its Object* (New York: Columbia University Press, 1983).

7   Lyn Schumaker, *Africanizing Anthropology: Fieldwork, Networks, and the Making of Cultural Knowledge in Central Africa* (Durham: Duke University Press, 2001), ii.

8   See, e.g., Victor Buchli, *The Material Culture Reader* (Oxford: Berg, 2002).

9   Carlo Ginzburg, "Signes, traces, pistes. Racines d'un paradigme de l'indice," *Le Débat*, no. 6 (1980): 3-44; Marc Bloch, *Apologie pour l'histoire ou métier d'historien* (Paris: Armand Colin, 1949).

10   Emmanuel Levinas, *Humanisme de l'autre homme* (Fata Morgana: Paris, 1972), 60.

11   Paul Ricoeur, *Time and Narrative* (Chicago: University of Chicago Press, 1988) 3: 125, citing Levinas, *Humanisme,* 59, 63 (page numbers in original).

12   Nancy Rose Hunt, "An Acoustic Register, Tenacious Images, and Congolese Scenes of Rape and Repetition," *Cultural Anthropology* 23, no. 2 (2008): 245.

13   Ricoeur, 266.

14   Fekri A. Hassan, "African Archaeology: The Call of the Future," *African Affairs* 98, no. 392 (1999): 393-406.

15   François Hartog, *Régimes d'historicité. Présentisme et expériences du temps* (Paris: Seuil, 2012): 154-7.

16   Shannon Lee Dawdy, "Clockpunk Anthropology and the Ruins of Modernity," *Current Anthropology* 51, no. 6 (2010): 761-93.

17   Zarina Bhimji et al., *Zarina Bhimji (Whitechapel Exhibition Catalogues)* (London: Ridinghouse/ Whitechapel Gallery/ Kunstmuseum Bern, 2012); Bogumil Jewsiewicki and Sammy Baloji, *The Beautiful Time: Photography by Sammy Baloji* (Long Island City, NY, Seattle, WA: Museum for African Art, 2010); on Mestre Paulo Kapela, see http://calvert22.org/events/

post-socialist-condition-in-angolan-contemporary-art; Jacob Dlamini, *Native Nostalgia* (Auckland Park, SouthAfrica: Jacana Media, 2009); http://nigerianostalgia.tumblr.com, see also: http://nigeriaworld.com/feature/publication/ kizito/040212.html; Chimamanda N. Adichie, *Half of a Yellow Sun* (New York: Alfred Knopf, 2006), *Americanah* (New York: Alfred Knopf, 2013); Guy Tillim, *Avenue Patrice Lumumba* (Cambridge, MA: Peabody Museum with Prestel, 2008).

18   Guillaume Lachenal and Aissatou Mbodj-Pouye, "Restes du développement et traces de la modernité en Afrique," *Politique africaine*, no. 135 (2014): 5-21.

19   P. Wenzel Geissler and Ann Kelly, "Introduction to Special Issue: Home for Science, Scientific Field Stations in Arctic and Tropics," *Social Studies of Science*, (2016, forthcoming).

20   Alexei Yurchak, *Everything Was Forever, Until it Was No More: The Last Soviet Generation* (Princeton: Princeton University Press, 2005).

21   Tim Edensor, "The Ghosts of Industrial Ruins: Ordering and Disordering Memory in Excessive Space," *Environment and Planning D: Society and Space* 23, no. 6 (2005): 829-49.

22   Charles Piot, *Nostalgia for the Future: West Africa after the Cold War* (Chicago: University of Chicago Press, 2010).

23   Edensor, "Ghosts;" Louise K. Wilson, "Notes on a Record of Fear: On the Threshold of the Audible," *Leonardo Music Journal* 16, (2006): 28-33 ; Elin Andreassen, Hein B. Bjerck, and Bjørnar Olsen, *Persistent Memories. Pyramiden – a Soviet Mining Town in the High Arctic* (Bergen: Tapir Academic Press, 2010).

24   See, e.g., Ahmed Kanna, ed., *The Superlative City: Dubai and the Urban Condition in the Early Twenty-First Century* (Cambridge, MA: Harvard Graduate School of Design, 2013).

25   Filip de Boeck, "Inhabiting Ocular Ground: Kinshasa's Future in the Light of Congo's Spectral Urban Politics," *Cultural Anthropology* 26, no. 2 (2011): 263-86; Martin J. Murray, *City of Extremes. The Spatial Politics of Johannesburg* (Durham: Duke University Press, 2011).

26   Joost Fontein, "Graves, Ruins, and Belonging: Towards an Anthropology of Proximity," *Journal of the Royal Anthropological Institute* 17, no. 4 (2011): 706-27.

27   See, e.g., Jamie Monson, "Defending the People's Railway in the Era of Liberalization: TAZARA in Southern Tanzania," *Africa* 76, no.1 (2006): 113-30.

28   Mariane C. Ferme and Cheryl M. Schmitz, "Writings on the Wall: Chinese Material Traces in an African Landscape," *Journal of Material Culture* 19, no. 4 (2014): 375-99.

29   See, e.g., James Ferguson, *Global Shadows. Africa in the Neoliberal World Order* (Durham: Duke University Press, 2006).

30   Jean-Paul Sartre, Michek Rybalka, et al., *The Writings of Jean-Paul Sartre* (Evanston: North Western University Press, 1974) 2: 174.

31   Helen Tilley, *Africa as a Living Laboratory: Empire, Development, and the Problem of Scientific Knowledge, 1870-1950* (Chicago: University of Chicago Press, 2011).

32   Meghan Vaughan, *Curing Their Ills: Colonial Power and African Illness* (Cambridge: Polity, 1991); Guillaume Lachenal, "Experimental Hubris and Medical Powerlessness. Notes from a Colonial Utopia, Cameroon, 1939-1949," in *Rethinking Biomedicine and Governance in Africa. Contributions from Anthropology*, ed. P. W. Geissler, R. Rottenburg, and J. Zenker (Heidelberg: Transcript Verlag, 2012).

33   To take the example of Southern Africa, see e.g. R. M. Packard, *White Plague, Black Labor: Tuberculosis and the Political Economy of Health and Disease in South Africa* (Berkeley: University of California Press, 1989); Shula Marks, "South Africa's Early Experiment in Social Medicine: Its Pioneers and Politics," *Am J Public Health* 87, no. 3 (1997): 452-9; Julie Livingston, *Improvising Medicine: An African Oncology Ward in an Emerging Cancer Epidemic* (Durham: Duke University Press, 2012).

34   John Iliffe, *East African Doctors: A History of the Modern Profession* (Cambridge: Cambridge University Press, 1998).

35   Didier Fassin, *When Bodies Remember: Experiences and Politics of Aids in South Africa* (Berkeley and London: University of California Press, 2007).

36   Ferdinand De Jong and Brian Quinn, "Ruines d'Utopies: l'École William Ponty et l'Université du Futur Africain," *Politique africaine*, no. 135 (2014): 71-94.

37   Kathleen Stewart and Anya E. Liftig, "Scenes of Life/ Kentucky Mountains," *Public Culture* 14, no. 2 (2002): 356.

38   See, e.g., Janet Carsten and Stephen Hugh-Jones, *About the House: Levi-Strauss and Beyond* (Cambridge: Cambridge University Press, 1995); Ruth J. Prince and P. Wenzel Geissler, *The Land Is Dying. Contingency, Creativity and Conflict in Western Kenya* (Oxford and New York: Berghahn, 2010); Knut Christian Myhre, "The Multiple Meanings of Moongo: On the Conceptual Character of Doorways and Backbones in Kilimanjaro," *Journal of the Royal Anthropological Institute* 20, no. 3 (2014): 505-25.

39   Edensor, "Ghosts," 830.

40   Walter Benjamin, *Walter Benjamin, Gesammelte Schriften Bd.5 1-2 (1892-1940) "Das Passagen-Werk"* (Frankfurt/M: Suhrkamp, 1991).

41   Robert E. Kohler, "Lab history: reflections," *Isis* 99, no. 4 (2008): 761-8.

42   Bruno Latour, *Nous n'avons jamais été modernes* (Paris: La Découverte, 1991).

43   Bruno Latour, "When things strike back: a possible contribution of 'science studies' to the social sciences," *The British Journal of Sociology* 51, no. 1 (2000): 107-23.

44   Mantha Diawara and Ka-Yalema Productions, *La maison tropicale*, Maumaus Escola de Artes Visuais / Jürgen Bock, Lisbon, 2008 (film, 58 minutes).

45   See, e.g., our shared explorations with "diggers" in Amani (this volume), or the experiment of co-authorship with retired nurses in Ayos: Guillaume Lachenal, Joseph Owona Ntsama, Daniel Ze Bekolo, Thomas Kombang Ekodogo, and John Manton, "Neglected Actors in Neglected Tropical Diseases Research: Historical Perspectives on Health Workers and Contemporary Buruli Ulcer Research in Ayos,

Cameroon," *PLoS Negl Trop Dis* 10, no. 4 (2016), doi:10.1371/journal.pntd.0004488.

46   On Kisumu, see also Kenneth Ombongi, "The Historical Interface between the State and Medical Science in Africa: Kenya's Case," in *Evidence, Ethos and Ethnography: The Anthropology and History of Medical Research in Africa*, ed. P. Wenzel Geissler and Catherine Molyneux (New York and Oxford: Berghahn, 2011): 353-72; P. Wenzel Geissler, "Parasite Lost: Remembering Modern Times with Kenyan Government Medical Scientists," in *Evidence, Ethos and Experiment*, 297-332; "What Future Remains? Remembering an African Place of Science," in *Para-States and Medical Science: Making Global Health in Africa*, ed. P. Wenzel Geissler (Durham: Duke University Press, 2014): 142-78; Ruth J. Prince, "Past Futures of Soviet Socialist Internationalism in a Kenyan Hospital," in *Beyond Realism: History and Anthropology of Africa's Medical Dreams*, ed. Noémi Tousignant and Wenzel Geissler (in preparation).

47   On Uzuakoli, see also Achinivu K. Achinivu, *Ikoli Harcourt Whyte, the Man and His Music: A Case of Musical Acculturation in Nigeria*, 2 vols.: *Beiträge Zur Ethnomusikologie* (Hamburg: Verlag der Musikalienhandlung Wagner, 1979); Stanley G. Browne and Lykle M. Hogerzeil, " 'B 663' in the Treatment of Leprosy. Preliminary Report of a Pilot Trial.," *Leprosy review* 33, (1962): 6-10; Joseph N. Chukwu and Uche M. Ekekezie, *The Leprosy Centre Uzuakoli (1932-1992)* (Owerri: Imo Newspapers, 1992); Ikoli Harcourt Whyte, *Abu Ekele Na Otuto. Songs of Thanksgiving and Praise : For Use by Choirs in the Worship of God : In the Igbo Language* (Umuahia: Methodist Church, Eastern Nigeria District, 1958); John Manton, "Trialling Drugs, Creating Publics: Medical Research, Leprosy Control, and the Construction of a Public Health Sphere in Post-1945 Nigeria," in *Para-States and Medical Science,* 78-102.

48   On Ayos see also Lachenal et al., "Neglected Actors;" Jean-Paul Bado, *Eugène Jamot, 1879-1937. Le médecin de la maladie du sommeil ou trypanosomiase* (Paris: Karthala, 2011); Guillaume Lachenal, "Médecine, comparaisons et échanges inter-impériaux dans le mandat camerounais: une histoire croisée franco-allemande de la Mission Jamot," *Can Bull Hist Med* 30, no. 2 (2013): 23-45; Wang Sonne, "Les auxilliaires autochtones dans l'action sanitaire publique au Cameroun sous administration française (1916-1945)" (Ph.D. thesis, Université de Yaoundé, Faculté des lettres et sciences humaines, 1983); Eugène Jamot, "La maladie du sommeil au Cameroun," *Bull Soc Pathol Ex* 18, (1925): 762-9; Philaletes Kuhn, "Die Geschichte der Schlafkrankheit in Kamerun und ihre Lehren," *Zeitschrift für Hygiene und Infektionskrankheiten* 81, no. 1 (1916): 69-137.

49   On Niakhar, see also Michel Garenne and Pierre Cantrelle, "Three Decades of Research on Population and Health," in *Prospective Community Studies in Developing Countries,* ed. Monica D. Gupta, Peter Aaby, Michel Garenne and Gilles Pison (Oxford: Clarendon Press, 1997): 233-52; Valérie Delaunay, Laetitia Douillot, Aldiouma Diallo, Djibril Dione, Jean-François Trape, Oleg Medianikov, Didier Raoult, and Cheikh Sokhna, "Profile: the Niakhar Health and Demographic Surveillance System," *International Journal of Epidemiology* 42, no. 4 (2013): 1002-11; Jean-Philippe Chippaux, "La zone d'étude de Niakhar au Sénégal," *Med Trop* 61, no. 2 (2001): 131-5; Ashley Ouvrier, *Faire de la recherche médicale en Afrique. Ethnographie d'un village-laboratoire sénégalais* (Paris: Karthala,

2015); Valérie Delaunay, Alice Desclaux, and Cheikh Sokhna, eds., *Niakhar: 50 ans de recherche en santé et population dans un observatoire rural en Afrique* (Paris: Editions de l'IRD, 2016 forthcoming).

50   On Amani, see: William Nowell, "The Agricultural Research Station at Amani," *Journal of the Royal Society of Arts* 81, no. 4224 (1933): 1097-15; Branwyn Poleykett and Peter Mangesho, "Labour Politics and Africanization at a Tanzanian Scientific Research Institute, 1949-66," *Africa* 86, no. 1 (2016): 142-61; Detlef Bald and Gerhild Bald, *Das Forschungsinstitut Amani: Wirtschaft Und Wissenschaft in Der Deutschen Kolonialpolitik Ostafrikas 1900-1918* (München: Weltforum Verlag, 1972); Mary J. Dobson, Maureen Malowany, and Robert W. Snow, "Malaria Control in East Africa: The Kampala Conference and the Pare-Taveta Scheme: A Meeting of Common and High Ground," *Parassitologia* 42, no. 1-2 (2000): 149-66.

51   P. Wenzel Geissler and Ann Kelly, "Field Station as Stage: Re-Enacting Mid-20th Century Scientific Work and Life in Amani, Tanzania," *Social Studies of Science*, (forthcoming, 2016).

52   Frederick Cooper, *Africa since 1940: The Past of the Present* (Cambridge: Cambridge University Press, 2003); James Ferguson, *Expectations of Modernity: Myths and Meanings of Urban Life on the Zambian Copperbelt* (Berkeley: University of California Press, 1999).

53   Richard Rottenburg, "Social and Public Experiments and New Figurations of Science and Politics in Postcolonial Africa," *Postcolonial Studies* 12, no. 4 (2009): 423-40; Vinh-Kim Nguyen, "Government-by-Exception: Enrolment and Experimentality in Mass HIV Treatment Programmes in Africa," *Soc Theory Health* 7, no. 3 (2009): 196-217; Erica Bornstein and Peter Redfield, "An Introduction to the Anthropology of Humanitarianism," in *Forces of Compassion: Humanitarianism between Ethics and Politics*, ed. Erica Bornstein and Peter Redfield (Sante Fe: SAR Press, 2011).

54   Joao Biehl and Adryana Petryna, eds., *When People Come First: Critical Studies in Global Health* (Princeton: Princeton University Press, 2013); Ruth J. Prince and Rebecca Marsland, *Making and Unmaking Public Health in Africa. Ethnographic and Historical Perspectives* (Athens: Ohio University Press, 2013); Tamara Giles-Vernick and James L. A. Webb, *Global Health in Africa: Historical Perspectives on Disease Control: Perspectives on Global Health* (Athens: Ohio University Press, 2013).

55   Geissler, "What Future Remains?," Vinh-Kim Nguyen, "Treating to Prevent HIV: Population Trials and Experimental Societies," in *Para-States and Medical Science,* 47-77, Manton, "Trialling Drugs."

56   Walter Benjamin, "Berlin Chronicle," in *Walter Benjamin Selected Writings, Vol. 2*, part 2 (1931–1934), ed. Marcus Paul Bullock et al. (Cambridge: Belknap Press of Harvard University Press, 2005): 611.

57   On historiographic operations as always situated in the present, see e.g. Ivan Jablonka, *L' Histoire est une littérature contemporaine. Manifeste pour les sciences sociales* (Paris: Seuil, 2014): 286.

58   Pierre Nora, *Les lieux de mémoire* (Paris: Gallimard, 1984).

59   See, e.g., in the case of science, Pnina G. Abir-Am,

"Introduction," in "Commemorative Practices in Science: Historical Perspectives on the Politics of Collective Memory," ed. Abir-Am, Special Issue, *Osiris* 14, (1999): 1-33.

60   Benjamin, "Berlin Chronicle," 611.

61   Ginzburg, "Signes, traces, pistes."

62   Jean Comaroff and John L. Comaroff, *Of Revelation and Revolution, Volume 1: Christianity, Colonialism and Consciousness in South Africa* (Chicago: University of Chicago Press, 1991), 53.

63   Ann L. Stoler, *Along the Archival Grain: Epistemic Anxieties and Colonial Common Sense* (Princeton: Princeton University Press, 2008).

64   Binford, *In Pursuit of the Past*, 19.

65   Luise White, "Hodgepodge Historiography: Documents, Itineraries, and the Absence of Archives," *History in Africa* 42, (2015): 317.

66   Sarah B. Farmer, *Martyred Village: Commemorating the 1944 Massacre at Oradour-Sur-Glane* (Berkeley: University of California Press, 1999); see also: Paola Filipucci, "Archaeology and Memory on the Western Front. (Ed.), Archaeology and Memory," in *Archaeology and Memory*, ed. Dušan Borić (Oxford: Oxbow Books Ltd, 2010): 171-82.

67   John Comaroff and Jean Comaroff, *Ethnography and the Historical Imagination* (Boulder, San Francisco, Oxford: Westview Press, 1992).

68   Nancy R. Hunt, *A Colonial Lexicon. Of Birth Ritual, Medicalization, and Mobility in the Congo* (Durham: Duke University Press, 1999).

69   Olivier, *Le sombre abîme*, 86.

70   Bruno Latour, *Reassembling the Social: An Introduction to Actor-Network-Theory* (Oxford: Oxford University Press, 2005).

71   Walter Benjamin, "Excavation and Memory," *in Walter Benjamin, Selected Writings, Vol. 2, part 2 (1931–1934)*, ed. Marcus Paul Bulloc et al. (Cambridge; Belknap Press of Harvard University Press, 2005): 576.

72   Yael Navarro-Yashin, "Affective Spaces, Melancholic Objects: Ruination and the Production of Anthropological Knowledge, Malinowski Memorial Lecture," *Journal of the Royal Anthropological Institute* 15, no. 1 (2009): 1-18.

73   Patrick Keiller, *Robinson in Space* (London: Reaktion Books, 1999); *The View from the Train: Cities and Other Landscapes* (London: Verso, 2014); Teju Cole, *Open City* (New York: Random House, 2011); Lauren G. Berlant, *Cruel Optimism* (Durham: Duke University Press, 2011); Kathleen Stewart, *Ordinary Affects* (Durham: Duke University Press, 2007).

74   Berlant, *Cruel Optimism*, 15.

75   See, e.g., Edensor, "The Ghosts," 328.

76   Stewart, *Ordinary Affects*.

77   See also Walter Benjamin, *Walter Benjamin: Selected Writings, Volume 4: 1938-1940* (Cambridge: Harvard University Press, 2003), 316.

78   Edensor, "The Ghosts."

79   Simone Fullagar, "Encountering Otherness: Embodied Affect in Alphonso Lingis' Travel Writing," *Tourist Studies* 1, no. 2 (2001): 179, cited in Edensor, "The Ghosts."

80   Edensor, "The Ghosts," 329.

81   *Ibid.*, 313.

82   On passivity in Blanchot and Levinas see Thomas C. Wall, *Radical Passivity: Levinas, Blanchot, and Agamben* (New York: SUNY Press, 1999).

83   Edensor, "The Ghosts," 840.

84   *Ibid.*, 834.

85   Emmanuel Levinas, *Zwischen uns. Versuche über das Denken und den Anderen* (München: Hanser, 1995, 1991): 154-66.

86   Edensor, "The Ghosts," 838.

87   Guillaume Lachenal, "Le stade Dubaï de la santé publique. La santé globale en Afrique entre passé et futur," *Revue Tiers Monde*, no. 215 (2013): 53-71, Biehl and Petryna, *When People Come First*.

88   Geissler, "What Future Remains?"

89   P. Wenzel Geissler et al., "Introduction: Sustaining the Life of the Polis," *Africa* 83, no. 4 (2013): 531-38.

90   P. Wenzel Geissler, Richard Rottenburg, and Julia Zenker, "21st Century African Biopolitics: Fuzzy Fringes, Cracks and Undersides, Neglected Backwaters, and Returning Politics," in *Rethinking Biomedicine and Governance in Africa. Contributions from Anthropology*, ed. P. Wenzel Geissler, Richard Rottenburg, and Julia Zenker (Heidelberg: Transcript Verlag, 2012), 13.

91   Edensor, "The Ghosts," 313.

92   Gaston Gordillo, *Rubble: The Afterlife of Destruction.* (Durham: Duke University Press 2014).

93   Jean-Paul Sartre, foreword to Franz Fanon, *The Wretched of the Earth. Pref. By Jean-Paul Sartre* (New York: Grove Press, 1965).

94   Noémi Tousignant, "Broken Tempos: Of Means and Memory in a Senegalese University Laboratory," *Social Studies of Science* 43, no.5 (2013): 729-53.

95   Edensor, "The Ghosts."

96   Nancy R. Hunt, "Espace, temporalité et rêverie : Écrire l'histoire des futurs au Congo Belge," *Politique africaine*, no. 135 (2014): 115-36; *A Nervous State: Violence, Remedies, and Reverie in Colonial Congo* (Durham: Duke University Press, 2016).

97   Geissler and Kelly, "Field Station as Stage."

98   Stewart, *Ordinary Affects*, 4.

99   Nancy R. Hunt, *Suturing New Medical Histories of Africa*, Carl Schlettwein Lecture, no. 7 (Berlin: Lit Verlag, 2013).

John Manton

Archives

A pause in the presentation, a *recursus*: What have we seen? What have we moved through? Papers scatter, drying in the hot, damp air at Ayos. Boxes of slides and folders of letters clutter a cool, dusty British attic. A shaft of light illuminates botanical samples arrayed in the drawers and desks of a laboratory in Amani. Let us take some time to consider the life of the record, a peculiar instance of the trace, at once set aside and disciplined, at once documentary and material, coursing through our investigations as an archival thrust and scaffold, at the same time as it is vestigial – merely indexical – in the aftertime of science. By means of collage, assembling stagings, brushes, and engagements with the past, we reorient our relation to the rhapsodic potential of material traces. While we work, as with paper taking on glue, or a sheaf of documents swelling in the forgotten damp, what is archival blooms in unpredictable ways within the uses we make of it, comes to surge and dwell within the histories we write.

As participants in this collective enterprise across a variety of African scientific sites, as historians, anthropologists, archaeologists, and artists, we are animated by an inchoate, loosely figured, but nonetheless generative shared *archival* sensibility. We walk among and nose through papers, maps, slides, each collection of which invokes resonances of the archival, denoting a sensibility with respect to conservation of the records and traces of past human endeavours. This is not ground we tread alone: the ways in which these records come to inhabit and unsettle conversations, provoke reverie, infuse collaborations, and disrupt commemorations are well rehearsed in recent African historiography.[1]

For all that we seek to plumb the affective resonances of traces for the intensity of their emanations,[2] and not so much their documentary content, we are not unconcerned with the fate of these records. We work with the *archive*; bounded collections, specific sets of documents arrayed together according to an organising principle, however minimal, shambolic, and happenstance.[3] We operate under the sign of the *archives* (singular), the institutional context within which multiple non-intersecting things called *archive*, separately and in series, are conserved and rendered (partially, negotiably) accessible. An archives – the institution – idealises the conditions in which the canonical traces of the past are mediated as history; beyond this, in the spaces in which collecting has not become canonical, the overabundant gardens, mothballed laboratories, and locked storerooms exert a sublime pull. Our ambulatory interest crosses, sutures, reproduces, and is unsettled by the institutional power relations which produce the boundary between the canonical and the scattered.

For Mbembe, the sepulchral reliquary of the archives, where records are collected and interred, gives way to a chronophagous statecraft which is predicated on denying the pervasiveness, integrity, and accessibility of the (archival) materials with which to construct alternative temporalities.[4] This abjection of custodianship, whereby the gatekeeper function becomes malignant, and the memorial function atrophies, is concealed by a procession of bland commemorations. The regime described by chronophagy – the rejection of temporalities antecedent to the state in its current incarnation – can be complemented by an *archivophagy*, arising amid termite husks at Uzuakoli, denoting the governance effects of regimes which actively abet the decay of records, the fallow of memory, and the degradation of temporalities of collective endeavour. The consequently contracted realm of postcolonial record-keeping, attenuated by custodial strictures within, and abjectly abetted decay without,[5] effects a baleful convergence of historiographical and political despair.

If we have shared a set of journeys and strategies across sites of science in Africa, and recognise at least tacitly an archival sensibility, how might we align this sensibility to our process, the intensities it generates, attuning all the while to currents in the documentary space we traverse? What are the gambits available to us? In the spirit of our open-ended unrecuperated assemblage – again, "[slowing] the quick jump to representational thinking and evaluative critique,"[6] – what follows is a propositional move through the at once totemic and insufficient form of the institutional archives, seeking to excavate the affective resonances of the historian's relation to the document and the archive, as well as to what is concealed, degraded, and occluded.

For the scholar seeking to extract sequence, series, affinity, or continuity among happenings and their traces through the human past, the archive has been key. For the artist, the archaeologist, the anthropologist, the historian, this urge produces at once and intimately a relation to the social and institutional space configured by the archival. The convergence of investigative practices on the archival, interrogating it within a variety of increasingly cross-fertilised traditions, spills out beyond and exceeds the archives as a specific place with particular and defined functions.

However, the totemic form of the archival is still given by the places in which, as Ricoeur writes, "the institutional character of archives is affirmed [...] the deposit thereby constituted is an authorised deposit," and where "the ideological character of the choice [...] presides over the apparently innocent operation of conserving

these documents."[7] The archives exerts traction to the extent that it performs a custodial role: the mediation of the custodian provides at once the necessary friction to stimulate labour, and the smooth guidance to direct this labour as utility.

As a place, the archives is at once playground and battlefield, a space at once domestic and alienating. It is a locus of scholarly self-fashioning, the momentary visitor effecting a fleeting transformation on the purposes of the archives as institution, corralling a selection of materials from an unfathomable and concealed whole, and infusing it with a sensibility at cross-purposes with the memorial and necropolitan impulses of the collection. Working at this interface, which behaves almost as a frontier, the process of matching and testing ideas is enacted, constructing investigators, managing the psychic risks of confrontation with fear and ignorance. The archives at once embrace and reveal. They excite a forensic sensibility, returning the scholar to themselves as detective – a fantastic process which is cosy, comforting and yet disorientating, engendering a heightened and receptive sensibility.

Much of the work of the historian leaves undisturbed the selective and custodial aspects of the archives as totemic form, as a place fulfilling a function within the ideal polis. Even within a perspective that critiques the partiality and the ideological nature and functioning of the archiving impulse,[8] it presumes an exalted status for those records that have been conserved, ordered, and rendered accessible. It prefers, among records and testimonies, those whose traces are most indelible. It takes the surface impressions, the terrain of documentary space, in which persistence is preferred to failure, and heaping and gathering more exigent than scattering, as given.

The archival encounter always attempts to evade the prescriptions of custodial fantasy. Gripped with the fever of what cannot be known, what is censored, and what will not be told,[9] the investigator seeks that which is at the edge of order, that which persists by chance, that which is all but scattered. However, even this bare persistence – materials that just about survive – encodes what Stoler describes as an exercise of power, a one-time gathering of documentary material, a means to describe and capture processes and practices.[10] The aspirations and the capacity of the archives to discharge its stated function, in respect of the state, the archival profession, and the contexts in which an archives is used, provide the frame for conceiving the ideal archival relation.

There is, consequently, a temporal unfolding within relationships formed at the archives, in which the researcher proceeds from a position of ignorance; indeed, the very existence of the materials which are indexed remains uncertain, indeterminate. Varying degrees of scarcity become manifest in negotiations between the custodian and the researcher, both in spite of and through the arts of concealment performed in respect of the ideal and impossible archival relation. One can view this as an active curatorial process, in which the intentions, expectations, and capabilities of both parties are constantly gauged and managed, and in which the pace of access to documents is performed according to a constant and continually replenished feint, preserving an agnostic state regarding the persistence of the archive. If it is presumed that the archival relation in fact conceals manifold deficiencies in memorial and organisational processes, and that the curatorial and custodial frontier consists in transforming this unfolding insufficiency into marginal satisfaction, it can be seen how the archives, in a very practical fashion, problematise the historical imaginary.

This has implications beyond the archives. The fragility of paper and tape, the discontinuity of institutional regimes, the rot that burrows beyond the custodial frontier and consumes the traces presumed to be persistent; all of these are processes which are unevenly distributed within the record of human endeavour across the globe. By extension, documentary space is not evenly accessible to the historian: some of its perturbations leave little recoverable record; some are oral, situational, relational. How do we find ourselves oriented within an expanded conception of documentary space? Can we say that we orient ourselves; that we have a say in our disposition with regard to what we encounter in the archives, and amid the traces and remains, the memorials and smouldering remnants of the past?

In any case, the relations that constitute themselves, canonically, around the totemic space of the archives creep out into conceptions of these traces and remains, of conditions of access, of the adjudged right to deploy them as narrative fragments, share and preserve them, and anchor them in documentary space. Alongside the narrative possibilities that excite the historian run destabilising contexts, authoritarian inscriptions, and mnemonic functions which artists invite us to challenge.[11] Among files, folders, photographs are read roads, buildings, landscapes. Folders encode data practices, and processes of audit and reconciliation; blueprints and photographs envisage, select, and enforce relations between utopian visions and recalcitrant materials; buildings reflect material choices and constraints, supervisory practices, and labour in dialogue with leisure, as joist, rafter, panel, brick, and plaster are yoked to purpose, plan, and process.

Enfolded within the broader archival encounter is the rich and manifold possibility of failure. Scholars and artists counterpoint bravura performance and careful orchestration, with baleful regret at accidental or deliberate destruction, at archival failure. Archival tropes are tuned to recovery, dramatisation, representation, surprise, and contrast. If scholars and artists are apt to fetishise the archival impulse, then when they are confronted with the ruined archive, with the ignored record, the ungathered tale, among the dispersal of brickwork, the unpicking of structure, they encounter the quotidian distribution of effects antithetical to the curatorial – anarchival – in which the documentary and archival at once attempt vainly to anchor historical endeavour, and founder in the face of decrepitude and vastness. Moving through the archives, stumbling into the archival, blinking in regret, elicits a desperate promise to act on forgetting and failing to remember.

1   Nancy Rose Hunt, *A Nervous State: Violence, Remedies, and Reverie in Colonial Congo* (Durham, NC: Duke, 2016). See also essays by Carolyn Hamilton and others in *South African Historical Journal* 65, no.1 (2013).

2   See introduction, this volume.

3   Luise White, "Hodgepodge Historiography: Documents, Itineraries, and the Absence of Archives,"*History in Africa* 42, no.1 (2015): 317.

4   Achille Mbembe, "The Power of the Archive and its Limits" in *Refiguring the archive* ed. Carolyn Hamilton et al. (Dordrecht: Kluwer, 2002):23.

5   Wale Adebanwi and Ebenezer Obadare, *Encountering the Nigerian State* (New York: Palgrave Macmillan, 2010): 4-5.

6   Kathleen Stewart, *Ordinary Affects* (Durham: Duke University Press, 2007): 4.

7   Paul Ricoeur, *Time and Narrative, Vol. 3.* (Chicago: University of Chicago Press, 1988): 117.

8   Michel Foucault, *The Order of Things: An Archaeology of the Human Sciences* (New York: Vintage Books, 1970).

9   Jacques Derrida, "Archive Fever: a Freudian Impression," *Diacritics* 25, no.2 (1995): 61-3.

10   Ann Laura Stoler, "Colonial Archives and the Arts of Governance," *Archival Science 2*, no.1-2 (2002): 87-8.

11   Charles Merewether, *The Archive* (London: Whitechapel Gallery with MIT Press, 2006): 10-7.

Noémi Tousignant

Half-built ruins

Blurred greyish heaps come into sight alongside the brand-new toll highway out of Dakar, Senegal. Speeding along in 2015, they barely sharpen into textures of cement blocks, the outlines of part-walls around rectangular orifices, staircases to surfaces sprouting bunches of metal rods. Further, at the provisional end of the highway (named, officially, "of the future"), an expanse of savannah is announced by billboards as a gleaming city-to-come. A herd of construction cranes are at rest. The highway is planned to continue, reaching near the arrested construction of the University of the African Future, an already-ruined remains of "an ever-emerging [Afro-] future," given form in a burst of the nostalgic yet cheerfully future-oriented megalomania of the government voted out in 2012.[1]

Frenetic and prestigious building projects that materialise as amputated edifices, cement carcasses, spectres of luxury, and perpetual construction sites are familiar features of contemporary African urban landscapes.[2] Deposits of volatile capital – of fleeting savings, roving corporations, illicit gains and political magic tricks – these are also stakes sunk into the skin of uncertain futures; they confuse genesis and residue, generation and dissolution, architectural action and futility, the built and the unbuilt. Is not such confusion what has made ruins so exciting to artists and theorists, gazers and voyeurs since the eighteenth century?[3] Here may be ruins that rise from the ground rather than fall from pinnacles, arrive, in the act of building itself, from the future instead of the past, an instance, perhaps, of what Robert Smithson called "ruins-in-reverse."[4]

Can the half-built be called a ruin? What would this mean for an excavation of Africa's present?

The iconic sites of the ruin art and scholarship that has exploded over the past two decades are in former meccas of modernity, now ruins of Fordism and Socialism, industrialisation and welfare.[5] Places where, it now seems, the arrow of time was once so certain; was crumpled by the fall into ruins; yet revealed to have always been pointing right here: to ruination. Places that are mostly not in Africa.[6] Pair "ruin" with "Africa" in a search engine, and find abundant references to ruination yet a curious shortage of ruins. Its physical scars – the gouges of open-pit mines, land stripped of nutrients and moisture, or landfills heaped with discarded electronics – are but the surface marks of centuries of ruining exploitation and abandonment: careful theft and extraction, careless disposal and squandering.[7] Africa, no doubt, has been ruined, time and again. But to depict the continent as one vast ruin, as under constant attack (like everywhere, but here perhaps more violently, more tragically) by the forces of ruination says nothing yet – as it seems the ruin should – about the built, or even about the half-built and unbuilt.

The recent explosion of ruin scholarship and its exhilarated rediscovery of modern ruin thinkers is inspired,[8] as we are, by the ruin as trace, as stumbling upon or rendezvous, between presence and disappearance. For the Nazi architectural theorist Albert Speer, this meeting could be scheduled. Ruins could be anticipated as the delayed capacity built into matter to proclaim that power once lived here; that though it may have waned, moved on, been evicted; it still stands, still looms, still impresses.[9] Yet the residual life of ruins escapes deliberate acts of material formation, destruction, and survival. The question of whose power was once here, of whose power still looms, becomes, in ruination, uncertain. If archiving, as Achille Mbembe argues, is an act of burial, the ruin – though often an actual or metaphorical grave – is inhabited by the undead; it remains active, in the resilient presence of built matter, which unpredictably releases its enchantments or its toxicity.[10]

While ruins had long stood for the pastness of the past, the inevitable transience of all glory and architecture, in the eighteenth century, Goethe and Piranesi looked on antiquity in Rome (which the latter called "speaking ruins") anew as "unhinged presence."[11] The paradoxical pull and elusiveness of matter-out-of-time disrupts sequence and containment, liberating a "folded temporality"[12] that vibrates with a history that is neither recoverable nor dead. For the romantics, ruins offered sublime views of the ungraspable, creating a distance in which paralysis could be released into pleasure. Simmel, around 1900, came back to the ruin as a more proximate point of equipoise of – with the power to fuse – thought and perception, historical time and built space, nature and culture.[13] As we stand before ruins, resisting the temptation to reconstruct (matter, history), other impulses beckon: the pornographic, the nostalgic, the diagnostic, for the seduction of decay,[14] futures now implausible,[15] and the present as truth of what Empires and modernity end up as: waste, illusion, and rot.[16]

What, then, are Africa's ruins? In the well-worn colonial myth, Africa's own pasts, pasts that were not historical, not even passed, were not only unwritten but also unbuilt. They had failed to gather up the eventful momentum of historical time into the mass of monuments, cities, or civilisation. Even the now celebrated precolonial ruin of Great Zimbabwe was long seen not as proof of Africans' capacity to build, for the monumental stone enclosure surely bore traces of foreign intervention, but instead of their assimilation to a landscape hostile to history itself.[17] Indeed, colonial experts in forestry and agriculture long cast African land practices as cyclical and destructive, failing to imprint the landscape with a durable, cumulative stewardship, and contented with moving through the ephemeral promise of huts, rainfall, tree-cutting, and ashes.[18]

It was with the recognition, around the mid-twentieth century, of Africans' capacity to enter historical time, and indeed that they already had, that late-colonial approaches to built pasts and futures emerged.[19] A new generation of (European) archaeologists set out on earnest hunts for artefacts, bones, and ruins,[20] while sociologists documented vibrant African modernities.[21] Tropical geographers (the mentors of André Lericollais, see: Niakhar, this volume) deciphered the deep, diverse marks of technique and organisation on and under the land itself, in the orchestration of the exchange of water and nutrients between tree roots, rotated crops, dung, and soil.[22] It was also the beginning of a building spree that was to extend the concrete presence of a newly generous and transformative colonialism. Roads, universities, administrative offices, hospitals, clinics, field stations, urban housing estates, sheds for the collective marketing of cash-crops were to be the marks of a developmental colonialism less reluctant to pay for durability, and slowly beginning to anticipate its remains. Indeed it is easy to forget how sparse, outside enclaves of white settlement and of mining and the unbroken lines of railway track that shuttled minerals and cash cops to sea, the built legacy of the prior, more nakedly extractive colonialism is. Though some governors' palaces and tile-topped bungalows remain solid, some even curiously un-ruined, in its sum, its scape, this pre-war colonial past appears as only half-built.

The twin late-colonial projects of construction and excavation, begun to save empires, turned, in French and British colonies at least, into the rushed planning of their posthumous legacies.

They were to be continued. New nations scrambled for history, thirsted for ruins, invested in museums and departments of archaeology, but digs are expensive, and soon there was no more money for fieldwork, for equipment, for salaries.[23] There was some building too, but so much more unbuilt: The blueprint of a hardly-built science-city built over by transnational collaboration in Kisumu (this volume), spaces cleared for laboratories that never broke ground, as in Amani (this volume), proposals for institutes lost in the archives, masterplans for capital cities relocated to arid hinterlands that only half made it out of architect's sketches,[24] colonial ruins, in Saint-Louis or Grand Bassam, that were never razed for redevelopment,[25] a commanding field station never built in Niakhar (this volume), because it was no longer time for *that* kind of colonialism. So many bold hopes did not make it to brick.

And so, in the present: half-built futures pile up, half-excavated.

A forensic approach to the African palimpsest marks out a postcolonial terrain of ruination without any real ruins of "its own." Here is a half-built ruinscape scarred by particularly violent and erratic trajectories of power and capital, from the ivory trade and turbo-capitalism to mansion-building dictators and global health gifts, which suck out, it seems, even the possibility of renovating and rebuilding in their wake, making durable only the showcases of their greed and generosity.

Or we can see ruins everywhere, sidestep hierarchies of anticipation even while sensing the reverberations of the durable, and look to bungalows, dying trees and uncut grass, hut-like research stations, laboratories built and unbuilt, brand-new hospitals that may never be filled, stalled construction sites, all equally as partial, uncertain, renewed openings for "vanished reality," including lost and elusive futures, "to

gain a foothold."[26] The intractably polytemporal fabric of ruins, of the strange sites and objects around which we stumble in this book, is, in a sense, "democratic:" its registers and radiates even the smallest acts of maintenance and repair, folds itself around the most awkward of accusations and hopes, gives up corners to the accretion of anger and death, ripples at hard-won, wondrous, and momentary synchronicity. Nothing in the present – not a story about past scientific friendships and heroes, not a bitter remark about precarious work contracts, not a brick or a grave – is allowed to be by itself. The resistance of matter is released as it is tamed. The present is attacked by pasts undeciphered, unfinished yet prolific; they embarrass and thrill, accuse and arouse, sadden and activate.

1   Ferdinand De Jong and Brian Quinn, "Ruines d'Utopies: l'École William Ponty et l'Université du Futur Africain," Politique africaine, no. 135 (2014): 71-94.

2   Caroline Melly, "Inside-out Houses: Urban Belonging and Imagined Futures in Dakar, Senegal," *Comparative Studies in Society and History* 52, no. 1 (2010): 37-65; Filip de Boeck, "Inhabiting Ocular Ground: Kinshasa's Future in the Light of Congo's Spectral Urban Politics," *Cultural Anthropology* 26, no. 2 (2011): 263-86.

3   Dariusz Gafijczuk, "Dwelling Within: The Inhabited Ruins of History," *History and Theory* 52, no. 2 (2013): 149-70.

4   Robert Smithson, cited in Caitlin DeSilvey and Tim Edensor, "Reckoning with Ruins," *Progress in Human Geography* 37, no. 4 (2013): 5, in presenting "half-finished buildings whose construction has been halted by malign economic conditions," as a "species of ruin."

5   E.g. Owen Hatherley, *A Guide to the New Ruins of Great Britain* (London: Verso Books, 2011); Tim Edensor *Industrial Ruins: Space, Aesthetics and Materiality* (Oxford: Berg, 2005); Julia Hell and Andreas Schönle, eds. *Ruins of Modernity* (Durham, NC: Duke University Press, 2010).

6   There are some exceptions, of course. Notably, the photographic works of Sammy Baloji and Guy Tillim (see introduction, this volume), and: George Steinmetz, "Harrowed Landscapes: White Ruingazers in Namibia and Detroit and the Cultivation of Memory," *Visual Studies* 23, no. 3 (2008): 211-37; Joost Fontein, "Graves, Ruins, and Belonging: Towards an Anthropology of Proximity," *Journal of the Royal Anthropological Institute* 17, no. 4 (2011): 706-27; Alfredo González-Ruibal, "The Dream of Reason: An Archaeology of the Failures of Modernity in Ethiopia," *Journal of Social Archaeology* 6, no. 2 (2006): 175-201.

7   Ann Laura Stoler, "Imperial Debris: Reflections on Ruins and Ruination," *Cultural anthropology* 23, no. 2 (2008): 191-219.

8   For a good overview, see DeSilvey and Edensor, "Reckoning with Ruins."

9   Mark Featherstone, "Ruin Value," *Journal for Cultural Research* 9, no. 3 (2005): 301-20.

10   Achille Mbembe, "The Power of the Archive and its Limits," In *Refiguring the archive*, ed. Carolyn Hamilton, et al. (Dordrecht: Kluwer, 2002): 19-27; Stoler, "Imperial Debris;" Paul Draus and Juliette Roddy, "Ghosts, Devils, and the Undead City Detroit and the Narrative of Monstrosity,"*Space and Culture* (2015): 1-13; Fontein, "Graves, Ruins, and Belonging;" Tim Edensor, "The Ghosts of Industrial Ruins: Ordering and Disordering Memory in Excessive Space," *Environment and planning D: Society and Space* 23, no. 6 (2005): 829-49.

11   Gafijczuk, "Dwelling Within," 154. See also Andreas Huyssen, "Nostalgia for Ruins," *Grey Room* 23 (2006): 6-21.

12   Gafijczuk, "Dwelling Within" 152.

13   Gafijczuk, "Dwelling Within."

14   See, e.g., Andrew Emil Gansky, " 'Ruin Porn' and the Ambivalence of Decline: Andrew Moore's Photographs of Detroit," *Photography and Culture* 7, no. 2 (2014): 119-39.

15   Steinmetz, "Harrowed Landscapes," also distinguishes between nostalgia and melancholia as affects towards the past mediated by ruins.

16   Taking this Benjaminian approach to the ruins of modernity and Empire, see: Gonzalez Ruibal, "The Dream of Reason;" Stoler, "Imperial Debris." On forensic ruins, see also: Gaston Gordillo, "Review Essay. Empire on Trial: the Forensic Appearance of Truth," *Environment and Planning D: Society and Space* 33 (2015): 382-8.

17   Martin Hall, "The Legend of the Lost City; or, the Man with Golden Balls," *Journal of Southern African Studies* 21, no. 2 (1995): 179-99.

18   James Fairhead and Melissa Leach, *Misreading the African Landscape: Society and Ecology in a Forest-savanna Mosaic* (Cambridge: Cambridge University Press, 1996); Henrietta L. Moore and Megan Vaughan, *Cutting Down Trees: Gender, Nutrition, and Agricultural Change in the Northern Province of Zambia, 1890-1990* (Oxford, James Currey, 1994).

19   Frederick Cooper, *Africa since 1940: The Past of the Present* (Cambridge: Cambridge University Press, 2002).

20   e.g. Paul Thomassey and Raymond Mauny, "Campagne de fouilles à Koumbi Saleh," *Bulletin de l'IFAN* 13, no. 2 (1951): 348-62; Nick Shepherd, "The Politics of Archaeology in Africa," *Annual Review of Anthropology* (2002): 189-209.

21   Georges Balandier, "Sociologie des Brazzavilles noires," (Paris: PFNSP, 1955); Lyn Schumaker, *Africanizing Anthropology. Fieldwork, Networks, and the Making of Cultural Knowledge in Central Africa* (Durham and London: Duke University Press, 2001).

22   Gillers Sautter and Paul Pélissier, "Pour un atlas des terroirs africains: structure-type d'une étude de terroir," *L'homme* (1964): 56-72.

23   Sheperd, "The Politics of Archaeology."

24   Lawrence Vale, *Architecture, Power and National Identity* (London and New York: Routledge, 2014).

25   Alain Sinou, "Enjeux culturels et politiques de la mise en patrimoine des espaces coloniaux," *Autrepart* 1 (2005): 13-31.

26   Gafijczuk, "Dwelling Within," 151.

Crab species identified by John Raybould in Amani and named after him; in Cumberlidge, Neil & Vannini, Marco (2004) Ecology and taxonomy of a tree-living freshwater crab (*Brachyura: Potamoidea: Potamonautidae*) from Kenya and Tanzania, East Africa. *Journal of Natural History* 38 (6): 681–93

Family POTAMONAUTIDAE Bott, 1970

Genus *Potamonautes* MacLeay, 1838
Potamonautes raybouldi, new species
(figures 1, 2)

Type material. **Tanzania:** HOLOTYPE (designated here): adult male (cw 55.7, cl 39.9, ch 20, fw 12.7 mm) (NMU KMH 11486) from water-filled tree hole in forest 500 m asl, near Zigi, 9 km from Amani, East Usambara mountains, coll. J. N. Raybould, April 1966; PARATYPES (designated here): two adult males (cw 40.5, cl 29.4, ch 14.2, fw 9.3; cw 39.6, cl 27.8, ch 13.2, fw 8.8 mm) (NMU TRW 1966.03.A.2), from water-filled tree holes in forest 500 m asl, near Zigi, 9 km from Amani, East Usambara mountains, coll. J. N. Raybould, April 1966; subadult female (cw 36.9, cl 26.4, ch 12.7, fw 9 mm), subadult male (cw 29.6, cl 21.6, ch 10.4, fw 7 mm) (NMU TRW 1966.03.B.2), from water-filled tree holes in forest 500 m asl, near Zigi, 9 km

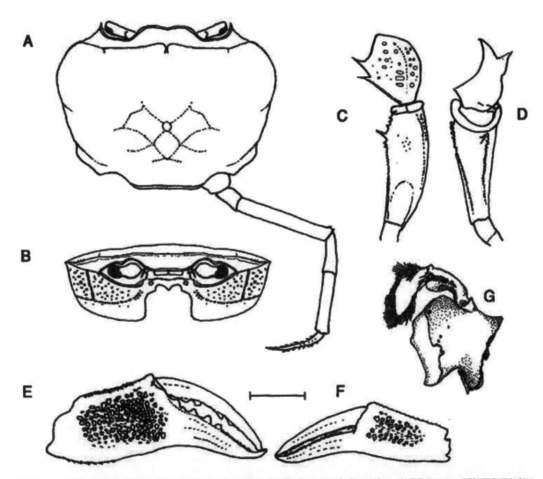

FIG. 1. *Potamonautes raybouldi* new species. Holotype, adult male, cw 55.7 mm, NMU KMH 11486, from Amani, East Usambara mountains. (A) Carapace and eyes, dorsal view; (B) cephalothorax, carapace and eyes, frontal view; (C) carpus and merus of right cheliped, dorsal view; (D) carpus and merus of right cheliped, inferior view; (E) right cheliped, frontal view; (F) left cheliped, frontal view; (G) left mandible, frontal view. Scale = 14 mm (A–F), 5 mm (G).

Echo [Amani Vanitas]

As someone who has been "looking North" in most of my research, I felt compelled to, at least for a change, to "look South." This was a while back, when Wenzel Geissler got in touch about travelling together to Amani Research Station in Tanzania.

This "looking" became, over a few months, a contemplation, ... a stunned wondering, as to why and how Amani has become, what it seems to be today: A relic of former colonial times, abandoned and still occupied. However glorious or glorified those times might have been and have become in hindsight: they are testing the dignity and livelihoods of many, past, present and future.

Listening to the ponderings and wonderings of a number of anthropologists along the way, I started to form a picture. A picture, stagnant and still, overlaid with voices and sounds. Voices from ambiguous times and places. All of it in a particular strand of slow motion, or rather more often "non-motion."

Fragmented questions intersected the scene ... "Why are there still hundreds of mice reproducing in a shed to allow the breeder to stay in employment?" "Who is using the post-office? Or the library?" ... "You are German, you must know where the gold is!" The gold – what gold!?

Wandering and wondering in the labs and protected forest area around Amani, I let the odd reality that was allowing the research station to be this hybrid, a living dead shell of former purpose, sink in ... When I started taking photographs inside the labs, a strange affinity to Dutch and Flemish Vanitas paintings unfolded. I was looking at still lifes: vessels, jugs, pots, a formerly functional array of plastic, lab-glass, polystyrene and paper records ... often sitting on dark, ... very dark wood.

Have any of the regularly passing school kids ever even seen this "still" world? If it wasn't for the daily routines and goings-on around these "still-lifes," what would we find in their place? Or: what would be left of them? If it wasn't for the government funding, protecting Amani as a colonial memorial, or a post-colonial remainder and reminder, it would most likely be looted, fall apart, overgrow and eventually disappear. Yet, there is still a post-office, various administration offices, even a functioning malaria test lab for the locals and of course the guesthouse we inhabited.

Why did it feel so different and subtly uncomfortable to be served three meals a day in Amani than anywhere else I have been?! Difficult to shrug off the exclusive, inherited position we were in here.

Vanitas is the Latin for vanity, in the sense of "emptiness" or a "worthless action." In the arts, *Vanitas* is a type of symbolic work of art, associated especially with still life painting in Flanders and the Netherlands in the 16th and 17th centuries.

But: here were no skulls, hourglasses, extinguished candles or rotting fruit; just the archived, disintegrating insects, dry rats and some moth-eaten curtains? Were the polystyrene cups taking place of the skull? Were they empty and worthless? – or ... actually stand for former wealth and incoherent values?

"Realm of Knowledge and Silence": a sign in the Amani library echoed around my head. The "freeze-frame-situations" in the labs and cupboards talk about the evanescence of *our* existence, there, and here.

By the time we left, I could not decide which part of the situation was more impenetrable or maybe less entangled: its past times, its current state or its future in our imagination.

Mariele Neudecker

Uzuakoli Leprosy Centre
Edited and written by John Manton

5° 39' N, 7° 32' E

Elevation: 120–150m

Location: Abia State, Nigeria.

Alternative names: Leper Colony, Uzuakoli; Native Administration Leprosy Settlement, Uzuakoli; Leprosy Research Unit, Nigeria. [Note: the term "leper" is outdated and stigmatising. Its use here reflects the historical record.]

Current Status: There is an active Welfare Department under the stewardship of the Methodist Church, which rehabilitates and repatriates former patients still resident at the Centre. The Medical Department acts as the referral centre for tuberculosis and leprosy for Abia State. It is largely non-functioning, and systematic research is no longer carried out at the site. Most, if not all, of the medical and administrative records dating from prior to 1982 have been lost or destroyed. The Chapel of Hope, at the centre of the complex, is dilapidated, though there are plans for its refurbishment.

Origin of the name: Lohum Imenyi is the closest village to the site, but the leprosy centre is named after the nearby town of Uzuakoli, corresponding to the site of a major pre-colonial market. Uzuakoli was a colonial rail halt and a site of Methodist evangelism and education, with its Methodist College, Uzuakoli dating from 1923. The Methodist origins of the leprosy centre may account for the continued use of Uzuakoli as its name.

Chronology

1932

Four years of leprosy patient activism, led by Ikoli Harcourt Whyte (born 1905) and John Nweke, culminates in Methodist Church and government collaboration to found a Leprosy Settlement near Uzuakoli.

The Leper Colony, Uzuakoli is inaugurated on lands leased from Lodu, Lohum and Nkpa communities. The medical superintendent is Dr James A Kinnear Brown.

1936

Dr Brown is replaced by Dr Thomas Frank (TF) Davey. Davey and his wife Kay expand research and pastoral care facilities, and instruct Ikoli Harcourt Whyte in musical composition and notation.

The Daveys remain at Uzuakoli until 1959. TF Davey develops Uzuakoli as a research site of international renown. A Concert Hall is built.

1945

The Nigeria Leprosy Service is founded, and Uzuakoli is brought under government management, together with mission-run programmes at Oji River and Ossiomo.

Uzuakoli is to specialise in chemotherapeutic research, with a full research service from 1948.

1949

Ikoli Harcourt Whyte is discharged from the leprosy centre, symptom-free. He chooses to remain resident at Uzuakoli, as a member of staff at the centre.

Ikoli Harcourt Whyte's repute as a composer and choirmaster spreads; choirs from across eastern Nigeria visit Harcourt Whyte in order to learn and spread his music.

1951

John Lowe, working at Uzuakoli, publishes 'Diaminodiphenylsulphone in the treatment of leprosy' in *The Lancet*, standardising dapsone dosage for worldwide adoption in the treatment of leprosy.

1960

Successful chemotherapy of leprosy renders large-scale leprosy settlements obsolete. Long-term residence and segregation become less common. Settlements are shrinking.

Nigeria declares its Independence on 1 October. Drs Stanley Browne and Lykle Hogerzeil replace Davey at the Leprosy Research Unit.

The work of Browne and Hogerzeil on clofazimine (also known as B663 or Lamprene) introduces a new option for the treatment of complications in leprosy. It is still in use today.

1967

Biafra secedes from Nigeria. Civil war follows. Uzuakoli is attacked in 1968. Dr Marcus Nkanno leads the patients into the bush. The Harcourt Whyte family also flees, losing many of the composer's original manuscripts.

The Research Unit at Uzuakoli ceases to function during and after the war. Nkanno is taken ill and dies in 1973. Medical services falter and life becomes difficult for remaining patients and staff at the centre.

1977

Ikoli Harcourt Whyte dies, as a result of complications arising from a car accident.

Harcourt Whyte's tomb is one of only two at the site of the Chapel of Hope, Uzuakoli Leprosy Centre. The other belongs to Dr Nkanno, the first Nigerian medical superintendent of the Centre.

1992

The Leprosy Centre, Uzuakoli 1932–1992 by Joseph N Chukwu and Uche M Ekekezie (medical and welfare superintendents at Uzuakoli) is published.

This volume is reprinted in 2014 to commemorate 50 years of German Leprosy Relief Association work in Nigeria.

2013

Much of the infrastructure of the leprosy centre remains in poor repair. A number of health and welfare related projects use and share the site with the tuberculosis and leprosy programme. The Chapel of Hope and Concert Hall are little used.

Five choirs sing the music of Ikoli Harcourt Whyte at an event in Abuja. These include the Achinivu Harcourt Whyte Choral Association, Arochukwu, and the Ikoli Harcourt Whyte Choir, Lagos.

A choral celebration takes place at the Chapel of Hope in 2015, to raise funds for its rehabilitation. Plans to beautify Harcourt Whyte's tomb, to re-establish medical research at Uzuakoli, and to set up a memorial music school are mooted, once again.

Musical memory and medical forgetting in Uzuakoli

The Leprosy Centre, Uzuakoli was once a key location in global leprosy research, but has been neglected since the beginning of the Nigerian Civil War in 1967. In its heyday, it was a charismatic scientific and cultural site, a garden of science and healing. Its architectural remnants are still in use, a material persistence and melancholic afterlife of the massive institutional mechanisms for leprosy control in Eastern Nigeria. This is evident both in degraded and destroyed paper records, and in the dissemination and performance of the choral compositions of its most famous former patient, Ikoli Harcourt Whyte.

By the early years of the 20th century, when the story of Ikoli Harcourt Whyte begins, southeastern Nigeria was a leading source of palm oil and rubber within the British Empire. Imperial rule was new to the area, which had been a patchwork of small states and loosely-aligned autonomous villages, still bearing many of the scars of centuries of slave raiding and forced labour. Leprosy rapidly became an object of fascination and puzzlement for the new colonial state, and the history of colonial administration in the area, in the short period between the 1910s and 1960, was marked by a disproportionate investment in building institutions for the management and control of leprosy.

Nigeria's huge leprosy centres, state- and missionary-funded encampments of thousands of segregated leprosy patients, offered opportunities not only for medical research, but for community reorganisation, and experiments in rural development and governance. The medical imperative – to control and eliminate leprosy as a threat to public health – was translated into an imperative of colonial governance, and a social experiment whose effects ramified through and were amplified by the music of Ikoli Harcourt Whyte.

While the records of past scientific endeavour at Uzuakoli have been of little interest to embattled successive medical administrators, grappling with the chaos of post Civil War and post structural adjustment public health, the echoes and resonances of song and music offer a striking contrast. Harcourt Whyte's music is a central component of the Christian Church musical repertoire in Nigeria and its diaspora, and has been recorded in Nigeria and the USA, recently reissued in mp3 format, subject to musicological studies in Nigeria's major universities, and recently performed in headline concerts in Abuja and Port Harcourt.

His life cut a path through the colonial history of Nigeria, the aspirations and disappointments of the independent state, and the dispiriting and calamitous experience of civil war. Thus, the recovery of Harcourt Whyte's story, and of his music, remains fraught with difficulty. At the same time, stories, histories, and trajectories of musical performance elicit and crystallise the ethical and ultimately redemptive potential of an alternative folk historiography of leprosy, its control, and the Nigerian encounters with science which it mediated. This restorative potential remains intangible, awaiting the galvanic coalition, the impulse that might transmute it into a socially, culturally, medically and economically productive aftermath of science.

It is more than simply trivial to say that destruction, a material event, happens in a place. Destruction is an ambiguous event, and can signify processes experienced as positive and negative, partaking as much in renewal as failure. Making and inhabiting place happens as much in relation to what is destroyed and superseded as to what is preserved in foundations, in the canon, and in the everyday.

John's script notes for radio documentary, *Uzuakoli in Music and Medicine*, April 2015

The failure of paper

Uzuakoli Leprosy Centre has generated a super-abundance of paper in its institutional lifetime. From the outset, even before it became a central institution of the newly-constituted government Nigeria Leprosy Service in 1945, the leprosy settlement at Uzuakoli documented a wide range of administrative, medical, and technical operations relating to the control of leprosy in the southern areas of Igboland. Founded by Methodist missionaries in 1936, its early super-intendents – in particular TF Davey – developed a considerable epidemiological machinery and chemotherapeutic research capacity which brought the settlement global renown. The patient records at Uzuakoli could imaginably comprise one of the most significant archives of medical work in Nigeria.

Selection of files from Records Annex, Uzuakoli Leprosy Centre, 2006

My visit took me to the Medical Department, where patient records were generated, used, and stored. I asked to meet some people whose names I'd been given, and did my best to explain what I was looking for. The notion that anyone would be interested in closed files, useless records, defunct material elicited the usual mixture of incomprehension and disdain, and, as usually happened, I was shown some recently closed files from the mid-1980s era of multi-drug therapy.

My companion, a social worker with the German Leprosy Relief Association, well known to the hospital staff, asked the same questions I had, and found that all of the old records were in a building to the rear, but that the key had been lost. She suggested they break into it, and a man and a woman went off to see what they could do. Before I'd managed to figure out what was going on, they came back with a small bundle of old files, which they laid down on the table and began to examine. They appeared relatively intact.

Sample file, Records Annex, Uzuakoli Leprosy Centre, 2006

"1961," the woman announced, and passed a file over to me to have a look at. "Clofazimine," I thought, and turned the first page. I saw first the network of holes, whose startling extent became apparent as I turned page after page, gaping, shedding dirt and termites onto the table and floor. My heart sank. File after file was passed to me. 1954. 1973. 1965. All in the same condition.

I asked to see where they'd found the files. I was led around the back of the building in question, known as the records annexe, to a broken window, where a bunch of files sat exposed to the elements. I climbed through the narrow gap, inside, where stacks of records were heaped along a wall under two open windows, a haul stretching back to the 1940s if not further. Each bound bundle I examined was hollowed out by termites, stuck together at the corners, in such a parlous and fragile state that I dared not disturb them. Bundles began to crumble at the touch.

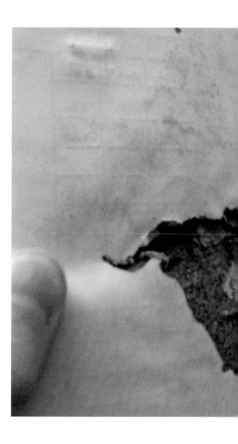

Records Annex, Uzuakoli Leprosy Centre, 2015

Sample folder, Records Annex, Uzuakoli Leprosy Centre, 2006

Sample file, Records Annex, Uzuakoli Leprosy Centre, 2006

The patients at Uzuakoli had fled the advancing front of civil war sometime towards the end of 1967 or early 1968. Whether the records had remained at the hospital or travelled with a conscientious member of staff, they had certainly survived one of the most vicious conflicts in modern Africa. Many patients survived and had returned to Uzuakoli by 1971, where some semblance of care seems to have been resumed. Thirty-five years later, visited by the depredations of successive civilian and military governments, the continual degradation of hospital and staff conditions, and the deprioritisation of almost all of a state's responsibility for its citizens, histories and memories which survived a catastrophic war had been eviscerated by the mundane action of accumulated neglect.

In what remained (and has since been lost), tantalising references abounded – to experimental drugs, to the social life of leprosy control, to the complex biology of infection and its effects on the body, to the interface between patient bodies and the gaze of doctor and nurse. Body maps, standardised descriptions, evidence of comorbidity with malaria, syphilis, and yaws, the dietary availibility of meat, family size, profession were all assembled in one location, sheaved with literature on marriage and the Christian life, offprints, sermons, scientific literature, settlement rules and regulations. This promiscuous piling, a storage without sorting, was no more than fertile ground for the life-cycle of the termite, and later, fuel for the fire which consumed the records annexe some years after my visit.

[Harcourt Whyte] was one of the first
patients to go [to Uzuakoli in 1932], and
all the experiments, scientific experiments,
to find a cure for leprosy, were tried out
on him, as a human guinea pig. So he spent
all his life in Uzuakoli, and Igbo became his
major language […] He was gifted […] He
became the composer of songs of worship
and wonder.

Interview with Professor Achinivu Kanu Achinivu, 17 and 18 March 2015

Soundings

Communal life has a sonic signature. Duress and choice give rise to a particular pattern of human association, given voice in a play of sounds and signals, calls and responses, interference and amplification... these reverberate through the temporal and spatial fabric of human enterprise.

If we become attentive to the rhythms of worship, of care, of dislocation, how different experiential domains converge, the reconstruction of communal association and family life, as these play out in particular spaces, we can attune to the performance of particular sonic repertoires, the habitual sounds and resonant silences of the clinic, the laboratory, the church, and the colony; of worship, of therapy, of domesticity.

This process – of attunement – is an exercise in understanding phase, duration, improvisation, selection, resonance and amplification, facets of human temporal and material experience which suffuse both the historical sequence and the historiographical imaginary.

In the case of Uzuakoli, this exercise can be divined as we follow the dispersal, transmission, translation, modification of music on its travels. The tutelary life of Ikoli Harcourt Whyte (recounted by Professor Achinivu) is captured in the dynamics of rehearsal and performance through which a choir comes to know its capacities, and to experience and interpret the intentions and readings of a composer, a conductor, a choirmaster. At the same time, the unruliness of music, its resistance to notation and insistence on the primacy of performance, continually disrupts our attempts to capture its history, and to write history through it.

John's script notes for radio documentary, April 2015

Achinivu Harcourt Whyte
Choral Association,
Arochukwu, 2015

He wrote music that touched on every aspect of life… *Through the Year with Harcourt Whyte* [an album recorded in 1982 by Achinivu's choir at the University of Nigeria] …

Four parts, four-part harmony – soprano, alto, tenor, bass – that, he acquired by studying Methodist hymn book, Hymns Ancient and Modern, revised church hymnary, sacred songs and solos… And then Dr Davey [the leprologist at Uzuakoli], while he went into the villages looking for leprosy patients and bringing them to the hospital, was also interested in the traditional music of the people, so he made recordings of those types of music, brought them home, and gave to Harcourt and said, "Listen to this, and write music that sounds like this, not the music that sounds like what you have in the Methodist hymnbook." So that's how… He did what Davey said; he listened and listened and listened, and in that way he began to develop his own style.

There was this tale… He was invited by [name unclear] choir, who were celebrating something, and they invited him to come and write a special song for them, and teach that song, and perform it, conduct it on the day. So when he arrived, he asked for blackboards, chalk, duster, and they brought all those, and he kept blackboards at the head of his bed. The following morning when they came they found the blackboards full of notes, and the story was that while he was sleeping, the angel of the Lord or some spirit whispered melodies to him, and he got up and wrote them down… which is possible. Inspiration. It happens to me sometimes, I sleep, I have some melodies, I just get up and write it down and sleep again. So, they came in the morning and saw the blackboards, three blackboards or so, filled with notes. That was it. In the evening, they assembled, he had harmonised the thing in parts, in four parts, he started teaching.

CD Cover, *Anyi bu ihe*, Achinivu-Harcourt Whyte Chorale, n.d.

LP Cover, *Oge di n'iru*, Harcourt Whyte Memorial Choir, n.d. [1970s]

LP Cover, *Through the years with Harcourt Whyte*, Christ Church Chapel Choir, 1981–2

Harcourt was very well known and appreciated. His music was number one everywhere at the time. He had his own choir, and his own choir was quote and unquote the best, the example that everybody looked up to… Emulating… So many choirmasters came to his choir, to sing along with them. I was one – I went to sing with his choir. [Names some famous choirmasters] – a number of them came to sing with him. These came from Uzuakoli… [One] had his own choir, in the Methodist Church, but he came to learn and then teach his own choir … And so, any piece they learned, they took back to their choir or choirs and taught them. So in that way, his music spread.

But there is a major problem that I am encountering now. That problem is that the people, those choristers from point of their level of education, did not copy music correctly. These, what I call them, diacritic marks – the stroke on the right side of a note indicating that it is of high pitch, or the one below on the right indicating that it's a low pitch. Many choristers did not put them, and that gave rise to different pitches … [Sings to illustrate differences arising from misplaced diacritics] And that's not what Harcourt wrote.

So that's one of the difficulties I had, so I tried to look up people like Elder Ndubueze Obioma, who gave me quite a number of his songs that he had. Many of them I do not know, so I had to sit him down to sing the melody to me. After singing the melody to me, I am then able to determine what the other notes should be, whether high or low or the same pitch […]

Interview with Professor Achinivu Kanu Achinivu, musicologist and choirmaster, holder of the named Ikoli Harcourt Whyte Chair of Choral Music, University of Port Harcourt, at his home in Arochukwu, Nigeria – 17 and 18 March 2015

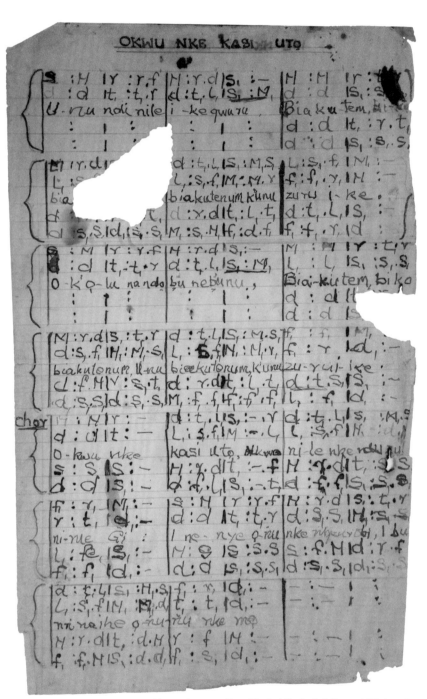

Manuscript score, *Okwu Nke Kasi Uko*, by Ikoli Harcourt Whyte, n.d.

Ayos

**Edited by Guillaume Lachenal
with John Manton and Joseph Owona Ntsama**

3°54'12" N, 12°31'34" E

Elevation: 650–700m

Location: Cameroon. Eastern border of the Central region, department of Nyong et Mfoumou.

Alternative names: Nkol'Nlong; Ajoshöhe (German).

Current status: Hôpital Régional Annexe, Ecole d'aides soignants, Ecole d'Infirmiers Diplômés d'Etat (Regional Annex Hospital, School for Nursing Auxiliaries, School for State-registered Nurses).

Origin of the name: Unclear. According to one informant, "Ayos!" is an onomatopoeic representation of the sound made by scissors at a medical circumcision. Thus the name Ayos may mark the medical origin of the town.

Chronology

1912

Creation of camp for sleeping sickness by Doctor Philalethes Kuhn on the site known as *Ajoshöhe*. 250 patients interned.

Massive programme planned to fight sleeping sickness in German Kamerun.

1914

World War One brings conflict between German and Allied armies in southern and eastern Cameroon. The camp is evacuated and serves as a *Gefangenenlager* (prison camp).

1916

Ayos is in ruins and bushes. "Only traces of the previous owners remain," according to French colonial doctors.

French colonial government takes over.

1918–1925

French colonial doctors, Dr Jojot and Dr Jamot, revive Ayos.

The Germans are actively forgotten.

1926–1930

Creation of the "Permanent Mission for the Fight against Sleeping Sickness in Cameroon," headed by Dr Eugène Jamot. Building boom in Ayos, which becomes a "medical city" including accommodation for nurses and a leprosy camp.

French doctors dream of the eradication of sleeping sickness and of the revival of the Upper Nyong region.

1932

Official foundation of Ayos Nursing School (*Centre d'Instruction Médicale*).

1937

Deaths of Eugène Jamot and Philalethes Kuhn.

Monument to Jamot built and commemorative ceremony held in Ayos.

1939

Commemoration of Jamot's 60th anniversary in Yaoundé. The German campaign to regain its former colony intensifies.

1950s

Modernisation. The French Colonial Development Fund (FIDES) funds major investments in "mobile" medicine. Dormitories and other buildings built in Ayos.

1960

Independence of Cameroon. Ceremony held at midnight in Ayos, involving several *Jamotains* (early nurses employed by Jamot).

Ayos is to become a medical school and University Hospital – an idea of French president De Gaulle.

1970

Death of Karl Kaledje, one the first *Jamotains*.

A new disease, Buruli Ulcer, is detected for the first time in Cameroon. All cases "curiously limited to the area of Ayos," according to French researchers.

1979

100th anniversary of Jamot's birth celebrated with several *Jamotains* present. Ceremony covered in the national daily paper, the *Cameroon Tribune*.

1987

1937, the 50th anniversary of Jamot's death, commemorated by a postal stamp.

Cameroon Tribune describes the decay of the site: "Everything is ruined. Crumbling little huts under palm trees."

1990

Biopic on Jamot, "La Nuit Africaine," aired on French TV, after filming in Ayos with local inhabitants acting as 1920s patients.

1997–1998

Rehabilitation of the "Case Jamot" (Jamot's old colonial house) by the French Aid Agency. *Comité Jamot* from France visits.

Ayos imagined as tourist site and museum.

2001

Epidemiological study of Buruli Ulcer in Ayos. International medical research resumes in Ayos, linked with the Neglected Tropical Diseases Initiative.

2005–2006

Rehabilitation of the hospital.

Destruction of most old buildings. Construction of a new hospital in Ayos funded by the African Development Bank.

The creation of a medical University in Ayos on the land of the former leprosy camp is under discussion in Yaoundé.

Views of the sleeping sickness camp (*hypnoserie*) at Ayos, 1924 (left) and 1928 (right)

Ayos: a century of biopolitics and commemoration

Ayos is a small town obsessed with its past. It is a site of exuberant, creative, recurrent and chronic commemorative activity, mainly associated with the figure of Dr Eugène Jamot, a larger-than-life doctor who worked in Cameroon in the 1920s – and who is still celebrated in France as a colonial hero. The landscape of Ayos displays the monuments left by this glorious past, but also the sedimented layers of a tougher history, marked by a long and continuing experience of epidemics and of drastic public health measures in disease control. Ayos is a site both of memory and medicine, and of seclusion and death.

The camp

Ayos was built as a *camp*, in the strongest sense of the term: a place of segregation, incarceration, experimentation and therapy. It was conceived as a "biopolitical" tool of the colonial state, whose function was to care – by means of excision and exclusion – for the life and death of a human population treated as a biological entity.

Ayos was created in 1912–13 by Dr Philalethes Kuhn, doctor-in-chief of the sleeping sickness service of the German colony of Kamerun. With its high, windy hills, the site was a strategic post on the river Nyong. Entirely navigable from Abong-Mbang to Mbalmayo (where the railroad connected with the harbour of Douala), the Nyong was at that time the main economic artery of Kamerun, notably enabling the export of wild latex collected in the forests in the south-east of the colony. As elsewhere in the region, the early-20th century rubber boom meant forced labour, violence, movements of workers, carriers and traders – and massive epidemics. The Nyong spread diseases just as it transported merchandise, and became the axis of a major epidemic of sleeping sickness. Ayos found itself at the middle of a pathological colonial ecosystem, and soon at the heart of a country-wide medical infrastructure.

The initial function of the *schlafkrankenlager* ("sleeping sickness camp") of *Ajoshöhe* was to concentrate and isolate people infected with trypanosome (the parasite causing the disease, transmitted by the tse-tse fly), in order to prevent further contamination. It kept the same role when the French took over most of German Kamerun after World War One and re-created Ayos. Mobile teams screened populations throughout the colony, and all cases of sleeping sickness considered incurable were sent to Ayos. For the government department assigned to deal with the disease, segregation was viewed as the key to population-scale preventive action. The system was initially inspired by the *konzentrationlager* set up by Robert Koch in Uganda in 1908 to fight sleeping sickness. The French called the camps *"hypnoseries,"* after the "leprosaria" used for leprosy patients all over the world. The whole space of Ayos – which had both a leprosy and a sleeping sickness camp – was organised as a biopolitical complex, with guarded wards for inpatients, laboratories, dispensaries, and a teaching theatre *(amphitheatre)*. It also included housing for the nurses, beautiful colonial houses for the doctors, and the associated infrastructure of water pump, generator, vegetable gardens, fields, fruit trees, swimming pool, football pitch, tennis court and cemeteries.

The imperial capital

The camp of Ayos became one of the most photographed places in the French Empire. From 1926, it served as the logistical base of the *Mission Permanente de Prophylaxie de la Maladie du Sommeil,* or "Mission Jamot," which was in charge of sleeping sickness control for the entire territory of Cameroon. Dr Jamot proved to be not only a charismatic leader and organiser, but also a very modern humanitarian *entrepreneur*. While French colonial action in the "mandate" of Cameroon was scrutinised at the League of Nations, and ritually denounced by German ex-colonial lobbies, Jamot skilfully harnessed a climate of imperial rivalry to secure significant funding from the French metropolitan state for his programme. With the help of graphic images, statistics, and heavily publicised and stage-managed conferences in Paris, he put Ayos at the centre of an imperial experiment, where French colonists could prove and document their humanism, benevolence and expertise.

Numerous pictures and films from Ayos displayed to young and old audiences in Europe images of crowds queueing for injections, debilitated bodies, big bellies, crazy and disordered movements, and haunted gazes. Most of the movie "Mission Jamot," presented in Paris at the 1930 Colonial Exhibition, was shot at Ayos. It cemented the glory of Jamot, who reinvented himself as the founder of Ayos, and the pride of the French pharmaceutical firm Rhône Poulenc, who sponsored the film. The sleeping sickness service of Cameroon used kilos of drugs from the firm, and Ayos served as an experimental zone for trying out new formulae.

Beyond press articles and postcards, the significance of Ayos in the French Empire also lay in its ascendance as a training centre. The sleeping sickness campaigns required the training of hundreds of highly specialised nurses, who took theoretical and practical courses in Ayos. As Jamot's methods were extended to the rest of the colonies of French West Africa and French Central Africa (AOF and AEF), the centre trained nurses of all imperial origins, from the French Congo to the French Sudan – it was one of the

cradles of a (short-lived) imperial "imagined community." The first Cameroonian medical doctors, who studied medicine in colonial Dakar and France from the 1950s, were all Ayos alumni. Beyond the medical profession, the nursing school catalysed the formation of an entire segment of the political elite of the independence years, including Prime Ministers Charles Assalé and Simon-Pierre Tchoungui.

The lieu de mémoire: *chronic commemoration*

When Jamot died in 1937, a commemorative monument was build on the top of the hospital hill. Philalethes Kuhn, the "real" founder of Ayos, died the same year, and was celebrated in Germany as a major theoretician of racial hygiene. The creator of the *lager* of Ayos had become a prominent Nazi doctor, following a trajectory which made almost too explicit the colonial genealogy of racialised European states of the mid-20th century. No monument for him, though – the role of the Germans is actively forgotten in the construction of the official (French) memories of Ayos.

The invention of Jamot as a colonial hero was swift: as early as 1939, commemorative monuments were inaugurated at Yaoundé, the capital, and in his native village of St Sulpice des Champs, in France. Jamot was an incarnation of a secular form of French universalism (he was a notorious "free thinker"), and of a colonial ethos of audacity and boldness – the image of the bush-doctor, laughing loud and working hard, hating bureaucrats and Americans/British/Germans, would inspire generations of French doctors. After World War Two, as a vast programme of social medicine based explicitly on Jamot's mass methods became a priority of French colonial policy, Ayos became a *passage obligé* for journalists and officials; commemoration was a form of imperial propaganda. By the end of the 1950s,

Jamot had streets and hospitals named after him all throughout Africa. His first book-length biography, written by a Cameroonian doctor, politician and Ayos alumnus, Marcel Bebey-Eyidi, was published in 1951 – to be followed by several others, including a TV biopic and numerous documentaries.

The successes of Jamot and Ayos as objects and sites of memory owe more to the *post*-colonial situation than to the celebration of the colonial past per se. From the late 1950s, Jamot became cherished as an early incarnation of a French-African relationship defined by ambiguous ties of friendship, familiarity and technical aid, which would form the key principles of the system of *La Coopération*. Certain details in the biography of Jamot helped, notably the fact that he had a Cameroonian wife and several *métis* children – including a daughter who married a prominent colonial doctor, Dr Plantier, who headed the hospital at Ayos in the 1950s. Jamot's name took on another meaning: he stood for the Frenchmen who loved and helped Africa from the beginning. He was a new model for a de-colonised relationship between Paris and its former territories; in Yaoundé, he even became the first "national hero" celebrated by the Cameroonian government of Ahmadou Ahidjo, in 1959. Ayos, where the French had built an "Ecole des Metis" for the mixed-race children of Cameroon, became the *lieu de mémoire* – site of commemoration – of this mythical French-Cameroonian "friendship."

From the 1960s on, commemorations in Ayos reinvented themselves as *Cameroonian* celebrations – all the more precious, to the French who sponsored and took part in them, for the fact that they were Cameroonian. Local actors – the families of locally established nurses, the mayor, the hospital staff – competed for the role of legitimate witnesses, interlocutors, and guides for the expatriates and government officials who would make excursions from Yaoundé.

A generation of local health workers called the *Jamotains*, who were said to have been the first Cameroonians to work with Jamot, became a central object of memory.

In France, retired colonial doctors and associations of inhabitants of la Creuse, Jamot's region of origin, organised the Jamot cult. Commemorations became transnational ventures, paired with donations of funds, hospital beds and football gear for the hospital, its workers, students, and patients. In the late 1990s, the French aid agency in Yaoundé funded the rehabilitation of the "Case Jamot," the superb colonial house which Jamot had built for himself on top of Ayos' highest hill, with stunning views over the Nyong and the whole medical complex. While the hospital increasingly approached ruin, it was hoped that the "Case Jamot" would became a museum and a tourist attraction. The fates of tourism and medical enterprise, ambiguously twinned in these twisted transnational logics of commemoration, continue to unfold, and to entangle buildings and bodies in nervous uncertainty and anticipation.

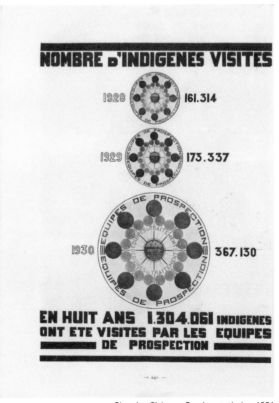

Sleeping Sickness Service statistics, 1931

Documents drying on the floor in the former pharmacy of the hospital, 2012

The Douala-Chad truck road, view from the hospital, 2012

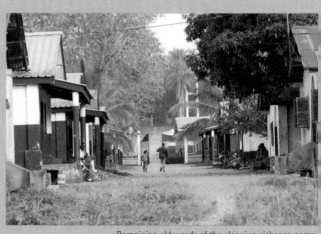

Nursing school and student dormitories, 2013

Remaining old wards of the sleeping sickness camp, now used for Buruli Ulcer patients, 2012

Stairs leading to the football field, 2012

Nursing school, classrooms building, 2012

Old colonial house, now used by the head of the nursing school, 2013

Kombang Ekodogo (born 1962) was the head of nursing *(surveillant général)* at the Ayos hospital in 2013. He guided our tours on the hospital site, taking us through locations and processes, meeting staff and patients, and describing practices and their histories.

Kombang was born in the leprosy camp *(léproserie)* of Ayos as the son of two patients interned in the camp since their youth. He was initially schooled by Catholic religious nurses at the leprosy camp, and later in the town of Ayos, where he frequently had to fight for the respect of "normal people." He was appointed as nursing aide *(aide soignant)* at the hospital of Ayos in 1995, and graduated as a nurse in 2002. He specialises in the surgery and care of Buruli Ulcer – a disease sometimes termed "the other leprosy" – and is part of several international research projects on the infection, where his expertise, surgical skills and tact with patients is precious. He still lives in the leprosy camp, where he has built a beautiful house for himself.

Daniel Ze Bekolo (born 1951), also known as Papa Ze or Mathusalem, was our guide in the town of Ayos and an extraordinary local figure. Notable by birth (into a powerful local clan, the Yebekolo) and profession (as District Leprosy and Tuberculosis Officer for decades, he toured widely by motorcycle to screen for new cases and care for old ones), he was a key actor in our research programme. We got his contact details from a well-known Cameroonian doctor in Yaoundé, who was in charge of several research projects working in Ayos; Ze Bekolo was his man on the ground. Charismatic, powerful and well-connected, he was both expert and renowned.

He knew the medical history of the site very well, having been a key nurse at the hospital in the 1970s and 1980s – a time when nurses performed surgery and critical care, attended births and prescribed drugs. Daniel Ze Bekolo was among the first nurses to perform surgery for Buruli Ulcer, a locally endemic, severe, debilitating skin infection caused by mycobacteria. He learnt the technique (including skin grafting) in the late 1970s, and has taken part in most studies of the disease following its "rediscovery" in the early 2000s in the context of the WHO Neglected Tropical Diseases initiative.

Although his familial lineage is relatively prestigious, and was established in Ayos several generations ago, Daniel Ze Bekolo was the first in his family to work in the health sector. His father, who worked as a builder on the hospital site, became a successful planter and trader, but did not go to school, nor become a *Jamotain* nurse. Consequently, Ze Bekolo has only one picture of his father: his ID card.

Jamot monument in Yaoundé, c.1960

Jamotains nurses, c.1950. From left to right: Amba Mbida Thomas, Emmanuel Bekala, Mveng Afana Moïse, Samba Luc

Eugène Jamot (1879–1937) was a colonial hero reinvented as Cameroon's first national hero. He has several homonyms in Ayos.

The *Jamotains* are a group of nurses commemorated for their participation in Dr Jamot's sleeping sickness campaign of the 1920–1930s. Many of them became nurses at the hospital in the second part of the 20th century and settled in Ayos. Their prestige, and the fact that several of them had marginal origins, whether geographically or socially, reveals the exceptional social mobility enabled by their engagement with the colonial health profession. Today, their descendants, such as Didier Messanga and David Mveng Akamba, play an important role in commemorations, drawing from extraordinary private archives and photographic collections.

Valentin Angoni (born 1973) works in Yaoundé as a driver at the *Institut de Recherche pour le Développement* (IRD), formerly known as the French Office for Colonial (and later Overseas) Scientific Research. He has been driving and arranging logistics for French and Cameroonian researchers for 15 years, all around Cameroon, in Central African Republic, and Congo. He has familiarity with research fieldwork in epidemiology, biology, geology, history and anthropology. He speaks several Beti languages, enabling mutual understanding with Yebekolo spoken in Ayos.

This is our first group visit to Ayos – well, Joseph and I have already been here briefly in 2005, but the proper fieldwork only begins now. And it begins with disappointment and melancholy. We were supposed to study a ruined colonial hospital, a green hill of old buildings and centennial trees. We have been funded on that idea: "an ethnography of medical ruins."

And as soon as we park the car we discover that everything is gone.

No more ruins, no more trees: the whole site of the hospital has been entirely "rehabilitated" by the African Development Bank, a Qatar-based financial institution. Simply put, the old buildings have been destroyed and replaced by a brand new, empty hospital. It's a figurative and literal eyesore, because of the reflection of the sun on the aluminium roofs and the new paint. I had been warned repeatedly, the week before, as I was making phone calls to organise the visit, that "nothing was left." The building boom that is transforming Yaoundé has arrived in Ayos, with its new architecture of cheap concrete and shining tiles.

Bricks

As we begin to walk around the hospital, with Daniel Ze Bekolo and two other hospital staff as our guides, I feel lost, estranged. I loved the site in 2005, and I had wanted to be back to spend more time in what was then an enchanting place – cool, quiet, spectacular. I don't even recognise it.

"I am destabilised," I tell them. "You cannot tell where you are!" They laugh. John [Manton], who is seeing the place now for the first time, watches the rest of us sharing our memories. We point at walls, at gravel, at empty spaces, at tree trunks. I tell them about the hundreds of pictures I took in 2005, suddenly precious – testimonies of something gone, which I can exchange with them.

New hospital, 2012

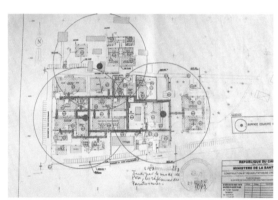

New hospital, site plan, 2007

Old hospital, 2005

End of the visit. We drive back from Ayos to Yaoundé. We chat about the destruction of the hospital with Valentin. Seems like a terrible waste. Why have they destroyed a site that attracted visitors (and historians like us)? And replaced it with a new hospital which seemed empty and not even functional?

Valentin says the right question is what happened to the bricks and steel sheets of the old buildings. "If you ask the students there, 'Where did the workers put the bricks?', they will tell you, 'They were loaded on trucks' – for big men in Yaoundé. Those bricks are worth a lot of money. And the walls were very thick. These are good bricks. When we are back in Ayos, I will go and ask the students, 'Where are the bricks?' I will ask them; I will say, 'I want them back!'" We laugh. "Destroying to 'share' the bricks," says Valentin. "*Tchip.*"

Guillaume's notes, Emini, 13 March 2012

This is becoming the running gag. Valentin is pursuing his own inquiry.

Everywhere we go in Ayos, we look for, and we find, the bricks – stockpiled in private homes and backyards.

In our rooms, on stupidly hot days and nights, we long for the old buildings with their big thick walls. They remained cool always, all year long.

Back in Yaoundé, we laugh at some Ministerial private palaces, with red brick walls. Here are the bricks!

Guillaume's notes, 25 March 2012

Guillaume It's been a massive investment, hasn't it?

Kombang Ekodogo Two billion CFA francs.

Ze Bekolo [pointing at trees and bushes]: Everywhere here, this is the land belonging to the hospital. We could have built anywhere. And leave what was there.

Kombang [We should have done] like where you live back home [in Europe]: "There is the old town, and the new town." We should have left the old hospital next to it. Instead...

Guillaume ... instead of breaking...

Kombang Exactly.

Hospital bursar [newly arrived in Ayos] But [surely] you had time to debate, before this was broken?

Ze Bekolo [loudly]: Not *before!* It almost caused a riot... People told us "We will build a hospital." And one morning, we arrive and we see people on the roofs [of the old building], stealing [steel sheets]...

"What are you doing?"

"We're building!"

"And as you build, you steal?!"

When they began to work on the roof of *Trypanosomés* [the oldest, German building of the hospital], I said, "Stop it, this is not normal." [...] I said, "How?? How can you break that?"

"We have been told to do it."

I said, "No!"

Joseph Owona Ntsama They did it badly *[les gens ont mal fait]*. People with a lot of money are always like that.

Guillaume [to Ze Bekolo, alluding to the fact that Ze Bekolo had been threatened by the authorities]: And so you were told to calm down?

Ze Bekolo I was "told" that I was stirring up the population. I am not stirring up the population...

Transcript of the recording of our walk around the rehabilitated hospital, 13 March 2012

Top to bottom: views of Ayos Hospital football pitch and buildings, 2012

Map of disappeared buildings and trees. Guillaume's notes, 2012

Nama Jean Bosco, 2012

This hospital, it used to be oil palm trees. When we had nothing to eat… We came to collect the palm nuts, which we broke. We oiled our feet, to be clean when we entered the primary school. Everything is gone. Why are those trees snatched? Whom did they bother? How?

Excerpt from the comments of Didier Messanga, son of Jamotain nurse Akamba Mveng Pierre, at the final workshop, 11 March 2013

Jean Bosco We, the common people, we have memories but we cannot respond, we cannot say anything. We notice and we put up with it. But inside it hurts!

Guillaume What was it that really attached you to the old hospital?

Jean Bosco First, Jamot was so intelligent that he built the hospital in a very beautiful manner! You know, we went there, it was a touristic place! There were patients of course, but one could go to take a walk... There was a road along the hospital, there were palm trees. And it was a place – I would say a holiday resort – one could wander over. […] I remember that at that time, when a sick person arrived at the hospital, from the way he was greeted he began to recover: as soon as he saw the hospital, health came naturally. The place was really appropriate for health. And hold on, this is not the case today. It is two different worlds, Mr Owona! Even if the buildings are new. *Tchip!* It doesn't bring that feeling it used to bring in the past.

Guillaume One was able to take a walk there, with one's family?

Jean Bosco Of course! One was able to take a walk there, it was so beautiful! I can tell you that on Sundays after Mass, even if you had none of your relatives at the hospital, you would go to the hospital for a walk… Everything was so tidy.

Transcript of interview with Nama Jean Bosco, son a of Jamotain nurse, 24 March 2012

Zero sum game (from Wikipedia)
In game theory and economic theory, a zero-sum game is a mathematical representation of a situation in which a participant's gain (or loss) of utility is exactly balanced by the losses (or gains) of the utility of the other participant(s).

Bricks remaining, Ayos Hospital, 2012

Mortuary of the new hospital, 2012

The new hospital is false

Jean Bosco And what hurts even more is that… Look, go and take a tour of that new hospital. You will see that some walls are already cracking.

Valentin I saw that. Where we sleep, up there.

Jean Bosco Big buildings that lasted for hundreds of years are broken, to build buildings that break in less than ten years! Why have we taken such a decision? My brothers, I tell you I don't know! *Tchip*. It hurts. I really wanted to tell you that.

Valentin Even the cupboards in the rooms… they are cracking already; there is wood powder coming out of them… They did that with false wood. They only put paint over it to cover.

Transcript of interview with Jean Bosco, 24 March 2012

View of the new buildings, 2012

Blaise I was working, I was doing the security for the post offices in Douala, when I heard on the radio that people were building in Ayos. I resigned, I said, "I am going to guard the things of my home place!" I started to work here in 2005. Until everything was built. I was the only security officer. It was over more than 200 workers who were here!

Guillaume Where did they come from?

Blaise They came from Douala, Nkongsamba, Akonolinga. Everywhere in Cameroon; From the east… without forgetting the native Ayos guys.

Guillaume The workers came from everywhere. But we have been told a lot about the breakages, that it has shocked people here.

Blaise The breakages?

Guillaume The breakages of the old buildings.

Blaise Oh yes, the breakages, it was "crazy"! Because in a way, the local people were against that. Things were broken everywhere here, there, up there. Even the dispensary was supposed to be broken, this is when the local people rebelled…

Guillaume And the materials of the old hospital, like the steel sheets and all that….

Blaise The materials from the old houses were taken by the District chief doctor. Or perhaps they put it in warehouses? But today, I don't believe if you search you will find anything. You won't find anything. It just disappeared by itself. But at that time I was not able to control – I was controlling the worksite and not the warehouses. It was state property. But I could see how it "leaked"…

Guillaume Did they break it up with pickaxes or bulldozers?

Blaise With the "Mac"… [miming a jackhammer]

Valentin With much care! To retrieve the bricks!

Blaise People directly took their bricks. You saw it, this morning when we were in that house: there was a pile of bricks there. People took a lot of bricks, a lot. The hospital staff, people from the neighbourhood, they

came, they took them away. I was not stopping them: as long as you are strong enough to carry, you take! Even the steel sheets, which were the so-called property of the state. It disappeared in no time. Was it during the night or during the day? I don't know.

Interview with Blaise Bekala, security officer on the 2005 building works, 10 March 2013

One night at the bar along the road in Ayos. We discuss Jamot and the hospital with a young man. We learn about the opposition of the townspeople to the destruction of the hospital. He alludes to witchcraft. "We opposed ourselves to the machines. The machines were going to have to go over us. […] One day a truck which was taking sand from the Nyong River for the buildings got stuck there. We said: 'You need to buy a beef,' to make it work again."

I ask, "What do you mean?"

"I am not into these kinds of things," he replies, not wanting to say more.

Valentin says it was some sort of mystical action against the truck.

Guillaume's notes, 23 March 2012

Tchip (to kiss teeth)

Tchippage, or kissing teeth, is a linguistic practice common in sub-Saharan Africa, the Carribeans, and among people linked to African, Afro-american, and Carribean communities in Europe and the United States. A *tchip* is a suction sound made with the mouth. Although it is semantically and technically highly variable, it generally expresses negative affects, such as strong disapproval, scorn, annoyance, disagreement, impatience.

Bricks make sense of the magic of the influx of capital that characterises the global health era, by connecting it to the political economy of an auto-cannibalistic state. They materialise the contrast between a past time of durability and efficiency and a new state of illusions, where buildings are crumbling before they are even inaugurated. The value of bricks makes sense of the apparent absurdity of spending so much for nothing, to build a useless and empty hospital. "Destroying for nothing" recurred in our conversations in Ayos. Destroying for bricks made more sense. Bricks were manifesting a (nostalgic) attachment to meaning.

Guillaume's notes, 2015

Roofs of the new buildings, 2012

What's the use of doing that? All this destruction? Everywhere you see these new would-be buildings that are useless, whose ceilings are crumbling all by themselves, while the hospital has not even been inaugurated. There used to be buildings with walls thick like *that*. They could have been preserved. It's not the space to build that was lacking, if one really has money to waste. [...]

We are natives, from here. It was a pride for me to stand where my father used to do injections. *Tchip*. But everything was broken, to build what you see here. What does this mean? Where is the medical equipment? When is the inauguration, ten years after the end of the building works? Why destroy everything, when the entire land down to the river Nyong is state property? It could have been built there, if one really had to spend money at all costs. Money that our children will have to reimburse, by the way. [...]

I can spend a year without going to the hospital. Because each time I go, I cry.

We did not need that. The old buildings that remain can be rehabilitated... It costs less. Really, you have to go and tell them in Yaoundé that it is our legacy... You are going to write history books, but our children will not be able to see anything, if everything is taken away. The earth blocks [bricks] that were taken away from the broken buildings, it is the local elites who got them back, to build their own houses.

We don't need these buildings which are of no use. Because everything that has been built, I can tell you that in 20 years... they won't last. Go see the ceilings that are already crumbling by themselves; they are made of plywood, of microscopic thickness.

So help us to tell to the people in Yaoundé that we want this memory to be kept. [...]

Those who will come after us in 2050, they should be able to find vestiges of the past. But we are destroying them. And without a reason. This is our current disgrace in Ayos.

Try to tell them.

Extract from the comments of Didier Messanga at the final workshop in Ayos, 11 March 2013

Pile of bricks in Ayos, quartier Château, 2015

Daniel Ze Bekolo Here it is: the garage.

Guillaume Oh! There was an old car when we were here in 2005. I took pictures of it. An old Citroën. There was an old car.

Ze Bekolo They removed it. It was with these old cars that we transported food for the patients.

Guillaume It was a museum piece.

Transcript of the recording of our walk around the rehabilitated hospital, 13 March 2012

Hospital garage and kitchens, 2012

Citröen truck, 2005

Guillaume So how did it work for the food?

Ze Bekolo In the times of the French, the hospital had a truck. The truck would go to the villages around and buy some bunches of plantains and bananas, and bring them back to the hospital. The patients were fed. Because the market in Ayos was not enough. Ayos hospital, that was something in those days! Pregnant women were there for one month! Even people from Ayos would come to the hospital to get some free food.

This is over now. It ended in the 70s, when I entered school.

Discussion at lunch with Ze Bekolo, Guillaume's notes, 8 March 2013

Present absences

Guillaume Can you explain to us how it worked, this old building of the pharmacy?

Désiré It was the state that bought the drugs: this was the system of the pharmacy, at the time of President Ahidjo [1960–82], the late President Ahidjo. It was only in the very serious cases that the sick were prescribed drugs that they had to buy themselves in a pharmacy. In most cases, the sick received everything here at the hospital pharmacy.

The system has changed. At the moment it is the opposite. Any sick person who arrives has to pay for the consultation first. He disburses something for the consultation. And on top of that he has to pay for the drugs.

Guillaume And tell me about the windows?

Désiré There used to be two windows. On the left was written *"Infirmiers"* ["Nurses"]. We, the majors, we would come every Monday morning, with the forms, everybody would order the quantity he needed in his ward. You pick up the drugs, you go, you arrange the drugs in the closets, and every morning you give each patient their treatment. The hospital also helped to feed the patients. There was a kitchen. It's not the case anymore.

Interview with Désiré Tipané, head nurse, Ayos Urban Health Centre, 28 March 2013

Akamba In the times of the *Jamotains*, it was free. The sick were cared for for free. The doctor prescribed, there was the pharmacy just across the lawn – the building is still there. And he just walked to get the drugs.

Guillaume This is why there were the windows?

Akamba Exactly! […] And I insist on *free* care. Because it *was* free; there were a lot of patients. At the time you could not say, "Beuh, I am not going to the hospital."

Guillaume And now the problem with the lack of patients is that it is not free?

Ze Bekolo The transition has been brutal, this transition at the hospital, from free treatment to payment – and what payments!

I remember an anecdote. When I was a little boy, we went to the hospital and we were given pills. I swallowed mine. But the mum of the boy next to me threw his pills away. She said her son was very ill and deserved an injection. [All laugh] I remember that an old nurse saw the women. Near the stairs, down there [pointing]. He called the woman, he said: "Madam, the pills you are throwing away today, there will be a day when you will have to buy them with money." This I *cannot* forget. I remember that day. You see that the transition has produced a sort of break.

Akamba A break. There at the hospital they ask you for money but you don't receive anything.

Interview with David Mveng Akamba and Ze Bekolo, 21 March 2013

Third and fourth image from the top:
Pharmacy with two dispensing windows, 2005, 2012

Fith and sixth image from the top:
Dispensary, 2012 and 2005

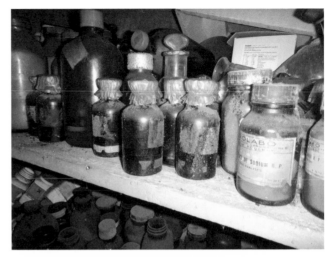

These old drugs are kept in the "Jamot dispensary," one of the few colonial
buildings preserved after the rehabilitation of the hospital.
They are regularly shown to visitors as remnants of the Jamot era.
All pictures, 2012

Joseph Owona Ntsama, Guillaume Lachenal and Jean Meno (left to right), entrance of the Ayos medical complex, 2005

Joseph Owona Ntsama and Guillaume Lachenal, entrance of the Ayos medical complex, 2012. Jean Meno was a nurse trained in Ayos in the late 1940's. He died in a few months before our visit

Details of the paintings, entrance of the Ayos medical complex, 2012

Guillaume Lachenal and Joseph Owona Ntsama, entrance of the Ayos medical complex, 2013

When we arrived somewhere, our guide Daniel
Ze Bekolo would always introduce us the same
way – speaking in Yebekolo so the series of
French names would ring very clearly:

"They came to study the history of medicine
in Cameroon.
But they were told that you cannot do the history
of medicine in
Cameroon without going to Ayos.
And that there is no
Ayos without Jamot.
And that there is no
Jamot without Jamotains.
And that there is no
Jamotains without
[Mbida Thomas / Minyono / Akamba / Kaledje /
Bekala / Samba]…"

GPS tracks from our tour in Ayos, 2012

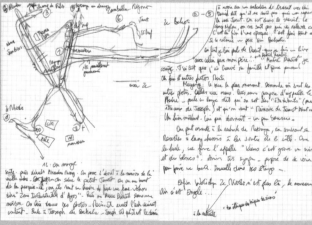

Hand drawn map of a tour in Ayos, 2013

Monument men

Ze Bekolo, guiding the visit to Jamot's swimming pool, 2012

Follow the guide

Once we had explained our project – we were looking for something vague, in between the history of Ayos and the memory of Jamot – our relationship with our guide Daniel Ze Bekolo became rather passive: he would sit in the front of the car, with the driver Valentin, the three of us packed in the back, and he would lead us to wherever he thought was important. He made a mental list of the people and places we had to see. The list, which we discovered gradually as we met the people, seemed quite straightforward – there was something habitual in our tour, which had clearly been done before. Just a year previously, a French TV crew had visited Ayos and followed a very similar path.

Sometimes, when people in Ayos talked to each other about us, they said, with the most unenthusiastic "business as usual" voice, "They came here for the memory of Jamot and all that…" (*"la mémoire de Jamot, tout ça…"*).

We sighed a lot during this fieldwork, impatient with our own incapacity to explain what we were interested in. And impatient with the obvious fact that we were following in the footsteps of many other "tourists" before us. Our fieldwork transformed itself. It became a permanent, shared, sometimes impatient, reflection on *how* we were guided: what maps, protocols, and social norms informed our touristic visit?

First days in Ayos

20 March 2012

Arrival in Ayos at noon. Meeting with the director of the hospital. We leave our luggage in the hospital in the "VIP" wards.

Interview in Akoun with Amba Mbida Benjamin (born 1934), son of Mbida Abada Thomas (1909–1971) and grandson of Akamba Mveng Pierre (1906–1996), two of the first *Jamotains*.

Interview in Ayos with Zangbwalla Minyono Gervais (born 1944), son of *Jamotain* nurse Minyono Mathieu-Ferdinand (1909–1968).

21 March 2012

First morning. Interview in Ebabodo with Mveng Akamba David (born 1939), son of *Jamotain* nurse Akamba Mveng Pierre (1906–1996), first Cameroonian *Jamotain*.

22–23 March 2012

Interviews with the staff of the hospital and nursing school.

24 March 2012

Interview in Ebabodo (Ayos) with Jean-Bosco Nama (born 1949), retired civil servant, son of *Jamotain* nurse Mveng Afana Moïse.

Visit and interviews in Camp Nylon (Ayos) with the grandsons of Bekala Jacques, *Jamotain* nurse.

25 March 2012

Sunday. Mass. Dinner at Ze Bekolo's house.

26 March 2012

Visit to the "Case Jamot."

Visit and conversation in Ayos with Markus Ondoa Kaledje, grandson of Karl Kaledje (c.1870–1970), *Jamotain* from Togo.

Interview in Emini (12km from Ayos) with Meyanga Samba and Samba Michel, sons of Jamotain nurse Luc Samba (c.1905–1992).

Excerpts from Guillaume's notes, 20–26 March 2012

Luc Samba, with a patient. c.1950

Jacques Bekala, c.1950

from top to bottom:
House of nurse Amba Mbida Thomas, 2012

Balcony, house of nurse Jacques Bekala, Camp Nylon, 2013

Portraits of Pierre Akamba, 2012

The pattern

As we followed our guide from house to house, from Mbida Thomas to Minyono to Akamba to Bekala to Kaledje to Samba, from *Jamotain* to *Jamotain*, we noticed other regularities, in addition to having to listen to the same story of Jamot, formatted by decades of commemoration and guided visits. There was the beauty of the houses, all of them among the most impressive in the town, a shared pattern in the concrete balcony that circled their verandas – the mark of a forgotten builder of the late colonial period, and an almost distinctive "*jamotain*" architectural style. And there were the pictures, the diplomas, the souvenirs on the walls.

All the families had collections of pictures relating to their *Jamotain* father or grandfather: beautiful official portraits of a young nurse wearing the colonial health service uniform. All the families had also hung on the walls framed diplomas and work medal certificates of their *Jamotain* elder. Frequently also, the official portrait of the first Cameroonian president Ahmadou Ahidjo was among the collection, as well as, of course, a picture of Jamot. Pictures, some of them very large, were exhibited to us swiftly; once more it gave us the impression that our interaction was of a habitual variety; only the younger members of the families seemed really curious to look at photos (and at us).

Daniel Ze Bekolo, during our visit to the Akamba family, 2012

Jamot and the six Jamotains.
Photomontage by Luc Léon Samba, c.1995

The photomontage

One series of pictures struck us as different: it was a set of enlarged portraits, apparently made from photocopies (although certain families had the original picture in their collection). They resembled proper exhibition panels. Joseph and I actually saw them in the Mayor's office when we visited the site in 2005. Among the panels, one was a photomontage. It was presented as the most precious and the most useful document for us. Blaise Bekala, the grandson of *Jamotain* Jacques Bekala, called it a "monument," without irony.

The "monument" was simple: at the centre, a picture of Jamot. And the pictures of six *Jamotains* making a circle around him. For each picture, the complete name and date of birth. We saw it, in versions of different sizes, in three different families. It was shown to us with pride; it helped, as a memorandum, those who told us the story of their father. Thanks to the "monument," it was possible to be precise about Jamot's date of birth and death, about the list of the *Jamotains*: it was possible to be a proper historian. For us it was a clear trace of a local commemorative initiative, with its remains now dispersed through the town – but who made it, and when?

Our tour in Ayos actually consisted in making the full circle on the photomontage: each picture of a *Jamotain* led us to a house, to a family, to a collection of pictures and documents, to a recorded interview with a version of Jamot's biography and a set of more intimate, filial, memories. In one week only, we had ticked the six. The monument was our map.

Jamotains

The photomontage illustrates who the *Jamotains* were. In a circular process, it distils from a tangled history a group of six nurses who constitute the *Jamotains,* whose status as *Jamotains* is proved by their presence on the montage.

The term *"Jamotains"* is loosely defined: there is no evidence that it was used at the time of Jamot. It is a historiographical and commemorative category; according to Cameroonian historian Wang Sonné, the term was first used in a commemoration organised by the Cameroonian government (and in subsequent journal articles) in 1979. For the historian, the "monument" is quite clearly a mystification: if the term ""*Jamotain*" designates the generation of Cameroonian health workers who worked during the heroic years of the Mission Jamot against sleeping sickness, then there are dozens, if not hundreds, of *Jamotains* to be displayed on the montage.

The making of this collective of six *Jamotains* followed another logic, which referred to the memory of a specific moment in the medical history of Ayos: the independence years, the 1960–70s, a time of plenty, when the whole hospital was run by a handful of prestigious nurses. They were successful planters and family men, at a time when cocoa prices were high. They were the elites of the new Cameroon.

Through the *Jamotains,* what is commemorated is thus not a mythical instant of colonial encounter, nor the traces of a great man; the memorial rather points to another, later moment of "emergence," the emergence of Ayos as a modern town in an independent Cameroon.

We pass by the grave of Karl Kaledje, for the third or fourth time today. I ask Ze Bekolo how many descendants of *Jamotains* are there in Ayos? He says: "a lot." "The *Jamotains* were the first to have emerged. So they had a social status and everybody wanted their friendship. Here when you want to be friend, you give your daughter for marriage, so that the *Jamotains* were greatly polygamous. Perhaps 15–20 per cent of the city of Ayos is related to them."

At lunch we discuss with John, moving between French and English. He says "'*Jamot*' is not a doctor. It is the name of a political process, of a moment of social mobility and class differentiation."

Conversation with Ze Bekolo, Guillaume's notes, 21 March 2012

Cosmopolitan Ayos

The photomontage is a who's who of Ayos. The birth and rise of Ayos as a "hospital-city" is a consensual narrative. There is less talk about the logical consequence of this history: the fact that Ayos can be considered a *cosmopolitan* place. Ayos is a microcosm of Cameroon and Africa, where old, respectable, families come from "elsewhere:" one *Jamotain* on the montage, Karl Kaledje, was born in Togo, thousands of kilometres away from where he married and settled, in Ayos. "The names remain," we were told by members of his family: West Africans patronyms – Kaledje, Koffi, Kwakou – are now common in the town.

Questions of land tenure and belonging are tense issues in Ayos, as elsewhere in Africa; they translate directly into economic issues in a region dominated since the 1930s by cocoa, and hit with dramatic severity since the late 1980s by economic crisis, currency devaluation, structural adjustment and the cocoa price collapse. In this context, the photomontage also produces a consensual history of the locality. Remembering Jamot and the *Jamotains* is not only a nostalgic distraction or a strategic attempt at capturing tourist/ethnographer rents: it functions locally as a largely approved way of discussing ethnicity, class, land tenure, individual status and collective progress. It serves as a common ground in the otherwise tense and fragmented social space of a semi-rural African locality in the aftermath of economic crisis and transformation.

Detail from the grave of Charles Kaledje, Ayos, 2012

This is what we found and how we found it: the story of a document, a photomontage, which we regularly encountered in Ayos until we understood that it served as the guide, memorandum and local map of our touristic visit. The photomontage authored and orchestrated our Ayos encounter.

Valentin Angoni (left) and Markus Ondoua Kaledje (right) in 2013

The photomontage as map in Ayos, 2013

We arrive in Emini, 12km from Ayos, at the house of Luc Samba, built for him in the 1950s by a French engineer. The building is beautiful. The two sons, Meyanga and Michel Samba, open the living room especially for us. It is a room for receptions, with beautiful modernist wood furniture. On the walls the usual portraits of Jamot and Luc Samba, the diplomas, the "Etoile Noire du Bénin" medal. There is the photomontage too, but a colour version of it. It is the "original:" the pictures of Jamot and the Jamotains have been delicately cut and pasted on the white background, some transfers lifting with age. The photomontage has a signature at the bottom: "Conception et Réalisation: Luc Léon Samba."

Next to it, there is another portrait, of a young man, with "Afro" haircut. Luc Léon Samba was the grandson of Luc Samba. He was a journalist, working in Douala, and composed the montage as "research" (recherche) on Jamot and the Jamotains. He is not here anymore to tell us why he did it and why he chose those six figures. He died prematurely soon after finishing this work, which now has a life of its own, of which this chapter is part. The photomontage in Emini is also (and perhaps firstly) a way to remember and mourn its author, a brilliant young man gone too soon, buried next to the grave of his Jamotain grandfather.

Guillaume's notes, Emini, 26 March 2012

The grave of Jamotain nurse
Luc Samba, Emini, 2012

Luc Léon Samba (right)
the author of the photomontage

Meyanga and Michel Samba in their father's house, Emini, 2012

Owona Atemengue Joseph (dark jacket) and his colleague Esseyi Laurent in Ayos, 1937

My father was in Ayos from 1937 to 1941.

Without clear reasons, I have long resisted the act of memorial writing, an act full of burdens from which I have taken refuge through self-censorship. To conjure someone who was my father from out of a fog, from such convulsive emanations, from fragile and fragmented recollections, to even piece together his long trajectory via Ayos to Paris is an intellectual challenge, but moreso a human and existential one. It forces me through this pile of eclectic, disjointed documents, to think in terms other than alterity and rationality, to attempt something other than organizing them into the frame of life history, claiming objectivity.

Joseph Owona Ntsama, 2015

Joseph Owona (1916–1971)

Anyways, for such a task there is not much: a few old photographs at different ages, students cards and diplomas; some vinyl records, a few books, his graduating thesis and scattered administrative references. Also, sounds; the music he listened to so attentively in Paris, the ambulance taking him off into the night…

Any document can be a starting point, but what it can yield, analytically, will depend on an intrinsic complicity with the "box of documents" and the sometimes palpable human shadows that preside over it, like secular guardian angels. As paradoxical as it might seem, it is with a sense of delight and jubilation that I throw myself into this task of deciphering documents that, for the most part, I was not part of the making of, not even as a passive witness. That is not where my difficulties end. There is no one who might explain anything at all who is still around: no men or women, no classmates from Ayos or Dakar, no close relatives, no nurse or doctor colleagues, no fellow soldiers. So I am getting ready for a strange conversation beyond the grave with a father who now "speaks" to me only through photos and written records.

Inhaling wisps of the past

And so it is a strange moment of communion between two souls: that of my father, transfixed in the unnamable trauma of death, and mine, in a constant but disordered motion of searching for something, I am not sure what… something alive and human; trying, relentlessly, to pin down an exasperated sigh, a malicious wink, the tempo of a breath… This is how I desperately "hunt down" my father's life, by inhaling the wisps and vapours striking off a surviving archive, an iconography, those bits of the surface of a life, refracted as a Manichean inheritance, polarised in the trials and tribulations of one orphaned at a young age. Iconographies become petrified in the time of the Eternal, of the departed who haunt our daily efforts to remember, always inflected by our desire for a story that makes sense. It's strange: I was not an abandoned child and yet I have to reconstruct my father's life, in the absence of family archives, by stumbling on the emptiness he left behind, by holding onto symbols and relics like these old records on the backs of which I find, in his handwriting, a note of the date and place of its purchase.

A life story without a testament

Joseph Owona or Joseph Owona Atemengue (some old documents include his second surname) did not leave a will, not even a few words jotted down or dictated, absolutely no written trace of any last wishes. Nothing. Absolutely nothing.

Joseph Owona was born on 18 August 1916 in Mefou-Assi (some documents give the name of the neighbourhood of "Mvog-Ada"), near Yaoundé (on the old Kribi road). He was the second of five children, four boys and a girl. His father Luc Fouda (Lukas Owona), second son of Fouda N'Kana, was of the great family of Tsungui Mballa and the clan of Mvog Ada. His mother, Suzanne Ngaoudi, belonged to the clan of Mvog Amugu, from Nkongoa in a place called Afap Akoung ("owl's wing"). Both parents were of the Bëti (Ewondo) ethnic group.

Family portrait. Left, Joseph Owona

1936

Owona Joseph (posted in Batouri) is candidate to the rank of third-class nurse on 1 January 1936, and is promoted on 20 January 1936.

Journal Officiel du Cameroun, 1 February 1936, issue 378, p.15.

1939

Graduated Infirmier Breveté

Diplôme N°3 du 2 septembre 1939, signé du Commissaire de la République Française.

1940

Owona Joseph, fourth-class nurse and third-year student at the Centre d'Instruction d'Ayos is named third-class adjunct health assistant, and posted at the filter-station of Yaoundé.

Decree of 12 Septembre 1940, Journal Officiel du Cameroun, 1 January 1941, p.31.

1942

Graduated Aide de Santé

Diplôme N°3/3 du 6 janvier 1942, signé du Directeur du Service de Santé.

1945

Graduated Médecin Africain, at Dakar (1945) alongside Marcel Bebey Eyidi, first biographer of Dr Eugene Jamot.

1959

"The first-class African Doctor of the second rank Owona, Joseph, currently occupying the post of Head Doctor of the Messa dispensary, is transferred to the authority of the Departmental Director of Public Health of Dja and Lobo to serve as Adjunct Doctor or the Sangmélima Hospital as well as Chief Medical Officer of the Urban District. Mister Owona will take up his new position after giving over his responsi-bilities to the African Doctor Malagal André. Signed on 27 November 1959 at Yaoundé by Charles Okala."

Decision n.1106 MSP/P. Article 3, File Vt 1/69, Cameroon National Archives, Yaoundé:

Graduation Certificate, *Ecole Supérieure de Yaoundé*, 1937

1960

Joseph Owona receives a third-class medal of merit as "African Doctor."

Decree n.2/PR/CHAN of 30 May 1960.

1970

Joseph Owona defends his graduating thesis, titled "Contribution to the treatment of genital haemorrhaging using a synthetic haemostatic agent," on 19 March 1970, supervised by Professor Jacques Grasset, chief of the obstetrics at the Maternité Siredey (Hôpital de la Pitié).

"Doctor of Medicine," File n. 2088 L, Faculty of Medicine of Paris

According to Ze Bekolo (25/03/2012), a *Jamotain* is anyone who worked with Dr Jamot. Yet many people worked with Jamot without being granted the honor of the *Jamotain* label; his grandfather, for example. Note that the *Jamotain* where not recruited from the traditional elite "bourgeoisie," that is, the nobility; they were, sociologically, the commoners who were allowed to work with Whites, unlike sons of chiefs who were barred by their social standing. For example, Mveng Afana Moïse, who, unlike most of the early *Jamotains*, was a pure native of the area and member of the great Yebekolo family, could not, like his predecessors, be called a *Jamotain*. It's amazing what this neologism stirs up; in the course of our fieldwork we meet all kinds of adventurers who, by any means possible, lay claim to some kind of "filiation" with Jamot.

Joseph's notes, 25 March 2012

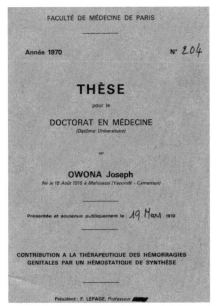

Cover page, Joseph Owona's 1970 Doctoral thesis, *Faculté de Medicine de Paris*

Nursing Assistant Certificate, Ayos, 1941

Diplomas

Joseph Owona grew up in the city of Douala, to which his parents had moved. He obtained his primary school leaving certificate from the *Ecole Régionale de Douala* on 1 August 1933. This allowed him to sit the 1934 entrance examination for the renowned *Ecole Supérieure de Yaoundé*, the institution that produced a native colonial elite to work under the French in the civil service. He came first. This granted him a territorial scholarship from the French state, and entry, alongside the next highest-placed students, to the school's health section. This exclusivity, but also surely their "magical" task of saving lives, gave a particular mystique to health students,

especially as they went on to study at the *Centre d'Instruction Médicale d'Ayos* and graduate with the title of *aide de santé*/"health assistant." An elite among administrative personnel, health assistants were reputed to be particularly attractive to the young black and métisse women of the Child Education Centre, or *"Cité enfantine,"* whose oft-cited and unequivocal marriage dictum purportedly ran: « *A défaut du Blanc, l'aide-santé* » !/ "If not a white man, then a health assistant!" Joseph Owona came first in his class for all three years of his studies at the École Supérieure, allowing him to keep his state scholarship.

I had the chance to meet with Ndakoa Mveng Thérèse (NDAKOA Thérèse on her identity card), the last widow of Mveng Afana Moïse (1909–1961), in her village of Ebabodo. Mveng Afana Moïse was a nurse in the disease control service and worked with Doctor Genet. When he died, he was posted at the pharmacy of the Ayos Hospital, where he "was in charge of the mixtures" (in the words of his son Nama Jean Bosco). She tells me my father was one of the nurses who embalmed him. And so it was a very emotional moment for me to shake her hand. I am not a doctor but for her, and even for her children... it's as if! Maybe they believe I will take my father's role when she, who is now very old, dies. This is rather strange and makes me feel uncomfortable.

Memory, apparently, carries great weight! And it is so hot right now! Jean-Bosco adopts us (he and I connect). Is my father tracing a path for us in this MEREAF project via this family that has survived the premature death of its head? What more can I do besides what I already know I must? I ask myself this. Guillaume is alert; John takes photographs; memory takes a step forward.

Joseph's notes, March 2013

Visit to Ndakoa Mveng Thérèse, 2012 (sitting with John Manton, top, and Joseph Owona Ntsama, bottom)

Student and registration cards for Joseph Owona in Paris, 1963 to 1965

Joseph Owona (1916–71)

As post-scriptum?

The cold rigidity of administrative records and these few faint traces, that's all there is. Hardly anything in the family archives, pillaged; photos of his thesis defence and his diploma of medicine disappeared, strangely, after his death. That is why I was so moved, so illuminated, by the widow of the *Jamotain* Mveng Afana Moïse. This old lady knew my father when he wore a nurse's smock. I never saw this, never saw him in a clinic in Cameroon, only ever in formal three-piece suits in France. I am sure I would not even recognize him in a photo from that time. Who knows what beautiful and sad stories of health-care in colonial times he might have told me, especially about those historical landmarks of Ayos, Dakar and Paris? "Ayos-Dakar-Paris," like a royal road that only a few brave native nurses dared to take, to become, even late in their careers, "Doctors of Medicine!"

I will always remember that terrible dance the Bantu dedicate only to great warriors, the *Esani*, danced with rage on the day of his burial, while for me, a "little Parisian," it was as if the drum rhythms of mourning, the *nkul ebanenda*, were refracted, in a strange musical alchemy, through the sounds of the well-known melody of Johann Sebastian Bach that my father loved so much: Violin Concerto N°2 in E Major, BWV 1042: Allegro.

Joseph Owona passed away on 3 March 1971 at the Hôpital Central de Yaoundé. He was only fifty-five years old.

Joseph Owona serves as first-class Corporal Army Nurse under the orders of the Doctor-Commander Garcin alongside: Laurent Esseyi, Bekala Jacques, Babatoura Abdoulaye, Etali Mathias, Messi Biakolo Etienne, Ekobena Abe Paul et Mbida Edjoa Gustave.

Service note n.4725, 6 September 1939, Cameroon National Archives, Yaoundé

The War. What Prévert called the "stupidity." I imagine my father lending his voice to the pathetic "Song of the partisans," standing to attention behind Commander Garcin. I also remember that record we listened to in Paris: "French Military Marches," on its B-side there were the tracks *"Le Régiment de Sambre et Meuse"* and *"Marche de la 2è D.B. ."* He had traced two crosses on that side, the sign he used to mark his favourites, as on other pieces of music he left behind.

Joseph's notes, March 2013

David Mveng Akamba

"We are used to these visits," David Mveng Akamba says politely when we first meet him. In our first two days in Ayos, we have gotten to know the couple of locals who act as quasi-official guides to any group of historians, medical researchers or photographers doing the Jamot tour. David and his little brother, Didier Messanga, are among them. They are sons of Akamba Pierre (1906–1996), a *Jamotain*.

March 21st, 2013

We are neither the first nor the last team to be welcomed to the family house. One of the largest in the town at the time, and still a superb U-shaped colonial-style house with large rooms, high ceilings, and verandas, it manifests the high profile of its builder. Pierre Akamba, *Jamotain*, was one of the key staff members in the local hospital in the 1950–1960s, and a successful cocoa and coffee *planteur*. He has had ten wives, 47 children and countless grandchildren – a recent Facebook page "the grandchildren of Pierre Akamba" estimates the figure at 195; it is almost hard to find someone in Ayos who is not related to Nurse Akamba.

As we begin the interview, David Akamba displays large framed pictures of his father, beautiful portraits of the young man wearing the colonial Health Service uniform, as well as souvenirs left some years ago by French visitors.

Views of our visit to David Akamba, 2012

When will independence end?

"Guten Morgen… You get out of here!" The younger brother of David, Didier Messanga, enters the room as we look at the pictures, voice recorders on the table and cameras ready. He is arriving directly from his fish ponds, wearing big plastic boots. "What are you doing here, is this an *exhibition?* Why on earth would they need to see these pictures?" The mood changes. David is embarrassed. "They are historians," he tries to explain. We are all looking down on our notes. "Wait, in Europe when one goes to a museum, he pays. Here what have you paid? These pictures are legendary!" Didier Messanga is loud and irritated.

Things get calmer after a few jokes. Soon we are talking about Paris and about his experience in France and Germany. General agreement is reached when it comes to lamenting the laziness of the French in comparison with the Germans. Although David, as the oldest brother alive, is the usual interlocutor for Jamot-driven visitors, the younger brother Messanga too has interacted with many foreign visitors in Ayos. But his record has more bitter notes than David's, a list of failed promises and lost contacts.

Messanga is locally known for his outspokenness, his work ethos and his experience abroad. He is nicknamed "the German" – a densely significant reference in the Cameroonian context, where the comparison with Germany has been used to provoke the French for more than 100 years now, and even more in Ayos, where the whole French commemorative industry is based on the active forgetting of the German doctors who first created the hospital, 15 years before Jamot.

We *know* we are not the first to meet the Akamba brothers – and we already know the faces of the two brothers. A month before our visit, on the

evening of 3 January 2012, the French-German TV channel Arte broadcasted the documentary "Médecins de brousse" ("Bush doctors") directed by Sylvia Radelli and François Caillat. The film combined old archival footage from French colonial propaganda, and interviews with French historians and medical doctors with a long experience of Africa (most of them fondly remembering the golden age of colonial medicine). The film crew had also travelled to Ayos, and shot beautiful images of the Ayos hospital. The film was not well reviewed: it was poorly plotted, and left reviewers impatient with its complacent use of colonial erotico-racist iconography. Even the most ardent fans of Jamot found it boring. Perhaps because I was annoyed that the ruins of Ayos had already attracted the attention of well-funded film-makers, I managed to download a cracked copy of the film, burned a few DVDs and took them down to Ayos.

The Akambas were interviewed the year before by the film-makers. Messanga knows the film had been shown on Arte – "everybody called me from Europe to tell me they saw me on TV." When I tell the two brothers that I have the DVD in my computer, they say they would like to see it. The film crew, who stayed only for a day, filming as much as it could, left with the promise to send back the film once it aired; but three months after the première, nobody in Ayos had heard any news from the film-makers.

Didier Messanga (top right) and David Akamba (bottom). Screengrabs from the film *Médecins de brousse* (2011)

Casimir Zengue Akamba

We are back with the DVD in hand. The Akamba sons form an entire neighbourhood in Mengana, two kilometres away from the city centre. Several sons of Pierre Akamba have had successful careers: while David was a relatively modest *fonctionnaire* (clerk) in the Cameroonian administration, some of his brothers studied or worked in Europe, and were able to build impressive houses around the father's.

Didier is not around, and David is at the house of another of his brothers, Casimir Zengue Akamba. The house, or rather the complex of houses, of Casimir is impressive by any standards. It is built on a promontory overlooking the Nyong plain, which is several kilometres wide at this point, with the kind of views which the colonial doctors loved so much in Ayos. The grass is neatly cut, the garden gently sloping down to the Nyong. It looks so nice that Valentin, the driver, has to ask if we may park on it. Casimir and David are sitting in a strange hexagonal building, a garden house with an inspiring architecture, mosaic on the walls, and a rooftop terrace; an ideal site for celebrations and barbecues.

We interrupt Casimir and David as they are watching a Premier League Football Game on satellite TV. We have no power and no running water where we are staying, at the hospital a few kilometres away, so a working flat-screen TV really looks like luxury. Casimir offers his own laptop to watch the DVD. He is in Ayos to relax for the weekend. He now works as an IT consultant, after a long career as an engineer at the National Electricity Company (SONEL). As the film starts

– with 1930s colonial music and images – Casimir asks: "What is the purpose? I mean: who ordered that film?" I insist that the film-makers are *not* my friends. "It only serves to justify colonialism," Casimir says, before going back to watch Wigan-Liverpool.

David is more interested, but rapidly asks if we could fast forward. "Let's forward… rather than listening to this big White here," he says while the screen shows a retired French doctor who talks of his passion for the "forgotten heroes" of colonialism. The experience is becoming annoying – to them, and to me, having already watched the film and being generally fed up with these eulogies of colonial medicine. "Ah, those white people, they only look for images of Africans with big bellies," comments David after a long series of shots of undernourished, terminally ill patients with sleeping sickness, taken from a 1930 film of Ayos. Fortunately, the moment arrives when David and Didier are interviewed – smiles on our faces as we watch David talking nicely in front of ruined colonial houses, explaining to the camera how great Ayos was "at the time of the whites;" and how destroyed it is now, with the traces of the old hospital almost completely erased. That moment past, we cut off the sound and let the now definitely boring film run in the background as we talk.

Casimir, the younger brother, teases David: "So you like colonialism, don't you?" Casimir is not enjoying the film at all; "this is all propaganda." He tells us about his experience as a Cameroonian student in 1970s France. He was brilliant in maths and science, which led him to enter the prestigious Classes Préparatoires of the Lycée Carnot in Dijon and then the highly selective Ecole Centrale de Lille. He remembers racism. He is shocked by the recent "colonial revisionism" (his words) in France, and the infamous law, passed under the Jacques Chirac presidency,

Views of our visit to David Akamba, 2012

about "the positive effects of colonialism." The benign memories of his elder brother about the white doctors in Ayos seem very naïve to him.

But David insists: there is such a contrast between the neat colonial buildings of the old hospital, and the "new" ones which have replaced them as part of the recent "rehabilitation" of the old hospital. Made of cheap materials, these are already degraded at the very moment they are finished. "It hurts to see that." In the film his brother Didier ("the German") is even more vocal: what happened recently to the hospital is a "total waste." What is gone was not only a useful infrastructure, but also something more intimate: their prestigious father's former workplace.

Joseph Owona Ntsama at Casimir Zengue Akamba's house, Mengana, 2012

Full time

"My father would always ask: 'When will Independence end?'" remembers David, as we are leaving. The nurse Pierre Akamba was a "tough man," whose word was his bond; brave and lucid enough, according to his son David, to denounce corruption and indiscipline, to tell newly independent Cameroonians that they were wasting a precious legacy. He was very critical of post-Independence politics.

"When will Independence end?:" I am not sure who is the original author of that sagacious joke; it is actually a classic punchline all through

Africa, where it has served to mock many authoritarian postcolonial authorities. But it captures well what David and Didier articulated in the film, and indeed what the Cameroonian commemorative initiatives about Jamot are all about. What it expresses is not so much a nostalgia for colonialism – the melancholic evocations that the French doctors and film-makers seem so pleased to find in Ayos. The old nurse Pierre Akamba was not only expressing his disappoint-ment at the failed promises of nationalism (and by contrast, the retrospectively desirable aspects of colonial tutelage). His apparently naïve question is richer – there is something of a proverbial wisdom in it: in only four words, it bends, crosses and distorts time and temporalities. It turns an historical event, "Independence," into a historical period, as if the moment had eternalised itself – like a DVD on pause. It expresses an impatient desire to see time restart.

That afternoon, as we watch a never-ending film that seems stuck in colonial time, in a superb house that makes tangible the trajectory of progress once embodied by the *Jamotains* as colonial auxiliaries, successful family men and nation-builders, David Akamba remembers this impatience.

The sun sets and the football game ends. Wigan wins against Liverpool, 2–1. A goal was denied to the infamous Luis Suarez, who was booked for a handball offense. And this is perhaps how Casimir will remember the afternoon.

Wigan-Liverpool FC – 24 March 2012 – 53rd minute screen grab from amateur Youtube video

"AYOS! AYOS! Area of misery and deaths, but also refuge and promise of life. How many of these poor, poor, human beings will have I seen? They are so pitiable with their skeletons underneath their thin and ash-grey skin; with their two eyes, alternatively firing diabolically or completely dull. AYOS! […]

Ah! I will not forget anytime soon the 'walk of the cadavers' which I saw during my first afternoon there. Sick people, already moribund, are lying in the sun, heating up. Time to go back to the huts. Slowly they are being put on their feet. Jerky moves. And here they are, almost all them, standing. Hands forward, like blind men, beating the void, […] skeletons who still have their skin and their eyes, they advance… advance. They reach you, hold out a hand which you shake, with such an emotion! They softly say 'Afternoon' ['*bezour*'], and pass by.

AYOS! Land of misery, realm of death, but also centre of the regeneration of lives."

Claude Legaiac, "Ayos," *Togo-Cameroun* (Paris), January 1930

Death and dust in Ayos

Looking for the graves of the few Europeans buried in Ayos was a classic attraction on our tours. They were easy to find, especially the monumental one of Dr Lagarde, who was buried on top of the hospital hill during World War Two. They elicited easy stories, and for us, easy pictures. What happened to the thousands of bodies of the patients of the sleeping sickness camp who died there was not mentioned to us spontaneously. We had to ask.

Grave of French military doctor Lagarde, Ayos, 2012

"Where are the graves?"

Joseph Owona Ntsama All those people who died...

Akamba In such huge numbers!

Joseph Do you have an idea of where they were buried? Is there a cemetery for the sick people of Jamot? Does that exist?

Akamba Oh yes! But it is now the forest! It is there at the brickyard [*briquetterie*]. It was at the brickyard where people extracted the bricks for Jamot's buildings. There was a field called Bandanglan.

Daniel Ze Bekolo Bandanglan! I don't know what it means.

Akamba What does it mean...? We just heard this name. You would die at the hospital, without a family, you would be taken there. At the time of the sleeping sickness, there were so many dead people. *En masse.* They had to bury quick quick. It was there, opposite the post office, down near the swamps. [...] It is now inhabited, people live there.

Ze Bekolo The only graves which have been respected are made of bricks, these are the graves of the whites. These are the only one who were respected, because they were...

Guillaume But how do you know that?

Akamba Because we are from here. Strangers don't know that. They see the houses, they cannot tell that there was once a cemetery. [...] Our primary school was down there at the crossroad. So the dead people coming down from the hospital, we would see how they were carried. [Laughs] When there was sleeping sickness it was every day. It has decimated populations. At the time of sleeping sickness, every day people passed by with one or two cadavers.

Interview with David Mveng Akamba, 21 March 2012

Quizzed about the location of the mass graves, people had no hesitations. There were two sites where bodies were buried. One was the "cemetery" in the colonial plans of the site, now along the asphalted road to East Cameroon. It serves as quarry to extract laterite (used to make roads). The story goes that one day a bulldozer opened up a mass grave. "It wasn't pretty," we were told. The other one, just across the small ravine, was called Bandanglan. It is mentioned in the 1950s French topographic maps as the "*Léproserie*." It is an obvious mistake, since the leprosy camp had always been (and is still) located on the other side of the hospital (to the south-west), in the lowland area bordering the Nyong. Ze Bekolo has no explanation of this mistake. Before Bandanglan served as a graveyard, it was the first brickyard, where the small red bricks of the colonial buildings were made from the red earth.

Guillaume's notes, 21 March 2012

"We are walking on graves"

Ze Bekolo Everywhere here, if we do excavations, we will find graves everywhere. I say everywhere here, because it was hundreds, hundreds. [...]

Guillaume And so these graves had no names?

Ze Bekolo No, they had no names. Nothing nothing nothing.

Joseph Without a cross.

Guillaume No funeral?

Ze Bekolo No funeral. You take a family of five, six, seven or eight people. Five get sick. One is brought to Ayos; he dies; then the other one is brought... If, for example, the mother or the father is gone first, then the children are helpless. When people from Bafia [a major focus of sleeping sickness, several hundred kilometres away from Ayos] were brought at this time, this was no easy job to bring them from Bafia. There was no vehicle. All traffic was through the river. My father had been a sailor – I don't know how to call that. "Sailor.".. I don't know.

Guillaume "*Piroguier*" [canoeist]? Or...?

Ze Bekolo He worked with the French. He would do the transport, Abong Mbang, Mbalmayo [place names], with dug-out canoes, to carry merchandise, before the roads.

Guillaume So when people were brought here, they were disconnected from their families?

Ze Bekolo Totally. So when someone died, what happened was... as we say now, "the common." It was the workers of the hospital who would bring the corpse, and they came to bury here. Dad told us... I haven't seen it. Mum would tell us a macabre story, where the people were so overwhelmed by the number of corpses that they were not able to dig sufficiently. They only made a small hole, maybe 40cm – even 40 is a lot. Thirty or thirty-five centimetres. Then they covered them with earth.

Guillaume It must have smelled…

Ze Bekolo The earth... Or is it... People say that something came. I don't know what came. It must have been animals, scavengers, and when people came one or two days later to bury someone else, they found... That was really disgusting. That wasn't nice at all. This is not good. Here.

If you see someone building [a house] here nowadays, it must be a stranger. An autochtonous [a native from Ayos] building here, this is not... [possible]. Me, I cannot build here. It is so anchored... Even if you do deep excavations here, don't be surprised if you end up with something in your hands. Here, around here: this is Bandanglan.

Guillaume "Bandanglan," what does it mean?

Ze Bekolo I don't know. How do the German say "cemetery"? This is not a Beti word. It's a foreign word that was transformed. This word has no meaning here. Me, I found this word when I was born.

Sound recording of our visit to Bandanglan, 22 March 2012

Quarry along the main road, 2013

Ze Bekolo knew Ayos and its many toponyms very well, but he had no clue how the site was named thus. *Bandanglan* means nothing in the local languages. "How do the German say 'cemetery'?:" back in France, I followed his ingenious advice. I googled frantically: *beerdigen*, "to bury," seems a very likely candidate. I wonder if Ze Bekolo knew it from the beginning.

Beerdigen
International Phonetical Alphabet:
[bəˈʔeːɐ̯dɪɡŋ̩]

Bandanglan
International Phonetical Alphabet:
[bã̀dã̀glã̀]

Carnage and commemoration

As we walked and talked about graves, it became clear to us that there was one point on which the colonial propaganda was not exaggerating: the scale of the carnage that sleeping sickness caused in the 1920–1930s, which is present in all oral histories of the region. *Carnage*: an old lady kept using this French word in Ayos, as she told us in Yebekolo about the history of sleeping sickness. The commemoration of Jamot follows the same structure: Jamot saved Cameroon from death; those who celebrate him are survivors; Jamot's premature death in 1937 was a sacrifice for the life of Africa. A corollary remains unspeakable: that the segregation of infected people in Ayos (and the containment of death itself by the camp infrastructure) was actually the key to the life of others and to the "survival" of Cameroon; that Ayos, for this reason, was at the same time a "vast cemetery" in itself. For the patients, the internment in Ayos then meant months, sometimes years, of seclusion and of uncertain medical treatments, and an anonymous death sometimes hundreds of kilometres away from home. The colonial doctors insisted their fate would have been worse in their villages, where, they said, the sick were expelled to live in small huts in the forest. In Ayos they had free drugs and free food.

Unknown grave, Ayos, 2013

"What do we owe Jamot?

You natives of Cameroon, you owe him your very existence. Without Jamot, Cameroon would be a vast cemetery, the regions of Abong Mbang, Akonolinga, would be desert, and the spreading disease would bring death to the furthest regions, which thanks to him have been preserved from it. Jamot is first and foremost the saviour of the black race in Cameroon. It is a reason [...] for you to associate his name with your parents', since you owe him life just as much as them."

Doctor-in-chief of Ayos, in a speech given to the nurses gathered in the amphitheatre on 5 June 1937, the day the news of Jamot's death arrived in Ayos

"This ceremony aims to celebrate the memory of our father, Doctor Jamot. This construction is a 'monument', which means that it will serve to transmit to our posterity the memories of the good deeds of Doctor Jamot for the black people of Cameroon."

Speech by writer-interpreter André Nkoumou at inauguration of the Monument to Dr Jamot in Ayos, 1937

"It was at the moment when we were falling into death that Jamot came. Ah! Sirs, if you had known the renaissance that followed the passage of Jamot and his teams; if you had seen children smiling and playing again; if you had felt confidence and hope coming back in our hearts; then you would know what Jamot means for us. If the region of the Upper Nyong is alive [...] we owe it to him. None of us must forget. It is a duty for Cameroon to make him one of its heroes and elective sons."

Speech by Jean Mabaya, Deputy at the Assembly of Cameroon, during the inauguration of the Monument to Dr Jamot in Yaoundé, 1959

Monument to Jamot (1937) in Ayos, 2012

On our way to Abong-Mbang [further east from Ayos, where I am conducting research for another project] I pass through Ayos with Valentin. We stop by to say hello at the hospital. A superb pharmacy has newly opened along the road, the "Pharmacie Jamot." There are some big public works going on near the hospital. The bulldozers and caterpillars are working on the road, adding new laterite earth to it. It is noisy and there is red dust everywhere. Their source of laterite is in the neighbouring quarry – the first Ayos mass grave.

As we drive around, we remember our discussions with the locals about Bandanglan, and we joke about it in the car. On his own initiative, Valentin stops the car near a worker and calls him. He makes up a whole story (I admire his ability to lie in such detail). He explains to the worker that he once was the driver of an Italian archaeologist (I don't know why he picked "Italian") who is interested in skulls and bones. Valentin says the Italian told him that the quarry of Ayos was a good source for skeletons, because of the many people who died in Ayos of sleeping sickness. The quarry made it convenient for an archaeologist. "So," says Valentin, "what I am saying is… where you take the earth, there are graves. This isn't good, is it?"

The worker is silent at first. Finally, he says he now understands why the whole work is going so badly – there have been problems with broken-down engines, and the weather has been so weird (it is still raining in mid-December, which has been unknown for decades); the public works have had weeks of delay. "This is all making sense suddenly," *"Maintenant je comprends ce qu'il s'est passé sur ce chantier."* A disturbed past has manifested itself.

I looked elsewhere during the whole conversation, as if I was not interested in Valentin's Italian experience. It was funny. Valentin was cunning, and a great liar, which is such a crucial

competency in Cameroon. It was disturbing also, for the worker and the two of us, to see the red dust now all over the neighbourhood. A floating reminder of a history of sickness and death, colouring and staining everything.

As we leave Ayos, we imagine, half joking, what would happen if we really were some Italian archaeologists interested in bones and skulls. We laugh, imagining the endless problems we would have with the local *gendarmes*, the impossible clearances we would have to negotiate, the things we would be accused of – for good reason. The idea of digging for bones is a

macabre, extreme, impossible version of our very research, which we like to present as an archaeology of colonial medicine. Our clumsy jokes are our way also to deal with the unsaid, the unspoken in the history of Ayos: the substrate of illness, disfigured bodies and death that lies beneath the glorious history of the hospital. Just like the monuments for medical heroes which mushroomed in the remains of the camp of Ayos, the cult of Jamot and the *Jamotains* conceals, is parasitic on, and inverts this history of sickness.

Guillaume's notes, 12 December 2013

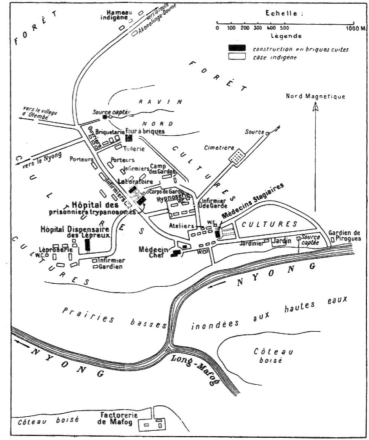

Map of the sleeping sickness camp of Ayos, 1921

Amani Hill Research Station

Edited by P. Wenzel Geissler
with René Gerrets, Ann H. Kelly, Peter Mangesho

5° 4' 60" S, 38° 40' 0" E

Elevation: 400–1100m

Location: Tanzania. East Usambara Mountains.

Former names: Amani Research Centre, East African Institute of Malaria and Vector-Borne Diseases, Agricultural Research Station at Amani, *Biologisch-Landwirtschaftliches Institut Amani* (Amani Biological-Agricultural Institute).

Current status: Subsidiary research station of the Tanzanian National Institute for Medical Research (NIMR), under the Amani Research Centre which now has its headquarters in Muheza in the nearby lowlands.

Origin of the name: "Amani" is "peace" in Kiswahili, the local *lingua franca*; the name was given by German missionaries who started the outpost as a retreat from the tropical climate. According to local legend, the first German settler, who was a woman, built her house on a nearby mountain which, on account of its rocky outcrops, was a preferred abode of ancestral spirits. After her house had been repeatedly and inexplicably destroyed by strong winds, she made her home on a lower ridge where she, eventually, found "peace." Another local story has it that the hilltop was originally inhabited by a local clan, which was paid 12 rupees by the Germans to vacate the site, and which was moved little by little to the valley below as the station expanded. In 2015, this clan — intermarried with descendants of immigrant staff of the research station — was defending its land rights against the research institute, on whose land they technically reside.

Chronology

1902

Amani Biologisch-Landwirtschaftliches Institut established by German colonial authorities. Director Zimmerman assembles an arboretum representing the entire German Empire, modelled upon older Dutch and British botanical gardens. Justified as a contribution to the productivity of the colony of Tanganyika.

1919–1920

After WW1, German East Africa is transferred to the British and named Tanganyika. Amani becomes the Amani Agricultural Research Station. German buildings, labels on trees, place names, and first names remain. Strategic cultivation of *Cinchona* trees is planned (their bark is used to produce quinine to treat malaria)

1949

The East African Malaria Unit (EAMU), established one year earlier in Muheza in the adjacent lowlands by Capt Dr Bagster-Wilson, seeks permission to move into the underused agricultural station. EAMU will contribute to public health agenda under the British Colonial Welfare and Development Scheme. Re-building of African staff quarters, now deemed essential for a modern colonial institution.

1951

EAMU moves from lowlands to Amani. Entomologist Mick Gillies arrives. Botanical gardens continue to be maintained. Institute cattle herd established. Eradication of malaria in Africa is the Institute's wider aim.

1954

EAMU becomes Institute of Malaria and Vector-Borne Diseases, and includes onchocerciasis among its disease foci. Experimental work. Field trials with new insecticides.

1961

Tanganyika independent. Internationalism. Tanzania's "*Uhuru* (Freedom) Torch" passes through Amani on symbolic tour and a monument is erected in Market Street, in Amani's former African staff settlement. Beginning of intense trade union activities.

1963

First article published with an African technician as a co-author. The "Africanisation" of qualified and scientific staff positions is discussed.

1964

Tanganjika reborn as Tanzania following union with Zanzibar islands.

1966

Amani's last British director, who leaves after a *fracas* with Tanzanian officials, is replaced by a Dutch director, Jan Lelijveld, possibly responding to Tanzanian opposition to British leadership. Emergence of new racial, gender and class relations, perceived as contrast to older British, "colonial" ones.

1967

Arusha Declaration – Tanzania's government embraces African socialism. Establishment of East African Community, under which Amani and other leading East African research institutions fell.

1971

Leljiveld ends his term as director. The first African director, Philip Wegesa, takes over the station at Amani. Continuation of existing lines of research; some attempts at plant-focused research.

1974–5

Plague research established under Dr Bukhari Kilonzo.

1976

Last resident British scientist, John Raybould, departs. Reduction of direct overseas funding for research at Amani. Transition towards individual research grants.

1977

Dissolution of East African Community. Some Kenyans and Ugandan staff have to leave Amani. Research activities continue.

1979

Amani becomes a Research Centre of Tanzania's new National Institute for Medical Research (NIMR) – to be funded through overseas collaborations.

1999

Amani celebrates its 50-year anniversary, with numerous overseas participants.

2009

Headquarters of Amani Research Centre moved from Amani Hill to Ubwari in Muheza in the lowlands.Centre consists of sites at Ubwari (Headquarters) Amani Hill, Gonja and Same. Most scientific staff are are now based in lowland sites. Core technical staff remain.

2015

34 staff members remain on payroll; 13 of these are "watchmen", most near retirement. No resident scientists; the official station director resides in the lowlands. Discussions about possible uses of Amani for research, higher education, tourism, or as conference centre. Former and current staff members privately engage in agriculture and tourism.

Amani: dream capsule suspended on a mountain

"It is my intention first to show you, by means of the lantern, the general appearance of the station and of the beautiful district in which it is situated. Unfortunately I have very few illustrations of our investigations. [...] We are, perhaps, unique among research stations in the extent to which we are self-contained. We erect and maintain our own buildings, make roads, construct our own furniture, provide our own electric, gas and water supplies, and run our own transport. For a time I even had the luxury of a private gaol, until a temporary prisoner discovered the weakness of its walls. We are provided with a post and telegraph office, a telephone exchange and a dispensary, but unfortunately no doctor."

Opening speech of the director, Amani Research Station to Royal African Society, 1933, in W. Nowell, The agricultural research station at Amani, *Journal of the Royal Society of Arts*, 1933, 81(4224):1097-115.

Driving up the winding road to Amani Hill Research Station in 2015, the rainforest suddenly gives way to the green lawns of tropical, yet unmistakably British, parkland. Within the clearing stand three flagpoles, a Tanzanian flag hanging from one of them, in front of the administration office, laboratory blocks and workshops, and a guest house, open but silent and empty, dilapidated but not derelict. Hedges are sporadically trimmed and gardens modestly tended; the sheets in an unused clinical examination room are laundered weekly; a Post Office worker keeps opening hours, yet few letters arrive or are sent; a man in a lab coat nurtures a burgeoning colony of white mice established by a scientist who left decades ago. The laboratories, each dedicated to a major "tropical disease" – plague, malaria, onchocerciasis – have their own, elderly attendants, polishing instruments and dusting specimens which are slowly disintegrating in their jars. A

Lane from "Lion Hill" along "Middle Ridge," overlooking overgrown pasture, 2014

maintenance officer presides over impressive but empty stores, enforcing procurement protocols and attendant paperwork; a permanently absent director posts rigid leave procedures on administrative displays.

Founded in the late 19th century by German colonial occupiers, Amani looks back at a long history of scientific experimentation and innovation, a bridgehead for advancement in forestry, zoology, chemistry and biomedicine. Amani's methods, findings and personnel have, at various points, been central to progressive imperial and post-colonial scientific endeavours. However, at 3,000 feet above sea level, surrounded by forest, the station's foundations as a remote sanatorium for exhausted Wilhelminian German officers, a tropical *Zauberberg*, persists in its later instantiations as hub of global scientific circulations. Under British direction, Amani's seclusion was amplified by its self-sufficiency: its independent hydroelectric dam and generator, power and water grid supplied the houses of all staff, and a hundred-head dairy herd provided subsidised milk and meat to staff. Racially segregated social clubs, and tennis and football competitions, ensured the socially-coherent running of the station as a world apart from the surrounding forest and from the teeming "tropics" of the African valleys below.

Poised on the surrounding hilltops is a group of spacious colonial bungalows, interspersed with large trees and hedge-flanked alleys, planted upon lawns of green grass – imported from Kenya, whence it brought its name, *Kikuyu* grass. On the terraced slopes and valleys below extends a more densely built-up settlement, which in colonial times was the African staff quarters – a world apart from the hilltops, yet connected to the same water and power supplies, comprised by one vision of segregated colonial welfare.

Amani's landscape is an assemblage of incongruous references to distant homelands and national idylls – Constable's England, Bavarian mountain huts, metropolitan academic buildings, modernist garden cities, and secluded scientific communities. The values and promises of home are ceaselessly projected onto the station itself – apparitions that remain forever out of reach. The metonymic capacities of this space to recall homes and reach out to the wider world reverberate through its scientific mission.

> "The year's work has also shown how suitable as a whole is the combination of a headquarters at Amani at 3,000 feet, with the field station in the Muheza foothills at 600 feet, and the intervening highly malarious low country, for the investigation and teaching of the facts about malaria and its control. While Amani provides surroundings in which it is possible to carry out laboratory work of precision and to do a prolonged day's work without undue fatigue to the European, the lower ground gives, for much of the year, a constantly recurring cycle of the interactions of the human and the mosquito phases of the malaria cycle."
>
> (Donald Bagster-Wilson, East African Malaria Unit, Amani, *Digest of the Annual Reports for 1952 of the Medical Research Organisations*, Nairobi, p.20)

In-between its phases of heightened scientific productivity, the station has been repeatedly mothballed – for example, in the immediate aftermath of the First World War, and during the years preceding its revival as malaria research station. The "contemporary" period from the late 1970s onwards, when Amani became part of the newly established Tanzanian National Institute for Medical Research (NIMR), has been also characterised by a gradual winding-down, a closing of projects and departure of personnel. One retired Tanzanian researcher compared this process to the onset of paralysis. Many of those who worked in Amani during its postcolonial heyday have memories of the station's views, its "beautiful" and orderly grounds, and well-appointed facilities, and recall a time of exceptional plenty and privilege. Yet, to those Tanzanians who arrived from the 1980s onwards, the cold wet climate, the isolated location disconnected from local circulations, and the absence of social, educational and economic opportunities, exacerbated by sharply declining funding, posed considerable drawbacks. Few African scientists posted here stayed for long, and many quickly moved their residence down into their primary field sites in the hot, malarious lowlands, inverting the British laboratory scientists' escape from climate, pathogens and local entanglements of half a century earlier.

Those who could not leave – owing to their subordinate position, or because they were born into local relations with people and land – sought to continue their regular rhythms of everyday life, between 8am and 5pm, and between the scientific station and what locally is referred to as Amani "camp" – the term used for the planned settlements built for the colonial railway and plantation workers. Some acknowledge the beauty of a landscape which reverberates with memories of a modern future that quickly receded from view, and a sense of indeterminate waiting – as lawns turn into bush, power supplies and water pipes break down, and work slowly comes to a standstill.

In 2015, many of the station's over 100 residential houses are empty – either abandoned, or held by staff who nominally serve at the station but reside elsewhere. The majority of those still living in institutional housing work in positions that do not allow them to move – as watchmen, gardeners or laboratory attendants – or have retired from such positions, still preparing to leave or waiting for pension arrangements. The longing to leave, and the preference for the hotter and more lively coastal towns, is a sentiment widely shared by these last Amani dwellers. Among these weary, waiting workers, one rarely finds the ambiguous permutations of *Heimweh* and nostalgia that saturate Amani for those who have long since left the place: "this place is dead," those who remain plainly put it.

The station's decline was both sudden and slow, depending on who you are speaking to: the colonials who took advantage of generous pensions immediately following Independence, or the African scientists who sought to resituate the station within the ambitious priorities of the emerging Tanzanian nation. But what resonates across all accounts of those who worked "on the hill" during the 1950s and '60s is Amani's evocative power as an aesthetic and affective project, where multiple, diverse, and often conflicting visions of homeland and history are at play. The disjuncture between the station as a place and as an idea is the station's persistent feature: as one of its former British inhabitants succinctly put it: "Amani will never be Amani."

Amani's salience as a dreamscape inheres in the perpetual postponement of its promise – it never quite becomes home, it never really changes itself or the world, and eventually one must leave it. That sense of curtailment and displacement is not reducible to colonialism's phantom limb. As Lisa Wegesa, the mother-in-law of the station's first African Director, Phillip Wegesa, whose small farm is not far from the station, comments: "Amani was so beautiful but now it is nothing of what it was. It is completely dead."

And yet not quite. Amani's stalled and sedimented temporalities – inscribed in the very layout of its buildings and design of its gardens – are all-too-tantalising. This hyper-textuality is risky: such picturesque remains and ruins, such clear monuments to forgotten futures, the sheer detritus of investigative clutter and epistemic things, can trigger a melancholic desire for authenticity already latent in the anthropological task. The ethnographer's projections upon such terrain are cast into sharp relief – walking along deserted paths between empty offices and laboratories, the bodily experience of fieldwork becomes pageantry of the past.

> "We moved into our bungalow that first evening. Like many other senior staff houses it was perched on top of a narrow ridge. [...] If there had been an international competition for the finest view in the world from a lavatory seat, I would confidently have entered ours. On a few clear days before the rains [...] just as the moon was rising, you could see the Indian Ocean as a narrow sparkling band, dividing the dark mass of the continent from the sky."
>
> (Autobiography of entomologist Mick Gillies, *Mayfly on the Stream of Time*, 2000, p.130)

Amani research station, central laboratory, around 1970

Inventory of all objects in the station, storekeeper's office, 2015

Crab specimens collected by John Raybould and colleagues during an excursion to Kenya, 2014

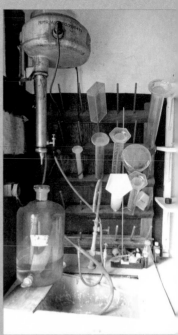

Drying rack, malaria laboratory, 201

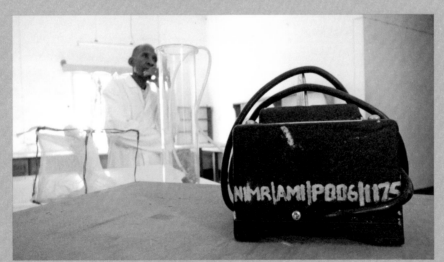

Micro pump used for 1960s fly rearing experiments, 2014

The power station attendant's family with the research station's generator that ceased working in the 1970s, 2015

Private photo album of Professor Frank Mosha;
laboratory images, mid-1970s

top: Row of abandoned staff houses in a "camp" of Amani in the forest, 2014
bottom: Collapsed former tea place in what was the African staff settlement, 2013

The family Borchart, after moving into Amani's *boma* or "Cathedral," 2015

The former shopkeeper of Amani's cooperative,
active until the 1980s, with the signboard of his shop, 2015

Aloys Mkongewa (born 1978), as yet unmarried, rents a house in the former African staff settlement or "camp" of Amani station. After spending his childhood and primary school years in Amani, and having completed secondary school, Aloys has worked since 2000 as a field technician and guide, variously assisting tourists, ornithologists, primatologists, botanists and pharmacologists, historians and ethnographers – being paid by the day. He recently bought land near the research station to set up a campsite business for European guests. Aloys' family history in Amani stretches back three generations, with ties to the station's first director after the Second World War, Donald Bagster-Wilson, who after retiring from active military service became a leading figure in British malaria research. Aloys was our assistant, as he had been for many before us. He knows Amani's people, flora and fauna, as well as the history of buildings and the landscape, and stories of the research station's inhabitants both living and dead. Unlike most people living in Amani's decaying institutional housing, Aloys nurtures some attachment to the place, and unlike most young people, he is bent on staying around.

John Raybould (born 1935) was fascinated by the natural world around him from his childhood in Surrey onwards. After studying biological sciences, he specialised in entomology and arrived in Amani in 1960, planning to study houseflies. He moved onto blackflies, and their ecological interactions with *Onchocerca volvulus*, the parasite which causes river blindness, and with river-breeding crabs, upon which the blackflies' larvae develop. This work was of relevance to the control of a debilitating tropical disease endemic around Amani, and allowed for systematic entomological, taxonomic and ecological investigations which gained Raybould recognition in wider entomological circles. Staying on after Tanzania's independence, he lived in Amani for much of his younger years, developed his research, and founded a family with a like-minded Japanese botanist fortuitously posted to map the flora of the surrounding forest. He left Amani in 1976, to apply his expertise in the West African river blindness control programme. After returning home to Britain at a time of scarce academic employment, he continued to use every occasion to pursue entomological research in Africa, and gained his living through gardening, which he regarded as a congenial continuation of his naturalist interests.

Tony Wilkes (born 1933) – or "Uncle Tony" as some African staff called him – is a British entomologist. Among colleagues, he is still known for his proficiency with a challenging method of age-grading, developed by Soviet scientists and imported to Amani. Wilkes grew up near Potter's Bar, then joined the army and spent time in Hong Kong during the Korean War. He came to Amani in 1958, and began a collaboration and friendship with Mick Gillies that would define his career across Africa. Wilkes' wife Dorothy (born 1933) raised two children in Amani and found a close friend in Agnes Gillies, who taught her how to paint.

Mick Gillies (1920–1999) grew up in London, the son of a renowned plastic surgeon. He attended Winchester and studied at Cambridge, and after medical service in the Far East, and several years as the doctor at the British Embassy in the USSR, he became the senior medical entomologist in Amani, where he worked from 1951 to 1963. Taking his leave from colonial service after Independence, he moved on to Sussex University. For his work on mosquito behaviour he received a number of medals and commendations, but his particular passion was mayflies, a species without medical importance, on which he became the world authority. His wife Agnes had been trained as a surgeon when she travelled with Gillies to Amani, leaving behind a Registrar's position in London. She raised two children in Amani and took up watercolour painting.

Phillip Wegesa (1930s–1982) came to Amani in 1963 as a junior laboratory assistant, having trained in his native Kenya. He worked with several British entomologists, including Gillies, eventually joining Raybould's blackfly laboratory. In early 1964, he was sent to the London School of Hygiene and Tropical Medicine to escort two cases of river blindness that were examined and treated in London. He used the occasion to have his own cataracts removed, and proceeded to obtain a Diploma in Applied Parasitology and Entomology, but did not proceed to do a PhD. Upon his return to Amani he continued to work on blackflies and river blindness. In 1965, Wegesa was the first African member of staff to be promoted to the position of Scientist and eventually Senior Scientist at Amani – designations previously reserved for white "officers." In 1971 he became the institute's first African director. He was forced to leave Tanzania after the breakdown of the East African Community. In Kenya he worked with the newly founded Kenya Medical Research Institute. He died in 1982 after a period of severe mental illness.

Tatjana Sergeevna Detinova (born 1911) stayed in Amani for six weeks in 1962, during a three-month journey on the African continent. Commissioned by the WHO, her brief was to teach a method of mosquito dissection which allowed the accurate determination of a mosquito's age, and could provide clues into the dynamics of malaria transmission and control. A prominent figure in Soviet science, she had developed the method with her collaborators in Moscow in the late 1940s, but because of the restricted circulation of Soviet scientific journals, this work only became more widely known after 1953.

John Mganga (born 1949) worked as a junior staff member at Amani from 1971 to the 1990s. Working as a field assistant, he contributed to research on malaria, river blindness and plague, working with Gillies, Raybould, Wegesa and the lead plague researcher, Dr Bukheti Kilonzo. While most of Mganga's work was focused on the field, he also participated in laboratory work. He is acknowledged in numerous publications authored by the scientists. After his retirement he continues to live with his wife and children in a staff house in Amani's formerly African (or "junior staff") settlement, splitting his time between here and a second home in a nearby lowland farming area.

Stephen Fedha (born 1940) joined "malaria", as it was referred to during the time of the (East African) "Community." After training in Gillies' lab, he worked extensively with Raybould on *simulium* research as a "fly-boy" (as the role was known, until Raybould officially renamed it "assistant"). His dexterity at catching crabs earned him the nickname "Dr Crab." He also worked on fly-rearing experiments carried out by Raybould in the laboratory, and epidemiological surveys performed by Wegesa, as is witnessed by acknowledgements and numerous photographs of field methods in published papers. Even 50 years later, he is particularly knowledgeable about the names and uses of various laboratory tools, and remains, despite a painful hip problem, a skillful collector of insect specimens. He has bought some land in the village next to Amani and retired there, successfully cultivating cloves and cardamom.

"The stairs," Amani's workers settlement, 2013

Wenzel   So what are your plans for the future?

Aloys Mkongewa   Ah, my plans… I like to stay in Amani for professional reasons, but we don't have many visitors here now, so the money is not enough for me to go to school. That's why I still am staying here in Amani and collect many informations about it. Because I believe that Amani will change some time, in the future. So when it changes I hope that I can collect the money and then I would go to school again. So many tourists will be interested to know the history.

So I can stay here in Amani with a profession. I want to stay in Amani for all my life. Only I would get a good job, maybe I could leave, because am suffering here, for finding a good life. But my interest is to stay here in Amani.

Conversation between Wenzel and Aloys Mkongewa, Aloys' house, Amani, 27 September 2013

Aloys, keeper of memories

First dinner

First evening in the Amani guesthouse, built by the Germans before the First World War. Dining room with large fireplace. Hardwood shelves with cheap 1950s novels – *Love in a Cold Climate* – and travelogues of the British isles – *In Search of England* – for the homesick lodger. We (Ann, René and I) sit at one table, several "local" people – staff? researchers? visiting civil servants? – at the other. Jehu, our driver, sits with them. (Awkward reenactment.)

After dinner, a young man from the other table introduces himself as Aloys. A good southern German name still current in these mountains, home to Germany's favourite potted plant, the Usambara Violet. Aloys is a guide and research assistant. He has worked for other researchers before us. Aloys' grandfather had, after working in Amani's botanical gardens, been cook to the director of Amani after the war, who paid school fees for Aloys' father, and whose children did the same for Aloys' older siblings, but then the contact faded. Aloys tried to find Bagster Wilson's grandchildren through Facebook, but got no reply. Yet.

Aloys empties a plastic envelope with photographs onto the table. I recognise a 1940s studio photograph of Bagster-Wilson, the first director of Amani after the war. Pipe, moustache, khaki. Some black and white pictures of young African men, some boys in school. Some faded colour pictures of white families in English living rooms, maybe in the 1980s. Some torn aerogrammes and letters.

Aloys was given these documents by his father, who has Alzheimer's, together with many "histories." He wanted Aloys to take care of these

First evening in Amani guesthouse, John Raybould, Aloys Mkongewa, 2013

images and letters, written to him and his father, Aloys' grandfather, by white women, first the wife and later the daughters of the famous British malaria scientist, Major Bagster-Wilson. "So that history does not get lost," the father had said; and also "to find these people again."

Aloys "likes history." He says he could not live in the village, in the forest outside Amani. He wants to be in Amani, the research station, where he grew up. It is here that he occasionally finds work as a guide. But would it not be more convenient and cheaper in a house outside? Cheaper, yes, but there are no connections – transport, internet. And he grew up in Amani. He likes the place.

Wenzel's notes, Amani, 19 September 2012

Letters and photographs related to the Bagster-Wilson family, which Aloys received from his father, 2013

My father has given me pictures

Aloys My father has given me pictures, do you want to see them?

Wenzel Yes.

Aloys Ok. See this one.

Wenzel Oh, this is Bagster-Wilson?

Aloys Major Bagster-Wilson, the director, yes.

Wenzel So how did your father get this picture?

Aloys The daughter sent it… This is her, the Mama Selina Emmanuel, the daughter of Doctor Bagster-Wilson and this is her husband, and these are the daughters of the daughter…

Wenzel And this was your father?

Aloys My father, yes, this was taken in the [institute] library in 1958. After finishing middle school. And this is my father when he was in school.

Wenzel Ah, this was still at school? He looks a confident man.

Aloys Yes, the picture was very nice. He got a camera from Doctor Bagster-Wilson, for memory.

Wenzel So he took these pictures with his own camera?

Aloys Yes. He got a camera and when he went to school he took his own pictures. He was very famous for that at the time… To use a camera at that time – it was very difficult, I mean… rare.

Conversation between Aloys and Wenzel, Aloys' house, 27 September 2013

Aloys' father as a schoolboy, 1950s

Captain Dr Bagster Wilson, first Director of the Malaria Research Institute; studio photograph, 1940s

Books, pamphlets and certificates bequeathed to Aloys by his father, 2014

Staff group photograph, Amani, late 1960s

That's where their history comes again

Aloys My father was born here in Amani, and got primary education in Amani primary school, built by the United Kingdom, and he passed to go to middle school in 1957, and completed standard [class] eight, but he didn't pass to go to Makerere university, so he just ...

He got big support from the mum [Mrs Bagster-Wilson]. And Doctor Bagster-Wilson found him work in Bombo [Hospital], 1961, after Independence. Later, we came back here to Amani, when I was seven, and then we were educated here and we are working here.

Wenzel How did your father meet Bagster-Wilson?

Aloys My grandfather worked at the coffee plantation, and later at the botanical gardens ... My father told me that... Mr Donald Wilson, he was very kind enough, he loved the people, especially the Africans, that's why when my grandfather could no longer work at Bustani [the botanical gardens], he gave my grandfather work in his big house there... . To feed the chicken and other things... to care about the gardens. The family was very was poor, so Doctor Wilson, as a support he paid for my father's school fees, because my grandfather was old and then there was no support, that's why he tried to help his son.

And later his daughter would help my father like that. She helped my brother like her father did to my father. So we will always remember and then we cannot forget... Even our children we will tell them.

My father... because he was very interested in history, he has given me this photo just to store it, save it, try to protect it. He said: "These people will find you maybe next time." I don't know. That's where their history comes again.

Conversation between Aloys and Wenzel, Aloys' house, 27 September 2013

East Usambara hillscape; from Super 8 by Jan Lelijveld, c.1970

And every morning I walked with my father

Aloys My grandfather was born 1895 and died 1978. He came from the Kilindu tribe. Many chiefs in Usambara mountains are from this tribe. He saw the First World War. He was carrying the burdens of the Germans. The Kariakoo [Carrier Corps]. After the war he was first teacher in a school under the British, and then he joined the [Amani] agricultural department, and worked there for a long time. Because he was educated. The first educated human around here in Amani.

At Amani later he was working to keep the labels on the plants in the gardens... he identified the plants and then he wrote the label and put it on the plant... [When the Germans left] my grandfather still worked there. That's why he had a good house for staff during that time. At that time it was a very... was very good. My grandfather's house was up there.

Later he became old. He was not able to continue with the work, so he went to Doctor Bagster-Wilson and applied for a simple work to keep him. That's when he was caring for the garden and fish pond and everything in the Boma [director's house; lit. "chief's home"].

And Doctor Bagster-Wilson asked my grandfather: "I want to help you for the education of your children, so ask them who is interested to be educated." The other two boys said no, they were not interested [...], but my father said he was ok. That's when he went to middle school.

And even after Doctor Wilson left, when he was in England, he sent money, [...] every month he sent the money. He sent it to our post office, through a money order, every month he received the money order from the Doctor Bagster-Wilson.

Later my father came back to Amani as clinical officer in charge. When I was in school, primary school, at lunch time I came to the clinic and then I went to get some food. Then he gave me money, and then I went to the hotel in Amani to eat lunch.

And every morning I walked with my father, because every morning he came to the dispensary, and I went to school. As we walked around he told me, "You see this, this was a place where there is something, and this and this and this. So you know this one... this was the house of Doctor Fletcher, this was the house of Doctor Raybould and this was the house of Doctor ...." And here it was where Dr John Raybould recovered my aunt's body from the river. And there he pulled up a vehicle from the swamps. And when we were in Amani station, he showed me that "this was the lab of Doctor John Raybould, and this is the lab of me, where I worked..." So [...] he showed me many things about the European time and even about Independence... And as I was walking, I learned the history from my father. First, I was so young I was not interested, but I... [Laughs] I learned the memory.

And sometimes when we were just walking around and he told me that during the European time Amani was a very beautiful place. And he knows very well. After seeing the changes he said that "Ah, nowadays Amani is... I don't know why Amani is going to become old?"

He told many things to me, many things. So that's why until now I am interested to still... to save the memory.

Conversation between Wenzel and Aloys, walking near Amani, 30 September 2013

Amani's dairy cattle; from Super 8 by Jan Lelijveld, c.1970

Tea estate workers settlement near Amani; colour slide by Jan Lelijveld, c.1970

Everything originated from there

Aloys My family was very close with the Europeans, during the European time here, he was working with the Europeans and also they helped him. Even when I was in class one [at school], I was asking my father about the history of our tribe, where we came from; about our family and other things, and from there he started to give me some information. Like the history of Doctor Wilson and our grandfather. Everything originated from there. Then he still remembered, he knew he was losing his memory, because he got a disease. But then he had a good memory... You cannot imagine, he had a good history, because he was educated then... He had many books...I think there are few people like him.

Dinner conversation with Aloys, Amani guest house, 19 September 2013

View towards Derema tea factory; from Super 8 by Jan Lelijveld, c.1970

He had a good history

Aloys wants us to meet his father, who, like the grandfather, had worked at the station. First in the lab, later clinic. The old man has Alzheimer's. As we are waiting for tea, Aloys tries to elicit his father's life story. The father's body turns rigid from concentration. His chest heaves. His gaze fixed on the distant past. He closes his eyes. His stretched hands move impatiently outwards and back in front of his face, as though trying to remove a mist, as he searches for a date. I apologise, feel awkward.

Aloys asks, repeats, listens patiently, and completes the father's sentences, when his frustration becomes too hard to bear. Retelling stories he has heard over and over again.

Occasionally Aloys gives me a look – "You see?" – as if to demonstrate the father's forgetfulness, or maybe to confirm his own secondary memory. Bearer of memories. Confluence of Mnemosyne and Lethe.

Wenzel's notes, 22 September 2012

He does not remember

Aloys He says that he began working with the East African Malaria Community, the Europeans, in 1959, which is true, I told you. [To his father:] When did you work with malaria [in Amani]?

Father [Pauses] I can't remember… [Smiles into the distance.] Doctor Mzangi. I worked with Doctor Mzangi.

Aloys You worked with Doctor Mzangi in 1961, didn't you?

[Long pause; the father's downturned hands gradually curve into a right angle above his knees, the fingertips tightly pressed against the thigh, trembling.]

Aloys He does not remember.

Father East Africa Malaria Community, we did many things; we shared ideas with the white people; we made things better [his hands search for words around his head]. Some of the whites were looking for mosquitoes near the road, some others near the stream. [Silence; chickens pecking.] Enough! I can't remember.

[Pause] I finished Amani primary school which was built by the British. At that time life in Amani was very good.

Aloys Better than now?

Father Yes, because all the places were… they were made beautiful.

Aloys He says nowadays everything is dirty and everywhere there is no good environment, but at that time everywhere was clean and the environment also was clean. And everybody was serious about everything there in Amani. When you work, you work seriously. I mean that, if you are working in the cowshed, you should make sure you work faithfully. When you are working in the garden, because this was Amani botanical garden, you should make sure you are working without cheating, without delay, without being lazy.

Father Yes, today it's really different. Because even the environment was… Even the trees were not cut in areas of the garden, it was forbidden; and the important trees were given names… But now it's all mixed. Even areas that should not have trees, you now find that trees are just there.

Aloys At that time, why do you think people were working seriously, and kept a good environment?

Father Because there were rules. So that, like as a pupil, you cannot cross and go through a white person's house. And when you come from school, there is a specific place where we got fruits, here at the bus down there, and there we ate. So every place was arranged, that students pass here, cows eat here, boreholes for drinking water, places of eating food. So you found that places where people stay were clean, no matter whether it was a white staying there, or people staying there. And there was just grass… But now people get in without… walk anywhere they want.

Aloys and Wenzel attempting to interview Aloys' father at his home in Muheza, 28 September 2013

Aloys attempting to talk with his father about the past; video stills, Wenzel Geissler, 2014

She was a housegirl of Mama Jacky

Ann Jacky Gillies [one of two daughters of entomologist Mick Gillies] said that your – is it your aunt? – looked after her and Susan [her sister] when they lived here.

Aloys Yes, she did but she is dead. She was a housegirl of Mama Jacky Gillies when she was born there, they called her Fatuma.

Ann In the book [Gillies' autobiography] [...] it talks about, maybe Jacky talked about it, how the hill where they lived, where your aunt pulled the pram... it's a very steep hill.

Aloys Yeah, Doctor Gillies, he wrote a book. Mama Jacky Gillies later sent me that book.

Dinner conversation with Aloys, Amani guest house, 19 September 2013

The free and easy life of the tropical home

"By the end of 1957 we were back at Amani. The girls were at an age at which they could enjoy the free and easy life of the tropical home. They spent their days in the care of the nurse, Fatuma, wandering round the grassy slopes of the research station, being taken to visit her friends in the Jr [ie "junior" – African] staff quarters and playing at games that their parents knew little about. One day after Fatuma had gone home, we were out for a walk on the edge of the forest. Aggie [his wife] was in front wheeling Jacky in a pushchair with Susie and me. It was at this moment that the cobra chose to cross the road in front of us and climbed unhurriedly up the bank. I steered the party away to safety distance but Susie who was the least concerned of any of us demanded to know where the snake had gone."

Mick Gillies, *Mayfly on the Stream of Time*, 2003, pp.194–5

Fatuma, Aloys aunt, Mrs Gillies and the children; probably driveway Lion's Hill, from Super 8 by Mick Gillies, late 1950s

Fatuma, Aloys aunt, Mrs Lelijveld and the Lelijveld's children; garden of the *boma*, from Super 8 by Jan Lelijveld, c.1970

"Have the fees *doubled* this year?"

Dear John Barnard,

Thank you for your two letters. I am glad to hear that Victor is doing so very well in school. But how have the fees doubled this year? Last year it was only 50,000. I have written to Dr Gardner and told him that I have sent you 48,000. I couldn't remember exactly how much was needed [though?] he sent me a letter, but that was all the money I had anyway.

We had Sophia and her children, four, five and one-year twins for three [months?]. It was very tiring and I am not as I was! But I love my two oldest grandsons. Nico who is four likes talking so much that if he had been here a little longer, he would have been a fluent Swahili speaker. In April my husband was able to sign an agreement with the cooperative, which was given our estate when it was nationalised…

Letter from Sylvie, daughter of Dr Bagster-Wilson, to John, Aloys' father; no date, early 1970s

Enclosed photograph of Dr Bagster-Wilson's grandchildren, sent to John, Aloys father, no date, probably 1970s

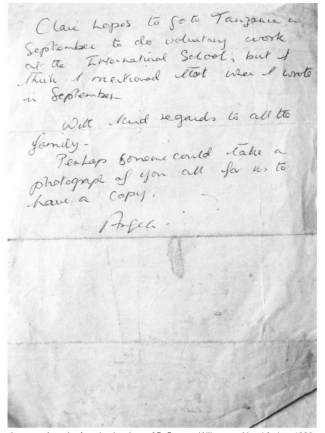

Letter written by Angela, daughter of Dr Bagster-Wilson, to Aloys' father, 1983

Pasture below "Middle Ridge," invaded by *Lantana camara*, 2014

Aloys at a prize-giving ceremony, Amani primary school, wearing the sweater given to him by Angela Bagster-Wilson, probably 1970s

View from the director's house or *Boma* onto "Lion Hill", c.1970

The beauty of lawns

Driving out of the station. Looking into the now-dense undergrowth, Aloys recalls that there had been lawns, covered with *Kikuyu* grass – low growing lawn grass imported from Kenya – interspersed with a few big old trees. To maintain *Kikuyu* grass, other grass species and shooting trees have to be regularly cut. If not attended to, local grass outgrows it. The institute had over 20 casual workers to do this, grasscutters, *"lantana"* – specialists in removing this exotic species – supervised by some permanently employed "hedge-cutters."

Aloys points at the valley, where the once-cultivated lawns had bordered dense rainforest. The boundary has given way to gradual transition. Aloys describes how all open space "within Amani," including the African housing in the "malaria camp," had been covered with lawns. Staff were then forbidden to cultivate bananas and tubers in the spaces between their houses. Aesthetically, African and white spaces where to be coextensive, contrasting to the forest.

Passing the Catholic Church, Aloys remembers how a Sunday tour to Amani, when he was a teenager living in a nearby village, was not something that one "just did;" it had to be well prepared for. "Like when you go to town." One would wear good clothes, clean and tidy, to visit Amani. On Sundays, after the mass, he and his friends would spend the day on the grounds of Amani, well-dressed, sitting or walking on the lawns and looking for strawberries – red succulent berries that still can be found here and there in the undergrowth.

The favourite sweater Aloys would wear on such occasions had been given to him by one of Major Bagster-Wilson's daughters, Angela, for a primary school prize ceremony. He still has the photograph.

Wenzel's notes, Amani, 13 February 2014

Staff assembly on the lawn, c.1970

This appreciation of a stretch of greensward

The lawn unquestionably has an element of sensuous beauty, simply as an object of apperception, and as such no doubt it appeals pretty directly to the eye of nearly all races and all classes; but it is, perhaps, more unquestionably beautiful to the eye of the dolicho-blond than to most other varieties of men. The close-cropped lawn is beautiful in the eyes of a people whose inherited bent it is to readily find pleasure in contemplating a well-preserved pasture or grazing land.

For the aesthetic purpose the lawn is a cow pasture; and in some cases today – where the expensiveness of the attendant circumstances bars out any imputation of thrift – the idyll of the dolicho-blond is rehabilitated in the introduction of a cow into a lawn or private ground. In such cases the cow made use of is commonly of an expensive breed.

The vulgar suggestion of thrift, which is nearly inseparable from the cow, is a standing objection to the decorative use of this animal. So that in all cases, except where luxurious surroundings negate this suggestion, the use of the cow as an object of taste must be avoided. Where the predilection for some grazing animal to fill out the suggestion of the pasture is too strong to be suppressed, the cow's place is often given to some more or less inadequate substitute, such as deer, antelopes, or some such exotic beast. These substitutes, although less beautiful to the pastoral eye of Western man than the cow, are in such cases preferred because of their superior expensiveness or futility, and their consequent repute. They are not vulgarly lucrative either in fact or in suggestion.

Thorstein Veblen, "Pecuniary Canon of Taste," Chapter 6 in *The Theory of the Leisure Class: An Economic Study of Institutions*, 1899, pp.133–5

Emerald green, flowing

Landscape design styles were another very important part of European borrowed baggage that arrived in the colonies. At the end of the 18th century and the beginning of the 19th century the most influential was "Capability" Brown. Lancelot "Capability" Brown edited nature and created an aesthetically perfect landscape. The topography was shaped in the form of a series of gentle convex and concave curves. Trees were planted in groves, groups or belts. An emerald green flowing lawn was one of the essential composition elements. He used only native deciduous trees […] and a few evergreen tree species. Brown's gardens were simply a productive working landscape arranged to be beautiful.

Maria E Ignatieva and Glenn H Stewart, in "Homogeneity of urban biotopes and similarity of landscape design language in former colonial cities," in *Ecology of Cities and Towns: a comparative approach*, edited by Mark J McDonnell, Amy K Hahs, and Jürgen H Breuste, Cambridge University Press, 2009, pp.408–9

Friesian cow, descended from the Institute herd, and senior staff bungalow, 2014

Writing landscape

"Now there," said he, pointing his finger, "I make a comma, and there," pointing to another spot, "where a more decided turn is proper, I make a colon; at another part, where an interruption is desirable to break the view, a parenthesis; now a full stop, and then I begin another subject."

Lancelot "Capability" Brown in conversation with Hannah Moore at Hampton Court in 1782; quoted in Peter Willis, *Capability Brown in Northumberland*, in *Garden History*, 1981, p.158

Pasture towards the "Bustani" workers settlement with cowshed, 2015

"Objects and words have hollow
places in which a past sleeps.
The places people live in are like
the presences of diverse absences.
What can be seen designates what
is no longer there […] Haunted
places are the only ones people
can live in."

Michel de Certeau, *The Practice of Everyday Life*, 1984, p.108

Aloys excavating a disused laboratory bottle in a banana field
that formally was the site of a bar frequented by Amani staff

The bottle

This was a bar

Walked from Amani research station to a nearby village. At a bend in the murram [laterite gravel] road, crossing a small bridge, Aloys pointed to an inconspicuous patch of ploughed land surrounded by banana plants and weeds by the riverside – presumably used to grow irrigated vegetables: "This was a bar." He crossed the stream and searched the terrain, pushing around the soil with his shoe, occasionally picking up some earth.

Dusting off some fragments of what had been the smooth concrete surface of the building's foundation, he explained: "I know my father used to drink here. Researchers came here after work." We kicked around the dirt for remnants of that time. Expecting to find a beer bottle, we found a 500ml apothecary jar.

Wenzel's notes, 11 February 2014

Beer after work

Wenzel So what did you do after work, when you started working at the workshop?

Mr Kimboi There were so many places around. Even here at Amani we had a club, but I usually went somewhere along the road. There were many places then. We went to drink beer after work. When we had our salary.

Nowadays people have no time. We must be busy after work, to find something to do to add money. The nearest place like this is 10 miles from here, now.

It has all changed. Life was better then. We were working for government.

Conversation with Mr Kimboi, car mechanic since the 1980s, Amani, 28 October 2015

Local people never came here

Wenzel What is this?

Aloys A bottle. There was a bar here – this is also "remains." [Giggles]

Wenzel This looks more like a laboratory bottle.

Aloys Yes a laboratory bottle, you see the numbers 5ml, 3 to 100 and also the rubber lid! Maybe they took some alcohol from the laboratory… spirits… to mix with local brew? Some people from the laboratory drank the spirits.

Ann Do you think it was maybe used as decoration?

Aloys I don't remember. My father told me only, and I saw the walls. I never saw the bar in operation. The name was "*Jirani*" Bar – "Neighbours' Bar." But the owner died, he was a lab technician. Mostly staff from East African Community used to come to drink after work, especially for the weekend. It was 1970s.

Local people never came here, because of the *mumiani* [vampire] issues. They thought if you come here, and you buy some beer, when you then get tired, the researchers take you. So the local people had their own bar – I think it was up there. But they didn't stay late there, because they felt uncomfortable because of the Amani staff who had their bar here at *Jirani* Bar. They feared them.

Wenzel So when you were a child in the 1970s, people were afraid of *mumiani* still?

Aloys Yes they were so afraid, it was not easy for a *mzungu* [white] to give a lift to an African; when you stop they run away, screaming, seeking for help – because they were not happy.

Wenzel Even you, you ran away?

Aloys Ah, me, my father told me about these things and I did not feel afraid.

Wenzel So are there any more remains here? Is this over there concrete?

Aloys No, you see when people dig, to plant vegetables, they remove the stones; that's why we only see the small concrete bits, because of the long time and people do cultivation here. [Picks up a piece]. That's another bit of cement, you see [knocks on it]: cement.

Conversation between Aloys Mkongewa, Wenzel and Ann while exploring the site of the demolished staff bar, 10 February 2014

Mumiani [vampires]

"Vampire stories reveal the world of power and uncertainty in which Africans have lived in this [20th] century. Their very falseness is what gives them meaning: they are a way of talking that encourages a reassessment of everyday experience to address the workings of power and knowledge and how regimes use them."

Luise White, *Speaking with Vampires: Rumor and History in Colonial Africa*, 2000, p.43

Amani "senior staff club" (?), interior, 1970s

Staff band performing at the "junior staff club" at the farewell party for Dr Lelijveld, 1971

Curious ritual

"When Sunday lunch time came round I left Detinova to carry on by herself in the laboratory, while Aggie and I went off for a session at the tin-roofed pavilion that served as our social club. It was the sort of place that could only exist at Amani. The forest came up to the edge of the tennis course, and there were times when shaggy, white and black colobus [monkeys] sat in the canopy and gazed down at their human cousins engaged in curious rituals with rackets and balls."

Mick Gillies, *Mayfly on the Stream of Time*, 2000, p.223

A wonderful game

Tony We had these tennis courts. And when we went back, for the anniversary, somebody realised that the tennis courts had been taken over. There was a… a toilet, made in the…

Dorothy In the corner, yes.

Tony Just where I used to execute a devastating top-swing lob!

Graham Yes. They didn't want to play tennis – but they were glad to have the club!

John Nowadays, the tennis courts are non-functional. You couldn't possibly play tennis on them because there are tree trunks on them.

Frances The only African I ever knew play on these tennis courts was Daniel Abaru. He was a Ugandan medical doctor – and he was a wonderful tennis player, actually! Jean Bonga [Dutch technician] was the best tennis player we had, and she couldn't find any partner, poor woman! And then *finally* Daniel Abaru from Uganda came, high-jump Olympic champion of Uganda, never played tennis in his life; she taught him, and within about a month they were ….

Vyvienne They were just *playing*. Yeah.

Frances …having a wonderful game, yes! So she was so happy. But he was the only tennis player. So, no wonder the tennis courts aren't used.

Conversation between former Amani scientists and technicians, staff reunion, Cambridge, 4 August 2013

We had two clubs

Mosha On the social side, in Amani we had two clubs; there was a club for Europeans up here and another one for Africans down there, and I could see those two classes when I came; but we conspired with Mwaiko and Kilonzo to try to penetrate through this, and thus in 1974 I was elected as chairman of this club [laughter] – of the European club and I encouraged a lot of…

Mwaiko Africans…

Mosha …Africans, including the junior Africans who would only have been comfortable down there, also to join here…

Facilitator So before that the club was exclusively for Europeans?

Mosha They didn't say it… they didn't say it but that is what it was… [laughter]

Kilonzo …in practice

Mosha …in practice….

Kilonzo …but in theory….(laughter)

Mosha That is how it was. But then I came across a problem, because people would just drink and sign and then at the end of the month they are not paying [laughter].[…] because it was the first time the Africans were exposed to this kind of things where they just drink and sign [laughter]. When they figured out it was free beer they became very generous: "Hey

Tennis competition, probably 1970s

Amani club, tennis courts, 2014

give him that whisky, and what they want!". Then find themselves at the end of the month, and they have drank much more than their salaries. So it became a bit of an embarrassment, that now we are trying to come to the club, but we have people who just drink and do not pay so that was a bit of a problem. So the challenge of transition, which I saw was in the club

[....] But in the science world there was no problem, because there was a lot of integration….

Conversation between former Amani senior scientists, Staff reunion, Amani, 25 April 2015

Eating duck

Mtoyi I think every end of year the former director, Phillip Wegesa used to slaughter a cow from the cowshed [of the Amani dairy herd], and we stayed together eat, drink and have fun, either in the 'cathedral' [the director's house], his compound or in the club. Actually we were working here as a family, we were very comfortable.

Mganga And in the early 70s when all of the Africans who served here were Mwaiko, Mosha, me and [unclear], the scientists, the African scientists at that time, we had some sort of nightly gathering what we called *kula bata* [laughter]. *Bata* means a duck, to eat ducks, yes, a kind of get together.

Conversation between former Amani senior scientists and technicians, Staff reunion, Amani, 25 April 2015

Amani netball team, early 1970s

Dinner party at the house of Dr Bukhari Kilonzo, 1970s

Mrs Lydia Frank, who worked in the bar in the 1960s, visiting the club, 2014

Frances Yeah, they were mostly Indian by the time we went there. And of course the Amani Institute staff as well. And it was really our only organised social life, that club.

Wenzel The club?

Vyvienne Yeah, it was.

Wenzel There were two clubs there, weren't there?

Frances Only one in my time.

Vyvienne Just the one.

Wenzel And what did you do there?

Vyvienne Drink. [laughs]

Frances We drank; we –

Vyvienne Played cards.

Frances We played cards; we had films that, as Katsuko says, they used to be hired and brought up.

Vyvienne Oh yes! The film once a month, yep.

Frances And the Tanzanians all loved *Carry on* films. Those were their favourites. [giggles]

Wenzel What films?

Vyvienne *Carry on*, those very – old comedy, very basic comedy, very silly English comedies.

Frances But they loved it! [laughs]

Vyvienne They loved it! So – I mean, it was an open night, you know, but – well, Ann and I, rarely went to them, because we weren't "amused" as they say! [laughs] But, yeah, they were always very busy.

Conversation between retired female scientists who worked in Amani in the 1970s, Cambridge, Amani Staff Reunion, 6 August 2013

Very colonial

Katsuko And if I could spare some time at eleven o'clock, I went to the library, wasn't it? It was a proper library.

Frances Coffee in the library, that's right.

Vyvienne I'd forgotten about coffee in the library.

Frances Yes, we always used –

Katsuko Yes, and they also had a club house [at Amani] and, occasionally they put a film on there, and so I was invited.

Vyvienne But the club house was more sort of tea-time, wasn't it?

Frances Well, you know it was an old, you know, colonial-type club. All these colonial places had their English club.

Vyvienne Yes, *very* colonial.

Frances And the members were, in fact, men from the tea estates, who had previously been British I suppose, but most of them weren't by the time we were there.

Vyvienne Yeah, they were mostly Indian, weren't they?

Wedding celebration in the remains of Amani club, 2014

Wedding celebration in the remains of Amani club, 2014

Only for drinking

Dr Lyimo I was just from University [in 1982]. […] I was met by the driver of the director, and we started to come up here. My first impression was: "Where are we going?" Because we climbed, and we go and go; I started counting how many corners – 10, 11! Then we arrived here and I said: "Oh, there is life up here!" […]

People were asking us: "You girls. What are you looking for here, why are you leaving Dar-es-Salaam and come to this place?" Especially the women discouraged us and told us we should go to town. […] They asked: "You are educated, why would you come here?" But I heard people talking about their work and I said: "Oh, this is interesting." […] And then I went to malaria resistance mapping. There was a lot of going out to the bush. It was cold… When the temperatures fell to 10° I could hardly function. I would just sit there with my legs folded under me on the chair and be quiet in a small office in this laboratory. In the beginning it was difficult because of the weather. […] And the social life, it wasn't attractive, there was nothing to

do here, not a party. There was this old club, but this was only for drinking.

Dr Edith Lyimo (born 1957), senior scientist; commenting on social life, Amani, Staff reunion, 23 April 2015.

One day

Saturday has come, the day of the wedding at the club. Since morning, music plays behind the iron sheets that enclose the site. Led by the old librarian, the schoolchildren carry chairs from the Institute library. A group of older women set up cooking stones under a tree. The guesthouse cooks brought along nice clothes for the evening – Lilian and Juma dance while cutting the vegetables for our supper.

At night, the hill lies in the complete darkness of a power cut. Only from the club at its apex comes music, overlayed with the sound of the generator; coloured lights outdo the moon. Inside the club enclosure, all the people of Amani seem to be assembled, transformed by the occasion. January, the guesthouse attendant, gently swings

as he wishes us welcome at the gate. Mathilda, the director's secretary, under an enormous, shiny headscarf, is the mistress of ceremony. Esther Kika, the star of the 1970s netball team throws a glance as she dances by.

After weeks of thick mist and silent drizzle, conversations about lost pasts, and search for traces, the party is more than pleasant. There is life in the remains – life that may draw upon past resources, but that has other destinations than the past. One day. The next morning, January sweeps the bottle tops from the wet asphalt of the broken tennis courts, and two little girls in checkered uniforms pick up soaked paper garlands on their way to school.

Wenzel's notes, 20 April 2015

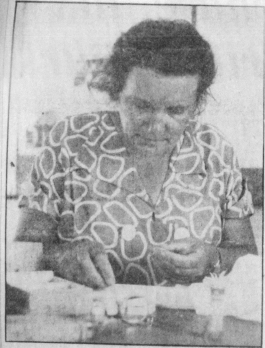

elp Dar

Soviet scientist visits Arusha

A SOVIET woman entomologist, who is a world authority on mosquitoes, Dr. T. S Detinova, (left) paid a brief visit to the Tropical Pesticide Research Institute, Arusha, during the course of a six-week stay in Tanganyika.

Dr. Detinova works at the Institute of Medical Parasitology and Tropical Medicine, known as the Mazzinovski Institute, in Moscow.

She is visiting Tanganyika and other parts of Africa as a World Health Organisation consultant and her work concerns the determining of the age of malaria-carrying mosquitoes by a technique which she developed in Russia.

During her tour she has found that she can apply the same technique for determining the age of the principal malaria carriers of East Africa. She has been working on this technique for 16 years.

Two children

In Tanganyika she is working mainly at the Malaria Research Institute at Amani. On leaving she will go to Brazzaville, the Upper Volta and Gambia before returning to Moscow, the whole trip taking two and a half months.

Dr. Detinova is married to an entomologist and she has two children. Her daughter, who is 25, is a biologist and her son aged 21, is studying at university to become a mathematician.

She has previously visited Geneva and London lecturing on her special subject for W.H.O.

● The age of mosquitoes has a great bearing on the control of malaria, as it is known that mosquitoes under a certain age cannot transmit the disease hence if they are killed before they reach that age the transmission of malaria cannot take place.

TODAY'S CAUSE LIST

Kenya man among five crash dead

READING, Tuesday.

MR. DONALD BRADFORD, 31, chairman of the Aero Club of East Africa, and four other people were killed in a mid-air collision between two light aircraft near here.

Mr. Bradford, a bachelor, who served with the Kenya Police in 1952 or 1953, was an electronic engineer with the Kenya Directorate of Civil Aviation. He was on leave in Britain, and was

APPEAL BY

Tanganyika Standard, 7 November 1962, Amani archive

As far as malaria eradication is concerned, it is hoped that the methods described in this monograph will serve as a starting-point in all countries for an extensive study of the age composition of mosquitoes in connexion with the epidemiology of this disease. I am convinced that international co-operation in this sphere will lead to the further development of the study of vector biology and thus to the speeding-up of global malaria eradication.

Vladimir Nikolayevic Bleklemishev, "Foreword" to *Age-Grouping Methods in* Dipitera *of Medical Importance, with special reference to vectors of Malaria*, by TS Detinova, 1962, p.11

Remembering a Soviet method

Age composition of malaria vector populations

On the 11 of September 1962, Tatjana Sergeevna Detinova flew from Moscow to Cairo beginning a three-month visit to the African continent. A Soviet entomologist whose recently-translated work was generating excitement among Western malariologists, Detinova had been commissioned by the World Health Organization (WHO) to supervise entomological work in a number of collaborating research institutions.

After a stop at the Regional Malaria Eradication Training Centre in Cairo, she flew to Nairobi and on to Tanga, on the coast of newly independent Tanganiyka. Failing to reach her contacts in the East African Commission, she commissioned a local driver – with no Swahili and limited English – to take her to Amani. Here, she spent six weeks working with Mick Gillies and Tony Wilkes on a new mosquito dissection technique, before travelling on to field stations in Brazzaville, Upper Volta and The Gambia. Despite stomach ulcers and perpetual visa troubles, Detinova completed three months of on-site training. WHO hailed her visit a great success.

Detinova's brief was to teach the "Polovodova method", a technique for establishing the physiological age of a female mosquito, which she had been working on for 16 years. It presented a huge improvement on earlier ageing techniques, such as attempting to qualitatively judge the wear of wing scales. Applied across a wide sample, the Polovodova method could provide clues into how many mosquitoes were living into old age, and potentially, offer critical insights into the long-term effectiveness of DDT-spray campaigns to control the disease.

The global malaria eradication campaign had been spear-headed by the US, and allied with an interest in winning the "hearts and minds" of local populations against the spectre of Communism. Yet after several years and large sums spent of the programme, it was unclear if this ambitious and vertically organised approach was having the desired effect. With the return of the Soviet Union to the League of Nations, the balance of power in the WHO was shifting, opening new opportunities to rethink current approaches. New directions which had worked well in the USSR were being considered: local health networks, sanitation methods, and community-based disease surveillance.

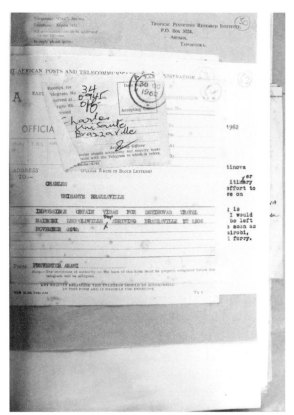

Telegram to L.J. Charles, Regional Malaria Advisor, Brazzaville from G. Pringle, Director Amani, 30 October 1962
Amani archive

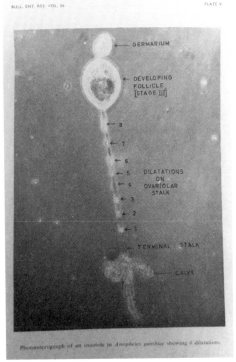

BULL. ENT. RES. VOL. 56   PLATE V

Photomicrograph of mosquito ovariole; in Gillies, M., and T. Wilkes. 1965. A study of the age-composition of populations of *Anopheles gambiae* Giles and *A. funestus* Giles in North-Eastern Tanzania. *Bulletin of Entomological Research* 56:237–62.

Cellular debris

The whole process of examination of the ovaries to determine the number of ovipositions consists of the following stages: One of the ovaries lying in a drop of physiological saline is immobilised on the slide by means of a needle held in the left hand; a needle held in the right hand is used to pierce the outer ovarian membrane in several places and then to remove it bit by bit. Where the membrane has been removed the ovarioles appear separated one from another […] The internal oviduct and the ovary are then pierced with the left-hand needle to immobilise them. The ovariole being examined is carefully moved aside from the internal oviduct with the right-hand needle […] It is possible to count the dilatations only when the ovariole has been preserved in its entirety and when the site of its connection with the internal oviduct is visible. If the pressure is carelessly applied, the ovarioles are very easily torn and then the total number of dilatations cannot be determined.

Tatjana Sergeevna Detinova, *WHO Monograph Series 47, part 1,* 1962, p.74

The process of perfecting this technique may prove very time-consuming, especially if the entomologist is working unaided. Under such conditions it may not be possible to deal with more than six dissections per hour, or approximately 30 per day. As a result, several contributors very naturally do not feel that they are yet in a position to commit themselves in the way of providing facts or opinions.

WHO, *Preliminary Appraisal of the use of Age-Grouping Methods in Anopheline Mosquitoes, WHO/Mal/264,* 9 May 1960

I soon spotted that the method of examination was a lot less systematic than her published accounts suggested. It was altogether more subjective affair, and when I started to do the dissection myself I found I was as much in the dark as ever. I could sense the beginnings of a difficult political situation. I saw myself being cast in the role of a Western scientist refusing to accept a Soviet discovery. Why else couldn't I see what was so obvious to her?

Mick Gillies, *Mayfly on a Stream of Time,* 2000, p.222

We have spent the morning at Tony and Dorothy [Wilkes'] house, looking through photo albums and picture frames arranged around the house, having tea, playing with the dog. When I ask Tony about his work with Detinova, he retreats to the backroom, returning with his dissertation. He opens the page with the microphotograph of a dissected mosquito ovariole, a diagonal tube with a bulbous head, intercut with numbers and arrows.

Tracing the tell-tale bumps with his finger and then mimicking the gestures of dissection in the air, he shows how he managed to string out the ovaries and carefully lay the specimen on the slide to be photographed. He recalled shaking with nerves in laboratory's dark room and the moment when the image emerged; how he ran to his supervisor and friend, Mick Gillies, shouting "Mick, look what I've got," and how they put their arms around one another. "It was," Tony said, "one of the best days of my life."

Ann's notes, 26 July 2012

Tony Wilkes demonstrating mosquito dissection, London School of Hygiene, 2013

Ann Do you remember Detinova?

Dorothy Oh, she was a lovely lady. She gave a wonderful book of Russian fairy tales to our daughter, Alice, who just loved them – she wanted to hear them every night. And she gave me the most beautiful amber brooch – amber from Russia. I wore it to a friend's daughter's wedding, just a few months ago. Let me see if I can find it… [Goes to retrieve the coat] … You see, here it is, isn't it lovely? Yes, she was a real sweetie.

Ann's notes, 7 August 2014

Dorothy's amber brooch, 2013

Dorothy & Tony Wilkes' framed photograph of Mick Gillies & Agnes "Aggie" Gillies, 2013

Tony shows us the double photograph frame: Mick Gillies in a classic posture with his pipe; his wife, Agnes waving from the corner of her house in Sussex. Tony becomes serious. "A great man and a great friend." It was Mick, the renowned entomologist, who had translated Detinova's work, but it was Tony who mastered the technique. Their professional collaboration was enormously productive; but it is their friendship that Tony emphasises.

One of our favourite tricks was to switch nametags at conferences. Some star-stuck student would introduce himself with no idea that it was not Gillies, the genius, he was trying to impress, but Tony, the oaf.

Dorothy shows us the album – a picnic with G&Ts, her brother's visit to Mombasa, her garden. Her mother did not want her to go; Dorothy was

pregnant at the time – she remembers looking out at her from the airport-bound coach: "her pale little face, clutching her handbag."

Dorothy Wilkes' friend and painting teacher Agnes Gillies at her easel in Amani, probably late 1950

Tony Wilkes, MRC Fieldstation Walikunda, The Gambia, c.1969

"But how beautiful it was!" She shows us some of her paintings: a series of shambas, dappled baobab trees, the Usambara mountains in the morning. She used to just sketch small things for fun, but it was Aggie, who inspired Dorothy to paint. "Her paintings," Aggie's daughter Jackie had said, "had a real voice." I dig out the Mick Gillies description of one that found its way into a Royal Academy Exhibition, that I jotted down in my notebook: "a spare but evocative picture of a tropical backyard, just a tap and the palm-like shadows of a half-seen pawpaw tree draped over the outside wall of the kitchen." Dorothy nods, "she had a gift, and it kept her busy. Something to do while the men where out collecting."

Not an easy person to get to know, Dorothy admits, but she realized over time they had become close. She was with her when she died: Dorothy was driving, and a car hit them coming out a blind drive. Dorothy was in a coma for days, with broken legs and ribs. "The poor children. Tony did not know where I put the [Christmas] presents so I had to tell them all where to find them in the house."

Ann's notes, 26 July 2012

Dorothy Wilkes showing her oil paintings of Amani hung in her dining room, 2013

Former head driver Mtanga, wearing his driver's cap, near Amani, 2014

The road loomed large in our lives. [...]

Mick Gillies, *Mayfly on the Stream of Time*, 2000, p.138

The head driver

Ali Shabani Mtanga began his career as a "turnboy" in 1938, helping the driver by loading the bags. His father had known someone in the head office and had asked to get his son a job. He worked for Amani before it became the centre for medical research, when it was still focused on agricultural studies. He drove four directors of the institute – they liked him because he was safe and fast. He would drive at night for [insect] collections and on long trips across the area and to the beach for the colonial doctors' wives.

Drivers' uniforms; Alib Abas – the local tailor who, like Ali Shabani Mtanga, lives in the same village in the valley below Amani – tells us were by far the most expensive. He was commissioned by Amani to make the uniforms for workers, drivers, and the scientists. Everything was khaki (sometimes different shades) but for the lab coats, which had to be white. It was important that they were dressed appropriately.

Ali kept his uniform neatly pressed in a plastic bag. And after donning them himself he lets Aloys try on the jacket – something that he does not allow his own grandchildren – he folds it neatly and carefully puts it back in the bag. The hat he keeps hung on the wall near his doorway; the precious badge reading "East African Commission" he has wrapped in paper and hidden.

Aloys smiles as he puts it on. He likes the way it looks and asks us to take several pictures "to remember this day."

Ann's notes, 8 February 2014

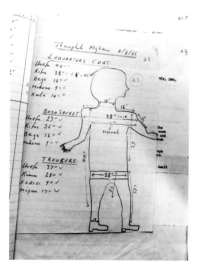
Drawing accompanying order for a driver's uniform, 1966, Amani archive

Kimurio, 23.4.54
Ramadhani Ngovi – Driver

Definitely no increment this year.

The above driver was caught by myself carrying passengers (3) on 21/9/54 between Gonja and Kihurio. […] He has previously been fined for this offence. I understand, and only the week previous I had warned the drivers and supervisors myself about it.
You may remember he asked for the increment, which was stopped for failing to take care of his vehicle, to be instated when you visited Kileo on 19.8.54.
    Please inform me what disciplinary action you consider necessary.

Hemingway, field officer.

Handwritten letter to the director (?); Amani Archive, Box 14, African Staff, Drivers: 127

Aloys putting on the old driver's uniform, 2014

A narrow escape

Between [the passengers] and safety ran a narrow track, a hundred years long. At the end of it was the Land Rover with Jonathan the driver nodding gently at the wheel [...] As he neared the welcoming refuge of the Land Rover, Tony [Wilkes] looked at the wide open back of the vehicle with the idea of diving headfirst into it before the lion could reach him. But by then, Jonathan had woken up, and, realising that something was amiss, had opened the passenger door in front to receive the stampeding [mosquito] catchers. After waiting some time more they decided to pick up the equipment they had left behind them, so the driver edged the Land Rover carefully down the grassy track to their abandoned catching site. The tubes and stools lay scattered on the ground, and their torches still shone out in to the empty night [...] They sat in the Land Rover and waited some more.

Mick Gillies, *Mayfly on the Stream of Time*, 2000, p.150

The last european director's car and its driver on the left, c.1970

Uniforms style

Circular No 31 of 1964: All Departments
Office of the East African Common Services Organization,
PO Box 30005,
NAIROBI

6 August 1964

UNIFORMS

Certain irregularities between Departments in the issue of approved items of uniforms have recently come to light. There have, in fact, been cases in which staff in certain departments have been issued with shoes as uniform without prior sanction from this office. Irregularities such as these can be a cause of strained staff relations when another group of staff, in similar circumstances is refused similar privileges.

In order to regularise the matter it has been decided to standardise on the times of uniforms to be issued to all categories of staff. I should therefore be grateful if you would let me have a list of uniforms issued by your Department to each category of Staff and the frequency of such issue. Any special departmental variations should also be indicated. When this list has been consolidated, a circular laying down the standard scale of uniforms for each category of staff will be issued. In the meantime, no additions or alternations to current authorised issues of uniforms should be made without prior authority from this office.

SECRETARY GENERAL

Amani archive, Box 14, *African Staff, Drivers*

Category of Staff	Frequency	Description
E.A. TRYPANOSOMIASIS RESEARCH ORGANIZATION		
Field Helpers	Annually / Replace when old / " " "	2 Overalls / 1 Pair Gum Boots / 1 Rain Cape
		Note: Issues of Trousers, Shorts or Jackets will not be made
E.A. FRESHWATER FISHERIES RESEARCH ORGANIZATION		
Motor Launch Crew: Cox'n	Annually / " / "	2 Blue Shirts / 2 Blue Shorts / 1 Blue Jersey
	Two years / " "	1 White Shirt / 1 White Short
	3 years / Replace when old	1 Pair White Sandals / 1 Peaked Cap
Boat Crew	Annually / " / "	2 Blue Shirts / 2 Blue Shorts / 1 Blue Jersey
E.A. DIRECTORATE OF CIVIL AVIATION		
Sen. Assistant Engineers/ Asst. Engineers/Technical Officers.	Annually	2 White Overalls or Coats
Radio Operators/Control Assts/ Traffic Clerks.	Annually / Replace when old / Annually	2 Khaki Bush Jackets with Buttons / 2 Khaki shorts or Trousers

Guidelines for the issuing of uniforms, 1960s, Amani archive

This is *mumiani*

Frances [looking at a picture] That's Ali Mtanga. The one sitting down at the side of the wall is Ali Mtanga.

Vyvienne Yeah.

Graham That's Ali Mtanga at the far corner?

Frances Yeah, that's right.

Graham This is *mumiani*'s [the vampire] day off.

Jan *Mumiani*'s day off!! [laughs]

Vyvienne One of them was the driver, wasn't he?

Graham Yeah.

Vyvienne That was the chunky second chap, wasn't it?

Graham Once we driving down from Amani to Muheza with Ramadhani Ali, do you remember, he was great fun; that was the driver, he was great fun. A real joker.

Vyvienne Yes. But a bit of an erratic driver. [laughs]

Frances Yes, indeed. And of course the windows were open, and I was in the passenger seat, and we saw a puff adder, and he said, "Oh, we are going to get this one!" He wanted to kill it. So he drove, and just for a moment, as we drove past it, its face was staring at me through the open passenger window! [laughs] Oh, gosh.

Conversarion between retired scientists who had worked at Amani in the 1970s, Cambridge, staff reunion, 4 August 2013

Research lorry in the field, Pare area, 1950s

Research lorry in the field, Pare area, 1950s

Land Rover in the field, 1970s

Car problems

The presentation of cars in stories, even stories about vampires, reveals popular ideas about the interaction between culture and technology, between bodies and machines. In many societies, automobiles generate their own folklore, becoming the vehicles of older symbols and associations, while their symbolic value is equal to their material worth. That vehicles could be controlled, modified, and transformed may have reflected the imagined powers of their manufactures or the real needs of their owners. Cars can take people away; monitoring and roads are ways of erasing boundaries and reclassifying space...What kind of being lives in a truck with curtained windows, and what kind of beings reproduce in the backseats of parked cars? Indeed the men who worked closely with machines – drivers, passengers, men who worked with electricity or mechanical shoves – rehearse biological or mechanical reproduction?

Luise White, *Speaking with Vampires*, 2000: 146

Dr Phillip Wegesa, first African director of Amani, shortly before his death, ca. 1982

Heritage?

"We are talking about Amani as heritage, of this magnificent Institute; but how does that relate to the African view of the Institute? Do they have any value on heritage that way? Because – in that sense, why did Philip [Wegesa, Amani's first African director] start taking down things? How does the idea of heritage for these old institutions register with Africans in general, with ideas about their, their continent, their future, their country? It might be that we have we have quite different views in that sense, er, quite different opinions."

Comments by Dr Jan Lelijveld, Amani's last European Director; Amani staff reunion, Cambridge, 6 August 2013

"Your humanism wants us to be universal and your racist practices are differentiating us; you are making monsters of us."

"Repressed rage, never managing to explode, goes around in circles and wreaks havoc on the oppressed themselves."

Jean-Paul Sartre, "Foreword" to The Wretched of the Earth by Franz Fanon, 1961, p.7 and p.17

"When the colonised questions the colonial world, this is not a rational confrontation of viewpoints. It is not a treatise about universals, but wild, insisting on absolute uniqueness. The colonial world is a Manichaean world."

Franz Fanon, The Wretched of the Earth, 1961, p.40

Tabula rasa

A clearance

At the centre of Amani research station is an
open space, a rectangular lawn framed by hedges,
onto which leads a set of ancient concrete steps.
There was once a building here, and the void is
not a result of ruination and decay, but a *tabula
rasa* – a product of action, erasure. The space was
once filled by a large laboratory, built for the
German agricultural station in the first decade of
the 20th century – according to some, the oldest
building of the station. It was torn down in 1973
at the behest of Philip Wegesa, who two years
earlier – a full ten years after political independence – had become the station's first African
director. Wegesa had been trained as a laboratory
technician in this building. When he, after
promotion through the ranks, was appointed
a scientific "officer," the last European director
of the station allocated the oldest laboratory to
his work.

Clearing where a German-built laboratory was demolished
to make space for new buildings in the 1970s, 2013

This director, who made way for Wegesa, was
a Dutchman who had studied with Wegesa in
London. He had been an acceptable transitional
leader both to the departing colonisers and to the
newly independent colonised. The last resident
European scientist at the station, John Raybould,
left two years after the demolition of the building. This was a time of "Africanisation," a time
of new circulations and spatial orders, imaginary ruptures and anticipations of change. A
period of new social relations and unfamiliar
spaces, infused with the pleasures of boundary
transgression – for both "African" and "European" inhabitants – but also an era of residual
oppression, carried forth in the enduring
Manichaean terminology of colonisation, and
of an unfolding peculiar, mimetic, violence.

Stairs leading up to the demolished laboratory, 2013

- 11 -

CHAPTER 2.

DEFINITION AND METHODS OF AFRICANIZATION

Africaniza-
tion

35. What do we mean by Africanization and who is an African ? These are terms, the use and application of which, have evoked strong emotions and yet very few Governments have defined them in clear and unmistakable terms. The definition which follows is, therefore, an attempt on our part to state what we mean in order to avoid misunderstanding.

36. Fortunately, we have in the Public Service Commission Regulations an authoritative definition of the term "African":-

Definition

"African means a person of African race domiciled within the Territories and includes an Arab who was born, and is domiciled, in the Territories and any person either of whose parent is, or if deceased was, an African within the meaning of this definition, who is domiciled within the Territories."

This definition has two qualifications, one of race, and the other of domicile. It includes a mulatto and an "Afro-Asian" domiciled within the Territories but excludes an African domiciled in either Central or West Africa. It also excludes a local European or Asian domiciled in the Territories.

37. We would, therefore, like to define Africanization as a staffing policy adopted by African Governments shortly before and after independence, which ensures, in the short term, that all key and policy-advising posts in the Civil Service are held by Africans, and in the long term, the reduction and ultimate elimination of the predominance of non-Africans at all levels of the Civil Service.

Africaniza-
tion often
attended by
employment
of more
expatriates

38. Africanization is not a wholesale displacement of non-Africans with Africans nor is it a policy of exclusion of non-Africans from Government employment. In many instances Africanization has been attended by the employment of more non-Africans. This is because independence is usually followed by rapid expansion of governmental activities to such an extent that available Africans are unable to meet increased demands particularly in the educational and technical fields. In the short term, however, Africanization involves displacement only in selective and sensitive areas.

Typescript "Report of the Africanization of the public services of the East African Common Service Organization," by JO Udoji, Esq., 1963, Amani library

"In the years preceding independence, 'Africanisation' took its leisurely course. It made little difference to our sequestered life in Amani."

Mick Gillies, *Mayfly on the Stream of Time*, 2000, p.255

Mick Gillies' laboratory team; behind Gillies (with pipe) are Phillip Wegesa (left) and Tony Wilkes (right), late 1950s

The staff at Amani, possibly at the departure of J Pringle, the last British director (holding a carving); in the front row, right of the director's wife is Wegesa, and to the director's left, Raybould, early 1960s

First "African" director

Dr Philip Wegesa, born in Kenya during the Second World War, came to Amani as a technician during the last decade of colonial occupation, when staff from all East African countries worked and rotated across a network of disease-specific research institutes. He participated in research on the parasitology of river blindness and the ecology of its insect vector, blackflies of the genus *Simulium*. He was supervised and trained by Dr John Raybould, the last British scientist resident in Amani. In the context of the Africanisation efforts preceding and following Tanzania's political independence in 1963, Wegesa and a fellow Kenyan technician travelled to London to accompany two river blindness patients that were to be treated there. He received training at the London School of Hygiene and Tropical Medicine, but while his colleague continued to do a PhD, Wegesa returned to Amani, where he was promoted and continued entomological laboratory work, and epidemiological surveys on river blindness and blackflies.

In 1973, a decade after decolonisation, and after the interim period during which Jan Lejliveld presided over the transfer to African scientists, Wegesa became the first African director of Amani research station. Together with his wife – a young woman from a neighbouring village who had worked as laboratory assistant – he moved into what was known as the *Boma*, the palatial director's mansion built around 1904. Half a century later, his widow recalled the experience: "Imagine, a small girl from the village in this big big house!" According to Wegesa's European colleagues, he had never liked the dark old building. Some attributed this to widespread local fears of German spirits, but others thought it altogether more a matter of style, recalling how Wegesa immediately removed the heavy Victorian hardwood furniture and replaced it with modern plywood designs.

Wegesa, his wife Joyce and Dutch visitors at the director's house, early 1970s

Phillip Wegesa, his wife Joyce, and an assistant in Wegesa's last laboratory in his hometown, around 1980

[When he was made a scientist], X got a bit too arrogant with it, and then Y went to the other extreme, and didn't really bother to do anything. As scientist he picked some losing questions, like: "Can you make insecticide out of orange peel?" [....] And – it's a very well-known thing in the literature that there are toxins and essential oils in orange peel and in most plants that can be useful pharmacologically or insecticidally – but he couldn't handle it. His intellectual ceiling was about capable of squeezing orange juice. And after writing a few, er, "reports" about whether the larvae died and so on [...] Well, we can't expect every one of them to be a winner!

Former Amani scientist in a discussion about Africanisation, staff reunion, Cambridge, 5 August 2013

Central laboratory, Amani (original construction German), 2013

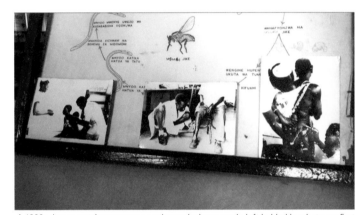
A 1960s demonstration poster on onchocerciasis research, left behind in what was first John Raybould's then Wegesa's laboratory. Wegesa demonstrating skin specimen collection, 2013

Specimens

Second day in Amani. Went with Raybould into his old laboratory. Took some time to find a key. A large Wilheminian room, dark hardwood furniture with late 19th century ornament, sunlight filtered by dusty windowpanes. Shelves on the wall covered with glass jars. Mostly of crabs collected by John and his assistants, between the late 1950s and early '70s; labelled with place names from around East Africa, mostly around Amani; also snakes' heads, whole snakes, collections of *Simulium* larvae. Much of the formalin has evaporated from the jars.

Wooden boxes with John's insect collections: houseflies from the '50s, lots of blackflies, as tiny as the pinheads that they are mounted on, mostly eaten by ants; some spectacular boxes of the biggest and most beautiful flying things you could imagine. In the drawers, notebooks with pencilled laboratory numbers, now incomprehensible, meticulously written by technicians, half a century ago; bundles of meteorological observation cards; a cloud atlas with glued in photographs of British cloud formations for meteorological description; several mummified rats of various sizes. Cupboards full

of – partly very toxic – laboratory chemicals, intricate glassware and measuring instruments. In large glass frames, the 1960s predecessors of today's conference posters, depicting aspects of river blindness research. One includes photographs of patients whose skin is snipped for laboratory examination. Patients and technicians are here equally nameless specimens; one of them is Philip Wegesa. This became Wegesa's laboratory, where he continued the river blindness work after Raybould had left, in 1974.

Wenzel's notes, 17 September 2013

Proposed laboratory

Heavy rain. Too much to walk in the forest. Searched through the institute library. In a cupboard filled with a random assortment of maps, we find a stack of architectural drawings, "Proposed Laboratory for EA Institute of Malaria and Vector Borne Diseases at Amani," dated 1975, by a Dar es Salaam architect. Detailed drawings of a multi-storey modernist laboratory building, various annexes, extensive residential housing, drainage and fixtures, all concrete and flat roofs, international style. Ground plans include the traces of the existing British bungalows, "to be demolished." The empty lawn beside the library – where Gillies' lab was, of which only a flight of stairs remains – and the large excavation behind it were to make space for the new laboratory block. Mr Otona, who was an administrator in the 1970s, explains while leafing through the drawings that the plans were never realised because of "the end of East African Community," and because there were no funds.

Wenzel's notes, 18 September 2015

Retired administrator viewing the unbuilt plans, Amani library, 2013

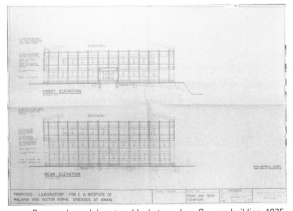

Proposed new laboratory block, to replace German building, 1975, Amani archive

Immutable mobile

The unrealised plans for a modernist edifice of national science travelled with Wegesa from Tanzania back to Kenya in 1977. Five years after the erasure of the old Amani laboratory, the East African Common Services Organisation, locally referred to as "the East African Community," to which Amani belonged, collapsed due to political conflicts, and all Kenyan citizens were abruptly forced to leave Amani. As an exile of sorts, Wegesa returned to Kenya at a time of renewed nationalist fervour (paradoxically heralding the liberalisation of economy, health and education) around the death of first President Kenyatta. While his family was put up in a hotel, Wegesa joined other younger scientists in a call for a new Kenya Medical Research Institute (KEMRI). This resulted in one of the first legal acts of the new president Moi: the Research and Technology Act of 1978, founding "para-statal" national research institutes to anchor research outside existing government ministries and universities.

After several months, Wegesa was granted permission to build up a national malaria research institute in Kisumu, a town near his original home area. Temporarily housed, with few staff and little equipment, in wooden barracks in the former "native" hospital, Wegesa weighed different options for the location of his new research centre. He rejected a large space adjacent to the new, Soviet-built provincial hospital near the town centre, and chose instead a large area of bushland outside town. There, he commissioned a young and ambitious Kenyan architect – known as the "first fully African" firm in Kenya – to draw an entire self-contained science city, a research "station" modelled on Amani not just in terms of its name and single-disease focus but also in its peculiar vision of space and architecture.

Covering 40 acres of insulated civic space, nesting the scientists' civic longings within a larger vision of the nation of science, the projected station comprised housing, schools, and sports and leisure facilities, integrating life and work and expanding the vision of a self-contained enclave of knowledge production. The modernist architecture resembled the earlier proposals for a new Amani – just larger. And the station was, like Amani, envisaged as lasting home for science and progress, sheltered from the circulations of urban social life; undisturbed; an orderly, ordering space, in sharp distinction from the irregularity of bush and peasant agriculture – the "field" of investigation – just as Amani's lawns had been enclosed by rainforest.

The station's perimeter was fenced, and the bush cleared, but within Wegesa's lifetime nothing was built. At the same time, in the same town, a group of younger Kenyan microbiologists recently returned from doctoral training in the US and also associated with KEMRI established a collaboration with the American Centres for Disease Control, and initiated what decades later became one of East Africa's largest research stations. Instead of executing the original blueprint, however, building work for this other "field station" was limited to laboratory and administrative buildings, without residential housing and civic infrastructure.

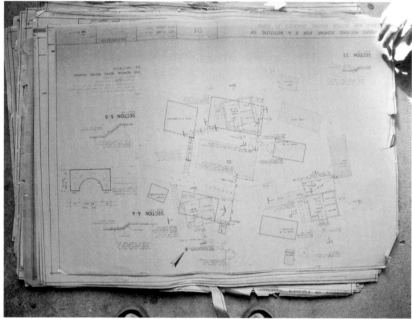

Proposed modern housing for senior staff at Amani, replacing colonial bungalows, 1975

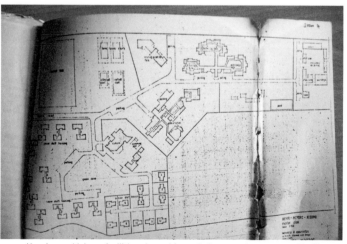

Housing and leisure facilities planned for malaria research centre outside Kisumu, Kenya, 1986

Home

Before any building work began at his new site, Wegesa fell ill. According to his colleagues at the small Kisumu lab, the once so gentle man of science attacked them, came to work bare-footed, threw about laboratory equipment. Eventually, he was diagnosed with schizophrenia and hospitalised at the notorious Mathare hospital in Nairobi. Released on medication, he remained formally on his institute's staff, and for a long while, "acting" directors signed documents for him.

His wife, who had left behind home and family in Amani, was employed as a technician; she assisted him in the laboratory of the new subsidiary "field station," established in a rented room in his home area. The family moved to his family land, into a spacious colonial bungalow, complete with fireplaces – unused on account of the much hotter climate – and decorated mantelpieces, strikingly similar to the colonial scientific officers' residences at Amani, which Wegesa had proposed to demolish for his vision of a new Amani.

As Mrs Wegesa recalled much later, he continued his research, and spent much time at night dictating to her research notes and experimental plans: "He had great plans, but nobody listened to him." His son, a primary school boy at the time, remembers how he used to walk everywhere holding his father's hand and listening to his stories and plans – and reminding his father to dress properly or put on his shoes before leaving their house. He recalled his father's kindness, and the pleasant smell of the small laboratory that Wegesa had set up, where he had helped his father sorting medicinal plants, grinding them, and extracting them with water.

In the end, Wegesa withdrew to his own lab, a mud-walled building in his village compound. There, now carrying the title of "Dr," he continued breeding mosquitoes for purposes known only to himself, and investigated medicinal plants the names of which had never been heard before. A large wooden signboard was posted by the roadside, emblazoned with the torch of Tanzania's freedom and African socialism, which had been carried through Amani on a national tour at Independence (and commemorated with a monument on Market Street in the African settlement). It read: "MASCRAFT:" "*Manyasi* [Kiswahili for 'traditional medicine'] African Science Research Foundation." Soon thereafter, and after marrying his wife, Wegesa died; ten years after becoming the first African director of one of the continent's major research institutes, five years after being expelled from it. The wattle-and-daub laboratory transformed, as such buildings do, into a termite mound. The family removed the signboard. Until 2014, it stayed under a stack of firewood in a chicken pen. In the time between my first and my second visit, someone began to chop it up for firewood.

Mrs Joyce Wegesa and her sons at home in Webuye, Kenya, 2014

Signboard of Wegesa's last laboratory where he worked on plant remedies and insecticides in the early 1980s, 2014

**Searching for the
laboratory**
(video stills)

Mrs Wegesa
That signboard was
somewhere there.

I remember the doors were here.

There was a tree here…

and he had just put the signboard
up there.

Yes, that is the stump of the tree, somewhere there.

It was here.

This man, I don't know, he had something.

Only that… nobody supported it, even I could not support him.

Dr John Raybould reading 1960s publications and explaining his methods, Amani guesthouse, 2014

"Reenactment's emancipatory gesture is to allow participants to select their own past in reaction to a conflicted present. Paradoxically, it is the very ahistoricity of reenactment that is the precondition for its engagement with historical subject matter."

Vanessa Agnew, "What is reenactment?," *Criticism* 46(3), 2004, p.328

Kidevu's return: reenacting mid-20ᵗʰ century science

Human baiting, crab-catching, artificial rearing

The forest clearing near Amani where the biting-catches were made. The two collectors are seated, while the two standing individuals are recording wind speed and light intensity, probably 1964

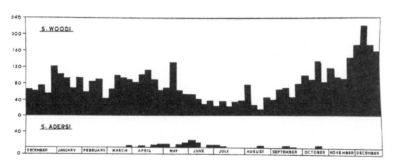

The number of *S. woodi* adn *S. adersi* collected during weekly 12-hour biting-catches at Amani between December 1963 and December 1964

Ramadhani Kupe and John Mganga, demonstrating mosquito catch, 2013

Biting-catch

Methods: A 12-hour biting-catch was carried out each week from the beginning of December 1963 to the end of December 1964 […]. All biting catches were carried out in a carefully selected clearing close to Amani (Fig 1), chosen because of the relatively large number of *S. woodi* females that came to feed. Collections were made by two assistants seated on a bench, in an unshaded area near the centre of the clearing. The collectors always wore shorts. Adult *simuliids* were caught while biting in 5 x 1 cm glass tubes with plastic caps. The time of biting of each fly was recorded. The collecting periods of the various assistants were alternated in such a way as to minimise the possible effect of one collector being more attractive than another to the flies. […] Throughout each collecting-period, records were taken at ten-minute intervals of temperature, humidity, light intensity, cloud coverage, wind velocity and rainfall. […] The effects of these meteorological conditions on biting behaviour have not yet been fully analysed, and this aspect of the problem will be reported in a separate paper.

In addition to the main study, certain other related phenomena were also investigated. Observations on the engorgement time and the size of the blood meal were made on a small number of *S. woodi*. The engorgement time was recorded to the nearest minute, while the size of the blood meal was roughly estimated as being small, medium or large according to the degree of abdominal extension.

John Raybould, "A study of anthropophilic female *Simuliidae (Diptera)* at Amani, Tanzania: the feeding behaviour of *Simulium woodi* and the transmission of onchocerciasis," *Annals of Tropical Medicine and Parasitology*, 61 (1), 1967, pp.76–7

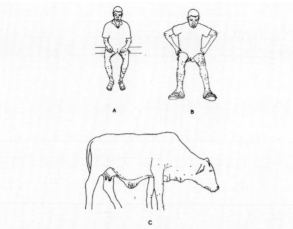

FIG. 2. The biting-sites of *C. bicolor* when feeding on man (A and B) and on cows (C): A, man sitting on a bench showing the biting-sites of 100 *C. bicolor*; B, man sitting on the ground showing the biting-sites of 100 *C. bicolor*; and C, cow showing the biting-sites of 50 *C. bicolor*. These drawings are semi-diagrammatic since it is not possible to portray all aspects of the body on a single drawing; biting-sites on the posterior aspects of the legs, therefore, are marked on the inside margin of the legs.

Methods

Biting catches using human bait-subjects were carried out at Amani during studies on *Simulium*. *Chrysops bicolor Cordier* formed a significant component of the biting-catches, and records were made for this insect also. […] To obtain further information on host choice and biting sites, biting catches were carried out in which two men and two cows acted as bait subjects. Each of the two collectors sat on the ground next to one of the cows, and recorded the precise biting side of every *C. bicolor* biting either himself or the cow. This was done by sticking a pin, in the appropriate position into a drawing of a man or cow. […]

FIG. 1b. *C. bicolor* immediately after feeding but before take-off; a drop of blood is visible on the skin at the site of the bite. (× 3.5.)

Ann. Trop. Med. Parasit., Vol. 61   PLATE V

FIG. 1a. *C. bicolor* resting on the ground. (× 3.5.)

Acknowledgements

I wish to express my thanks to Dr G Pringle, late director of the East African Institute of Malaria and Vector-Borne Diseases, for his advice and encouragement; to Mr ASK Yagunga, and Mr J Mganga for their conscientious assistance throughout the course of the investigation; and to Mr K Madeni, Mr S Fedha and Mr RA Kupe and other members of the institute's staff for their invaluable help.

John Raybould, "Studies on *Chrysops bicolor Cordier (Diptera, Tabanidae)* at Amani, with particular reference to feeding behaviour," *Annals of Tropical Medicine and Parasitology*, 61 (2), 1967, pp.167–8, 173

Enacting anachronicity

Reenactment shifts historical accounts from representation to presentation; its grasp of the affective tenor of the past is lost, in fact we did not gain much of any insight into the mundane realities of work in the 1960s and '70s. But rather what it does produce is a resonance of ethos, a reflection on purpose. It opens the past, not merely to diverse readings but also to imaginations of possible outcomes, makes us read the past not just through traces, but equally through absences and gaps. This is an eventuality that lies at the heart of the ethnographic endeavour – not as "witnesses" of the past, but as co-producers of present pasts.

The power of reenactment seems to inhere in its anachronicity – the tensions it introduces between immediacy and theatricality, authenticity and artifice, representation and desire. These performances open up the work of science, not simply by accessing "tacit" – or affective –dimensions of past experimental labour, embodied history, but also by exposing the faultlines between past routines and present realities.

The reenacting of colonial science, as an event in the present, disrupts straightforward narratives about the promises and shortfalls of scientific progress, provoking questions about the sentiment and stakes of research in "the tropics."

Ann's notes, 14 November 2013

John Raybould examining black fly specimens
collected in the early 1960s, Amani guesthouse, 2015

John Raybould and Stephen Fedha attempting once more to collect
Simulium at old collection site, 2015

Returns

John Raybould returned twice to Amani with us. Once as our witness of past explorations, the second time on his own last expedition. On both occasions, we performed (or re-performed) the same scientific procedures with the original cast, on site: collecting blood-feeding insects from one's body, collecting crabs and the fly-larvae on them, preparing materials in the laboratory.

The first time, we conducted literal reenactments as ethnographic experiments: we asked Raybould and his former local assistants to reenact the scientific method sections of research papers that they had published in the 1960s. The same people, the same sites and tools, fifty years later. These reenactments of written scripts from the past served us not so much to *add* tacit, embodied, emotional and relational dimensions of documented past events, as some historians attempt, but to shed light on the ethical and political tensions in our relationship with the past, and the experience of loss and decay – and to provoke and sense unexpected constellations, excess that moved beyond the script, and created new insights – such as, e.g., when John in an unobserved moment, disposed of the animal specimens that we had collected during demonstrations, taking great care both not to unnecessarily harm the animals or upset the natural species distributions, or to reveal to his assistants the scientific irrelevance of this reenactment.

While the relation between text, action, effect and observation was less predictable than a mere re-staging of an old script, the second re-performance, two years later further challenged the boundaries of past and present: John staged – if this indeed is the word – his own last blackfly

expedition to Amani. This time, he pursued an actual scientific aim: after attending the British Simulium Group's definitely last meeting in 2015, John had informally been asked to collect, should an opportunity arise, once more some few black-flies from Amani for a colleague's genomic research. Our project brought this unlikely opportunity about. By contrast to the previous re-nactments, this collection had a scientific purpose and was mandated by an organisation, albeit one that, according to its own last "Bulletin" had concluded that on account of dwindling membership, "there was little point in continuing the group."

Quite apart from the problem that such ad hoc private collection of biological materials for a friend sits uneasily with contemporary regulatory frameworks, this revival of scientific work complicated the notion of re-performance. What did we actually observe when the five old men (as had been the case in the 1960s, John participated in the man-baiting catch) one more time, and presumably the last time, did what they once had done together? A biographical encore or coda, a return, or a closure? While this was not a mere demonstration, it was replete with references to the past, as well as anticipating itself as future past, as the last time to be remembered. The presence of an acclaimed photographer (however, one without any naturalist leanings), complicated this further, making the protagonists lapse in and out of demonstration mode, alternatingly concerned with the verisimilitude of their actions to an older "reality," and with the quality of their future specimens. Specimens that they collected although, they confessed, the technicalities of genomic research were beyond their understanding.

View into the abandoned senior staff bungalow inhabited by the Gillies in the 1950s, 2014

"What if time (re)turns? What does it drag along with it?"

Rebecca Schneider, *Performing Remains: Art and War in Times of Theatrical Reenactment*, 2011, p.4

Mrs Gillies and children (?) bathing in Sigi River rock pool;
from Super 8 by Mick Gillies, late 1950s

Performing time: what boundaries to reenactment?

As we studiously reenact experiments conducted half a century earlier, our fieldwork is colonised by performances of pasts – collective and personal, some externally imposed and others playful. Performance can rekindle traces. Tracing remains has performative effects.

Having a meal in the century-old research station guest house, among European visitors, served English breakfast fried on a broken iron stove, cast in Sheffield. Opening abandoned laboratories, together with attendants older than the apparatus they had left behind in their youth; digging with them through drawers of pre-war German cupboards, looking for something they had long forgotten. Explaining disused instruments to a local secondary school-leaver who never saw the research station – or for that matter, any laboratory – in operation. Perusing a library that stopped collecting in the mid-1970s, for a paper acknowledging – for the first time – an octogenarian assistant's contribution to fly taxonomy. Squatting on the library floor, reading job applications by village boys of the '50s, interspersed with 1960s inter-library loan slips requesting papers from Soviet colleagues across Cold War boundaries, and lists of subsidised milk rationings to 1970s staff families.

Negotiating some daily pay for the old men, who had been assistants half a century earlier, and whose first question to us was what "research" we had brought. Hiring, as field assistant, a young village man whose father had been a research assistant, and whose grandfather the cook for the scientific director, who had paid the father's school fees. Visiting the young man's father suffering from Alzheimer's, and hearing the father's and grandfather's stories from the son's mouth. Or speculating with him about the purpose of an overgrown concrete basin adjacent to the imposing former director's villa, which may have been the director's swimming pool, or a fishpond, or a mosquito breeding site – or all or none of it.

Seeking insects, birds and lichens in the forest, together with the 90-year-old bearded white man, who was born in my father's birth year; helping him with his shoelaces (which I never did for my father) after fly-catching in rocky streams; sharing in a smile over his shoulders, as he explains to a village chief that he "was just looking for flies."

Swimming in the rock pool he discovered when half my age. And being confused with him by villagers, who only eventually accept that I, on account of my beard, must be his son. Or searching, together with Ann, guided by images and autobiographies, through the remnants of European domesticity – a giant bath-tub marked "Armitage Shanks," deposited in the garden; barely-discernible rows of geraniums and cyclamen; an ornate wooden dressing table covered with cobwebs left behind in an abandoned English bungalow; resting on the collapsing veranda, overlooking a Constable-style vista of undulating pastures dotted with Friesian cows and what from a distance appear to be old oaks.

Such engagements with place are not about recording evidence of the past, traditional

The authors bathing in Sigi River rock pool;
polaroid by Mariele Neudecker, 2014

Wenzel being greeted as the "Kidevu"
(bearded), 2014

John Raybould explaining the use of
crab traps to Wenzel, Bristol, 2012

archaeology, nor do they bring the past "to life," allow witnessing mundane habits or historical affect. Rather, they are performances of temporality in a present event. Projecting desires in time, inverting time, imagining pasts and evoking past hopes; playing at roles, dreaming and remembering dreams, we break open the surface of the present. Drawing ephemeral lines between present and pasts, we attune our senses to the making of time itself, and of our selves in time. The anachronicity of our experience does not lead to a stable representation of the modern, scientific 20th century past that we came to study; instead, it places the synchronising apparatus of that past formation in its idiosyncratic beauty amidst more ordinary modes of searching in and for time.

Moving beyond the silent stage of Amani where every action appears reenacted, one recognises the performance of temporality across all our fieldwork practices – maybe any ethnographic fieldwork? History inheres here in the mundane pleasures of visiting and conversation, and every gesture carries an echo, a diffuse resonance: staying with elderly scientists in quintessentially grandparental English homes, sleeping in the rooms of their now adult children, conversing over teacakes and early evening drinks about bygone days, sharing, ambiguously, in post-

imperial nostalgia and anachronistic turns of phrase. Making reference to past events that had no bearing on our lives; even retelling, as with our own grandparents, stories that our interlocutors had forgotten; and leaving their homes entangled in their lives and memories that we had suddenly woken.

In what we at first had thought of as mere elicitations of historical narratives and facts – "oral history" – we performed time, rekindled past feelings and emotions about the past, in those who were more than mere informants, and in ourselves. Like all ethnographic fieldwork, our short-lived participation in old scientists' lives enacted other modes of being. But (maybe) more than traditional ethnography, this performance enmeshed times past and present. British living rooms became like Amani's hillscape, landscapes of remains, which we momentarily coinhabited; weaving unpredictable patterns between past and present.

What applies to the temporality played out between people extends to engagements with things. Landscape, buildings and rooms, objects are from another time, carry traces, remain what they have been without ever returning to it. Sheltering from the rain under the veranda of a ruined colonial bungalow, listening to drops gathering in the disused and displaced bath-tub, moved outdoors as a cattle trough. Dropping into a rock pool after a day of *Simuliid* larvae collection. Joining, through the fragment of a historical letter, a correspondence between long-gone strangers.

Temporality then is a matter of shifting constellations emerging from action, some more coherent, most fleeting, non-aligned and incoherent. Moments of imagining time that take shape in relations, and that can create affective bonds, make momentary temporal collectives – coevalness – but can also remain incommensurable, reasserting contradictions, procuring embarrassments, conflict and struggle.

If temporality is (re-)performed in events, in movements between one another that set traces in motion and leave new traces behind, is there a limit to reenactment? And, if temporality indeed is performed, does one ever inhabit the same time as the other in more than a mere physical sense – is one ever "coeval" in the ethnographic encounter, as Johannes Fabian admonished us, apart from in the fleeting moments in which one agrees at playing at the same temporality?

Esther Kika and John Mganga preparing the inventory of their laboratory, video stills, 2015

Working through remains

When reenacting Raybould's 1960s papers, we performed past work, executing "Methods;" shedding light on the context and resonances of past action. But how are we to enact the action itself, reconstitute "work"?

Work, back then, was frequently described in terms of its "seriousness," its "conscientious" execution of precise instructions. Wasn't this also John's concern last year, when he secretly returned the crabs that we had caught into the stream, without his former assistants noticing, so as to avoid that they realise that this fieldwork hadn't been "serious"? (It was reflected also in his insistence on delivering the crabs back to the very stream they were collected from, in order not to disturb local ecology.)

At the same time, African technicians' work was fragmented into tiny functional bits, which each technician was trained to execute to perfection; very narrow task-scapes.

Wenzel's notes, Amani, 23 March 2015

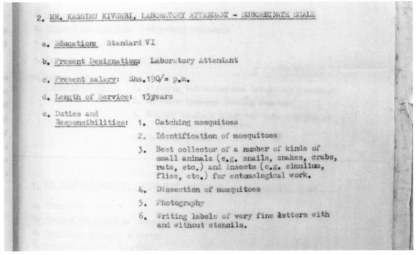

Entry into the staff record of Kassimu Kivumbi, "Laboratory Attendant – Subordinate Scale," early 1960s, Amani archive

Work

Key to the success of scientific collections and experiments was the execution – with maximum "fidelity" – of prescribed actions; accurately repeated over long periods of time, according to a defined speed and rhythm, aiming for complete coverage and faithful recording.

Commitment to "serious" work – measured by adherence to rules, absence of error, and timing – was instilled as a virtue, and became a source of satisfaction and pride for some. Recall, for example, the dis-satisfaction of Mr Mganga, John's octogenarian assistant, at having to use an inappropriate (and French) 1980s recording form for his 2014 reenactment of 1965 fly catches. Or the exclamation of Mrs Mathilda, the last Institute secretary, yesterday, in response to my questions about how it feels to have nothing to do in her office: "It is painful. We were trained to work so hard. We even typed confidential reports up to midnight. I was the fastest typist – I liked typing!" Punching the air with ten-finger typing, she went on: "But I leave my house at 8.30am, for my daily programme – so work continues."

How does one reenact this: not the past script, but the essence of the work it entailed, rekindling the affect and relations it entailed? Seriously.

Wenzel's notes, Amani, 23 March 2015

Laboratory drawer opened during the preparation
of the inventory, 2015

More challenging than anticipated

Again heavy rain today. When I arrive at the central laboratory, John's old lab, at 8.30, they are already there: John Mganga and Stephen Fedha, old men who assisted John in the 1950s; Esther Kika and Martin Mwaiko, the current elderly caretakers of the laboratory; and Mrs Mathilda, the director's secretary (since 1987). Mathilda is cleaning the typewriter with oil and a small cloth; the others have found their lab coats and are ready for today's task: the laboratory inventory.

I explain the work: to examine, record and photograph every object in the room, taking each wall in turn, working from upper left to lower right. The list is first handwritten by the laboratory attendants and then typed up by the secretary. We work from 8.30am to 1pm, and from 2pm to 5pm, aiming to finish the room.

The work is more challenging than I had anticipated:

What is an object? Is a cupboard full of half-eaten 1960s files one object or a myriad? Upon closer examination, files stuck together by bat excrement and time become re-differentiated, referring to different decades, different projects and diseases, different scientists and assistants.

Can objects be counted as group of a class – glass cylinders, used test tubes, meteorological day records – or should each be described in turn – 1.5l glass cylinder, 200ml glass cylinder with lid?

What if objects break up, if parts are found in different places, or when objects dissolve into waste? A diagram that is half-eaten by rats, a crumbling rubber tube?

What if objects cannot be named and nobody recalls their function?

Or if an object requires a long story: glass ball, approximately 3-inch diameter, used to bundle daylight for

detailed examination of morphological patterns on mosquito wings?

And what about objects that don't belong, or even offend sensitivities and disturb remembrance: three mummified dead rats in a drawer, behind a cloud atlas, and an early 1950s rainfall notebook (soaked in toxic anti-mould and insect tincture, half-eaten)?

The inventory progressively breaks apart the sedimented whole of the central laboratory into fragments – into the original components and objects, and beyond that into the products of their decay.

Writing these objects proves challenging. Many terms have only ever been used verbally. Mathilda types – it seems to me, mercilessly – precisely what the attendants have written.

At several points, I am compelled to go over procedures again. Split the overarching task – to name all objects – into smaller and smaller components that structure the work without imbu-ing it with wider meaning. First take object from shelf; place on surface; photograph; write; return. At one point, after explanations and discussion, Mganga and Kika start a wall all over again. Feeling very awkward. Slightly too much reenactment. At one point, one of the old men asks me whether he can go for a short call. Another one asks, before lunch, to go for a drink of water. (Should I have stopped reenactment there?)

Stephen Fedha is most knowledgeable about the laboratory objects. He knows the names of many a strange apparatus, and the others go across the room to ask him, get spellings and functions. Behind his back, Mganga chuckles over Fedha's expertise. On two occasions, he throws small objects across the room at Fedha's back.

Mganga and Fedha find exercise books, which they filled in the late '50s with the rows upon rows of neatly pencilled microscope counts of some parasite

– the books do not contain labels or indices. Some objects still evoke, 50 years later, some admiration – the microscopic camera proudly labelled "Leitz;" the crystal ball for mosquito morphology; the shiny skin-snipping set.

The whole morning, rain kept dripping through the roof, gathering in small pools on the black and white tiles of the laboratory floor. At lunch, we each went our way, to continue an hour later, slowing down under the afternoon's warmth. By 5pm we are almost finished, pushing through the last glass cupboard together, to get home. Mathilda will finish typing tomorrow.

Wenzel's notes, Amani, 23 March 2015

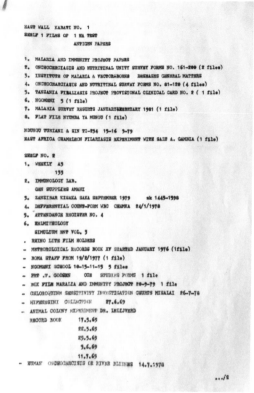

Typewritten inventory of central laboratory, first page, Amani, 2015

Mrs Mathilda's restored typewriter, 2015

Mrs Mathilda, typing up the handwritten lists provided by the laboratory workers, 2015

160

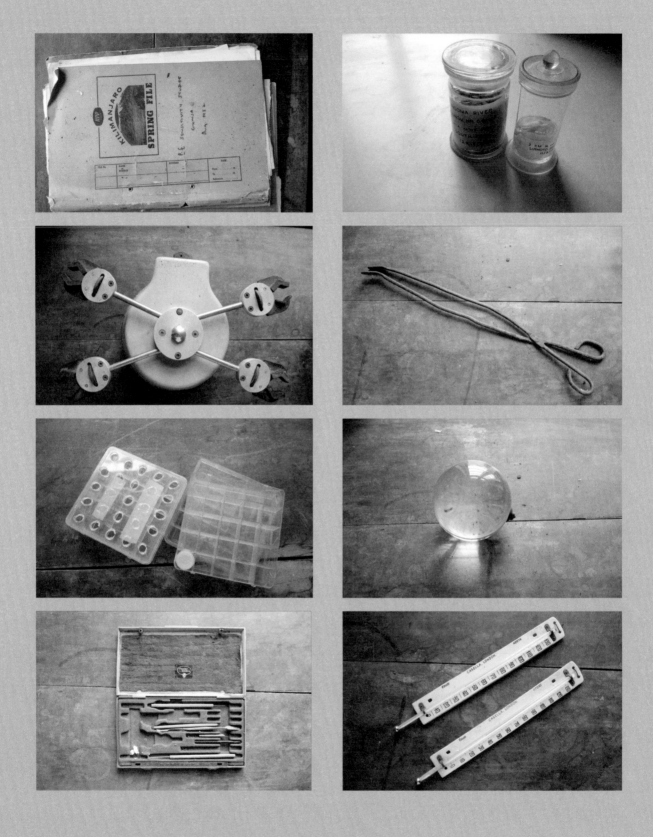

18 of 3561 objects photographed for the inventory, 2015

Derema, hole inside German mansion, 2013

Zomba   You see, they went there in there.

Mbonde   Eeh.

Zomba   They have destroyed the concrete right here, to find out if there is any money.

Mbonde   Ah.

Zomba   They have destroyed it right here.

Mbonde   Yes.

Zomba   You see?

Interview with local resident Mr Zomba,
walking around German mansion in Derema, 24 July 2014

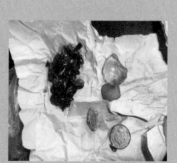

German relics offered to René
by a treasure diggers, 2013

Treasure diggers

Sigi Wood carving railway station, 2013

German remains

Still waiting for research clearance for "Memories" project so only scouting permitted. Decided to get a deeper sense of the site and asked Aloys to show Mbonde (my research assistant) and me old structures, especially those dating to its German period. What meanings are attributed locally to such remnants of German presence? Aloys' face lit up when I asked him to show me German-era remains – he appears keenly interested in the history of the Amani Institute, the local ethnic group and the Eastern Usambara Mountains more generally. Together with Mbonde, we hopped on two motorcycles and drove the 7km down the curvy,

Sigi Wood carving train station, 2013

pockmarked road to Sigi, and visited the recently restored former German railway station near to entrance gate of the Amani Nature Reserve.

Aloys explained that the building nowadays serves as the Visitor Centre for the Amani Nature Reserve. The door was locked, Aloys got key from a staff member. We entered the building – I was struck by a smell, stale and musky. Spiderwebs along the ceilings, dried-out insects on the polished wooden floors; some dusty, crooked-hanging exhibits. Several remnants of German period: distinctly carved (restored?) woodwork, and, a (poor) reproduction of a photograph of men posing at a bowling alley. Outside, along a trail towards the fast-flowing Sigi river, Aloys showed us crumbling remnants of the German-built water collection reservoir, used for steam trains. I asked Aloys if such sites associated with German activity mean anything to local people today. Aloys exclaimed yes, and said that some people (allegedly) unearthed valuables at or near such German sites. He did not know of any recent treasure digging near the ruined dam, but would take us to other sites with recent activities.

Back uphill, Aloys drove straight to the spot along road flanking northern edge of Amani Hill to show a hole dug into the reddish soil that is large enough for an adult to stand in, about 2 metres

Sigi *Kegelbahn* (bowling alley, around 1900

deep. Unknown people had dug it few months earlier (summer 2012). Aloys explained that in the Eastern Usambaras people have been digging for "German treasures" for several decades, but on Amani Hill digging only became possible after the scientists departed in 2005 because guards used to protect the area and chase intruders away. This hole was located under a former toolshed. When I asked why this specific location, Aloys said that he heard diggers looked for particular signs that could indicate treasures might be buried there. Growths of finger palms were one of the signs that diggers looked for (because it is not a native species, but a tree imported by the Germans). Aloys did not know if the diggers had actually discovered treasures from this hole. He knew diggers and could arrange for us to talk with them.

Rene's notes, 12 November 2012

Amani Hill, hole, 2013

Tombstone of a German doctor, 2013

Magoda, a flower indicating German treasures, 2013

Digging inside German-era mansion, Derema, 2013

Today we will visit tombstone of German doctor some 4km from Derema, adjacent to site that, people say, hosted German-era clinic or hospital. Aloys and Mbonde had visited the site several weeks ago. Sparked my curiosity, also because I had not read anything about any such hospital in the archival record. Beautiful ride on motorcycle past remnants of Derema water mills, through tea plantations and forest fringes. Mbonde did not recall the location of the site, but after asking several times, local people pointed us into the right direction. Off the main road, we drove 1–2km along a narrow path that sloped along hills where tea was planted. Mbonde parked motorcycle and we climbed some 50m to cleared spot in tea plantation where damaged gravestone stuck out of reddish soil. Carved and polished gravestone, looks like polished granite. Script in German. Smudged with soil, so difficult to read. Washed with drinking water and filled carved-out letters with mud to make text visible. A physician (Dr Med.) named Felix – family name not visible on tombstone.

From the tombstone we walk about 200m toward the forested fringe on top of a hill crest. Ahead, a hedge-like row of distinct bushes on right-hand side, some carrying yellowish-orange

flowers that I had not yet seen before. Behind the bushes, Mbonde explained, was the location of a German-era hospital. We walked along the perimeter – dense bushes, uneven terrain, almost impossible to penetrate without a hatchet (which we had not taken along). Many holes and other signs of digging. Aloys had told us before coming here that local people had been digging here for decades. Difficult to photograph due to tree cover and darkness. Site exudes unique atmosphere, also because the special flowering trees grow only in this area.

Enough time left before sunset to swing by the German villa at Derema-1, to check out the state of the building, if any new holes have been dug. As usual, some kids were playing soccer on the field facing the mansion. We parked motorbike and exchanged greetings. The kids continued playing as Mbonde and I walked around the house to spot any changes, as we have done during the past two years whenever we were in the area because this house is known to attract diggers. We notice a new hole: a wall to the basement has been broken open. The hole was quite narrow, but a slim adult or child could fit through.

From the breached wall, we walked

around the house to the room where the floor had been breached several years ago. Last time we visited, one could look into the basement through this hole, but this time it had been largely filled with soil. Clearly a sign of continued digging in the basement, however so far we've had no luck so far in identifying let alone contacting the diggers. We casually asked some kids about latest digging – they had no idea.

Rene's notes, 30 September 2014

Derema mansion, new hole in basement wall, 2013

Holes and ghosts

After the scientists left Amani Hill Research Station in 2005, for newly-built, modern laboratories in the lowland towns of Tanga and Korogwe, various groups of "diggers" were delighted that they would finally get an opportunity to start digging for treasures. Of course, some guards remained at Amani to patrol the compound, but since most staff had moved elsewhere, it had become quiet enough for diggers to commence their secret, nocturnal activities.

Digging in the Eastern Usambara Mountains is an all-male activity, usually involving teams of around three to six men formed around a shared goal: to search for, excavate and sell treasures and other valuables dating from the period of German colonialism. Members of a digging team vow to share both the burdens and the fruits of their labour, which also has an important ritual dimension, since buried treasures are protected by potent Swahili and German spirits who must be "treated properly." Otherwise, buried valuables will be rendered invisible or otherwise irretrievable. To avoid antagonising these protective spirits, diggers must refrain from polluting activities such as sexual intercourse or drinking alcohol before and during digging. Furthermore, at various stages they pay a traditional healer to help identify where the treasures are buried and which treatment (often, a combination of medicines and potent words) may be needed to appease the spirits. Only when all steps are followed correctly can treasures be extracted successfully from the hole.

Identifying areas that might contain German-era treasures is easiest with a map indicating where items are buried. Diggers heard that such maps exist, but since these were made around a century ago by Germans, they have never seen one. Lacking maps, diggers therefore scour the environment for possible signs, often – though not always – near tangible remains of former German habitation such as (ruined) houses, roads, dams or wells. They also look for more subtle signs, for instance the presence of exotic flowers or plants such as the fan palms in the photo above. To diggers, a cluster of fan palms near to a site of former German habitation – in this case an abandoned toolshed belonging to the Amani Research Institute – indicated that valuables might be buried there.

One moonless evening about 2–3 years ago, a team of diggers assembled on the road snaking along Amani Hill. After verifying that no guards were around, they initiated the first crucial steps by identifying where treasures might be hidden. To treat the spirits that were protecting these valuables, the diggers had requested help from a trustworthy traditional healer, whose sizeable fee they paid by pooling financial contributions. The healer prepared a special *dawa* (medicine) that he smeared on diggers' spades and machetes, uttering potent words during the treatment. The *dawa* was dual-purpose: it enabled treated tools to "detect" the German-era treasures but also appeased the spirits that protect these valuables. Immediately following his treatment, the traditional healer departed. Then team members began digging into the wall of the hill, slightly below the left-most cluster of fan palms. After several hours of fruitless digging, they went home and returned the following day. Again their efforts yielded nothing, and when the hole was about three metres deep, the diggers stopped digging.

The diggers agreed that the healer must have been off a little when indicating the likely location, so they started digging about two metres further to the right, at a spot similarly covered with finger palms. They returned to the new site several nights in a row, and the resulting hole was much wider and deeper than the first one. Again, however, they unearthed nothing but soil, roots and insects.

The men did not give up. Some diggers have been digging for 30 years without finding anything of value. Yet sometimes, diggers are lucky and unearth something of value – German coins such as *hellers*, or *rupia*, much more valuable and sought-after. Some digging teams are said to have found gold and diamonds, but also motorcycles and tractors that were in working order. Recalling such successes often inspires team members to continue digging, but also a strange event which prompted a change of plans.

En route to Amani Hill for nightly digging, the diggers ran into a friend who told them the following story: he ran into two young *wazungu* (whites), a male and a female, who were walking out and about deep in the night. The *wazungu* asked him to show them the two holes where diggers had been working, examining each hole briefly with a flashlight. The male then pulled an ancient-looking map out of a coat pocket, and began walking toward *mifinesini*. At this junction, the *wazungu* climbed down the shrub-covered hill, halfway down as the brook. After about 20 minutes, they climbed back to the road, carrying three metal tins in their hands. The diggers' friend recalled the strange light these tins emitted; it was impossible to see what could be inside. Both *wazungu* were smiling and chatting loudly in their unintelligible language. The male handed the friend some coins. After saying *asante* (thanks) they placed the tins in carry-on bags, mounted their motorcycle, and drove off into the night. They were never seen or heard from again. Some people say they became very rich.

The diggers took the story as a sign; they had been digging in the wrong location. This was a familiar problem. Almost all diggers agreed that the German spirits which protect treasures are both cunning and tough. Moreover, since contemporary traditional healers were not as skilled as those in the past, very few knew how to prepare medicines that can successfully treat German spirits. Hence German spirits continue to confound African diggers, whereas *wazungu* often succeed in unearthing treasures.

Inspired by the story about the two young *wazungu*, the team retraced the steps of the foreigners, and stopped at a site where the soil appeared to have been disturbed quite recently. The team began digging, with spades and hatchets, but since they did not find anything valuable or promising, they decided to recruit professional help.

Hamisi, a digger, suggested they seek help from a friend at the Ministry of Natural Resources in Dar es Salaam. The team supported his plan. For about US$300, Hamisi's friend agreed to investigate the site with professional equipment borrowed from the Ministry. Upon reaching Amani, Hamisi and his friend met with the other diggers and together they went to the spot where the two *wazungu* were said to have retrieved the luminescent tins. Hamisi's friend carried a device that resembled a typewriter, with an antenna. He explained that it was not a metal detector but something different, and made approving sounds when the device beeped as he traversed the area. The scan confirmed the presence of buried treasures and he advised diggers to obtain help from a *mtaalamu* (an expert, in this case a traditional healer) to facilitate digging.

The diggers agreed to save around US$200–300. Several weeks later they had accumulated the sum. They contacted a *mtaalamu* with a good reputation, who prepared *dawa* which he sprinkled over the topsoil. The healer then told them to dig until encountering a sign – such as an arrow or a slab of concrete – which would indicate that the treasure was nearby. At that point they would have to contact another healer who could prepare a special *dawa* to calm the spirits protecting the treasure. Then the treasure would be theirs to collect.

Pleased with the steps taken, the diggers started
digging, night after night. When the hole was
about 12 metres deep, the diggers came across
an arrow-like piece of wood. They were elated,
for this could be a sign that something of value
was buried there. Once again, they stopped
digging, and planned to save up sufficient
money to pay a healer who could treat the
German spirits that are protecting the treasures.

Amani, giant hole downhill from
director's house, 2013

Amani view, Mlinga mountain and coast line, 2013

Derema, 12 March 1903

§ 1. The German East Africa Society
represented by _____ transfers free of charge to the
Imperial Government of German East Africa represented by
_____, a plot of land located in Amani, for the estab-
lishment of a Biological Agricultural Institute in Amani.

§ 2. The land gifted, which excludes an area of about 130
hectares that are designated for locally residing natives, as
indicated in the accompanying map, covers according to
previous measures about 250 hectares.

German National Archive; GNA R1001.8650, p.105.

The botanical garden

Amani Biologisch-Landwirtschaftliches Institut, around 1900

Demarcation

It seems essential to me that natives retain the land they have been cultivating, so as to ensure that the availability of a tribe of capable workers for the Institute.

Letter from the Imperial Governor of German East Africa, Count von Goetzen, to the Department of Foreign Affairs, Colonial Department, Berlin, 16 September 1902

An experimental station

[...] Important for choosing the location of the experimental station [ie, Amani] was the proximity of large plantations and the fact that, to meet the most immediate needs, a house was available that had been used as a sanatorium for convalescents [...]

In the immediate vicinity of the station building one finds an assortment of useful plants and seed beds, and farther away are special cultures. That way the institute will serve its primary purpose, advancing the cultivation of useful plants. For the first plantation, the Royal Botanical Garden has sent 859 species of tropical useful plants as well as 208 other tropical plants. These were planted shortly before my arrival in Amani, and are developing well according to the latest report by Professor Zimmermann, especially the rubber plants we sent, *Kickxia* and *Castilloa*, as well as *Cinchona* bark trees. Professor Zimmermann's relations with Java, and similarly the procurement of plants and seeds by Professor Dr Volkens and Dr Busse during their stay in Java, will significantly contribute to the multiplication of valuable cultivars; I myself was able to contribute ample seeds of Japanese Camphor trees.

Adolf Engler, *Das biologisch-landwirtschaftliche Institut zu Amani in Ost-Usambara*, 1903

A model of biological-agricultural institute

Java has been in many ways a model of the biological-agricultural institute at Amani. [...] The Botanical Gardens in Buitenzorg had to fulfill a dual function, namely: to be both a "centre for "pure," free-from-practical-utility, detached science" in the colonies, as well as a station that finds practical answer to questions.

Detlev und Gerhild Bald, *Das Forschungsinstitut Amani*, 1972, pp.44–5

Amani's potential for producing quinine

Quinine is a drug derived from the bark of a tree called cinchona. The supply of this drug, essential to the efficient functioning of mankind in the tropics, comes almost entirely from the Dutch island of Java. The fact that the British Empire required about eight million lb. of the bark has led to considerable investigation to see if it is possible to break the Dutch-monopoly. Cinchona bark sent to London from this Territory has been stated to equal the best Javanese bark, which helps forward the encouraging opinion that quinine may be produced profitably in this country.

Tanganyika Times, Saturday, February 2, 1929

Overview of Amani botanical and forestry plantation, copied 1922, from older German original

Mbomole Hill, Japanese camphor trees, 2014

Sigi chini, tagged para rubber tree, 2014

Little rain during the last couple of days – looked promising for walking through the former botanical garden with Mr Mbalawe. After breakfast, we packed the camera, sound recorder, bottles of water, and drove by motorcycle to Mlola. Journey took little over an hour. We parked motorcycle along road, climbed to Mr Mbalawe's house. His wife, sitting outside in the shade with several other women, was pounding flour, and greeted us as we approached. So did Mr Mbalawe, who, pointing at dark clouds, said that rain might once again mess up our plan. We left promptly, descended to the road, and discussed the plan with Mr Mbalawe: to walk through the former botanical garden and to retrace what was happening there in the 1970s, when people were still working there and maintaining the garden.

While walking along the road, Mr Mbalawe explained that, back then, the area looked like a plantation or a garden. Each plot was dedicated to cultivating one species. Mr Mbalawe would point in different directions: over there used to be breadfruit trees, in that direction areca nuts, there teak. The plot where bamboo used to be cultivated still contained a lot of bamboo, but in other areas there seemed to be few if any traces of prior cultivation. To my untrained eye, those areas looked pretty much like other parts of the

Memory walk

On agenda today: visit with Mr Mbalawe, the former forest officer of the Amani botanical garden, to plan a "memory walk" in the area. Some months ago, Mr Mbalawe had agreed to this plan but rainy weather has prevented its implementation so far. No electricity and poor mobile phone signal in Mlola, where Mr Mbalawe lives, so we will drive there by motorcycle. Located along the Sigi River, at south-eastern edge of the former Amani estate, Mlola can be reached by a very poor road.

Weather played havoc – yet again. It was dry in Amani but downhill in Mlola it had rained. Road is in terrible shape, mostly rocks and pebbles, very bumpy

ride. Parked motorcycle on roadside, asked a kid to watch it. Terrain probably too slippery for planned walk through Amani estate.

Mr Mbalawe greeted us warmly. We chatted, his wife served us tasty clove-flavored spiced tea. Pointing at pregnant clouds, he said what we knew already: rain is likely today, would it make sense to postpone our plan? We agreed to postpone: filming will be difficult when the steep and rocky terrain is wet and slippery. We'll try again on a later date, preferably after a couple of dry days. Exchange greetings, return to Amani.

Rene's notes, Amani, 2 October 2013

Amani Nature Reserve, a very diverse mix of trees and plants.

After about 500m, we veered off the road and entered into the forest proper. Mr Mbalawe led the way. No visible trail, steep and slippery due to wet leaves. Fallen trees and thorny thickets made some areas difficult to pass. Filming difficult. A botanist by training, Mr Mbalawe enjoyed talking about trees but had relatively little to say about the workers or social activities. A former plot with rubber trees contained plenty of old and young trees. Mr Mbalawe pointed at the bark of some trees, which showed signs of cutting to harvest latex milk.

Rene's notes, Amani, 6 October 2013

[Approaching plot where rubber trees used to be cultivated:]

Mbonde So these plots contained rubber trees?

Mbalawe Yes.

Mbonde Then you go to another plot?

Mbalawe (mumbling) You'll find, uh, coca cola.

Mbonde Coca Cola?

Mbalawe Coca nut.

Mbonde Kola nut?

Mbalawe Yes.

Mbonde Then you continue... you find another plot?

Mbalawe Maybe households.

Mbonde Ah.

Transcript of walking interview with Mr Mbalawe in Amani Botanical Garden, 6 October 2013

Mbomole cinchona grove, 2014

Mbomole viewpoint, tea plantation, 2014

Cinchona boom

Upon returning to Amani, Mbonde stopped motorcycle to show me a hideout used by smugglers during the 2009 'cinchona boom.' Almost invisible from the road, it sits off a "mouse trail" (KiSwahili: *njia panya*) that snakes downhill onto the coastal plain, bypassing the checkpoints where police officers inspect traffic for outlawed goods.

Not permanently inhabited, the dwelling sometimes serves as a restaurant where residents consume local alcoholic brews and freshly grilled pork – activities frowned upon by part of the population, hence the remote location. Two 'regulars' had offered the owner Tsh 10,000/- (US$ 7) to hide bags with bark during the 2009 cinchona boom, a generous payment that ensured no questions were asked.

Middlemen paid up to Tsh 15,000 (US$12) per kilo of cinchona bark during the 2009 boom, when locals debarked and decimated thousands of threes during nightly forays into the forests. Officials never discovered that 1200 kilograms of cinchona bark had been hidden in the restaurant. When the coast was clear, porters carried 80kg bags of bark on their backs, downhill along the *njia panya* to a house in *Kisiwani*, a village just outside the gate to the Amani Nature Reserve. A known criminal protected by 'friends in high places' owned this house, so we decided to halt the study here.

Rene's notes, Amani, 8 December 2014

Mbomole, recently debarked cinchona tree, 2014

Dar es Salaam (1944), wartime manufacture of quinine, 2014

Large-scale debarking of cinchona hybrida trees:

This activity surged during the beginning of September 2009. The cinchona bark reportedly is used to make tablets. This illegal trade was halted in a joint operation with paramilitary soldiers. Thirty bags containing 80kg of cinchona bark were seized [and burned].

Report by Director Amani Nature Reserve to Tanzanian Ministry of Natural Resources and Tourism, February 2010

Final visit to Amani. Frustration mounting: unable to resolve key aspects of 2009 cinchona boom, when most trees were decimated in the Amani Nature Reserve: What makes cinchona bark so valuable? Why did those financing the operation pay up to 30 times the going market rate? What were the destination and the purpose of the estimated 3000kgs of bark?

Rene's notes, Amani 20 February, 2015

Below is the attached snap showing 30 barks of *Cinchona* arrested during the operation are burned.

Burning illegally harvested cinchona, 2009

Niakhar

Edited by Noémi Tousignant

14°34'48" N, 16°34'48" W

Elevation: 6m

Location: Senegal. Sine Region, Department of Fatick, District of Niakhar, 135km east of Dakar.

Prior and alternative names of overlapping areas: Sine Saloum Study, Sob Terroir Study, Ngayokhem Permanent Study, Ngayokhem Population Laboratory, Population and Health Programme in Niakhar, Niakhar Study Zone, Niakhar demographic/health/environmental observatory.

Current Status: Health and Demographic Surveillance System (HDSS) run by the French State Institute for Development Research (IRD, formerly ORSTOM).

Origin of the name: "Niakhar" was the name both of a district chosen for demographic observation in 1962, and of that district's main town. In 1972, Senegal's districts were subdivided into rural communities, one of which was also named Niakhar. In 1981 a research station was built in the town of Niakhar. In 1983, ORSTOM delimited a new observation zone around 30 villages that has since been labelled an HDSS. This zone is also called Niakhar, although it does not include the town or rural community of Niakhar.

Chronology

1962
Pierre Cantrelle introduces repeated demographic observation to the Niakhar district as part of the Sine Saloum Study, a Senegalese State initiative to improve civil registration.

Demographers imagine rural Africa before this study as "*terra demographica incognita.*"

1964
Cantrelle is hired by the French State's Overseas Research Office of Science and Technology (ORSTOM).The Sine Saloum Study continues.

1965
André Lericollais and Joseph Diatte conduct a "*terroir*" study of Sob, in which they conduct fine-grained surveys of land and resource management.

The study's finding of land "saturation" will justify government programmes of assisted migration.

1967
After the Sine Saloum Study, annual census-taking continues in Ngayokhem administrative unit, a reduced area of Niakhar district. It is renamed "Ngayokhem Permanent Study."

Longitudinal data series created by the Sine Saloum Study are to be preserved and extended "for as long as possible."

1974
Annual observation in Ngayokhem stops.

1977
Annual observation in Ngayokhem is resumed to offer the possibility of full records of reproductive life for women whose birth dates were recorded by the Sine Saloum Study are who are about to reach puberty.

1981
Demographer Michel Garenne and fieldworker Michel Ndiaye purchase land for a research station in the town of Niakhar. The costs of land and building are shared by Pierre Cantrelle and three further fieldworkers, Tidjane Sene, Takhy Diop and Emile Ndiaye who have been working for ORSTOM since the late 1960s, and now have permanent contracts.

Garenne is seen as reviving Cantrelle's legacy. He envisions the future of Niakhar as a study zone for world-class, interdisciplinary health research, including vaccine trials.

1983
Routine data collection is extended to 30 villages for a study of child nutrition and mortality, and in preparation for vaccine trials.

Eight of these villages have been followed since 1962.

1985
Sob is studied again as part of a research programme initiated by Lericollais to revisit old fieldsites. He and Diatte return to measure changes in tree density since 1965.

1987
A major measles vaccine trial is implemented.

Some villages refuse to consent to vaccination and blood-sampling. Garenne's final report blames "bad memories" on earlier health studies in the area.

1987–1997
This is a decade of intense activity; a larger fieldwork team visits each family compound weekly for the measles trial, then a pertussis vaccine trial. A team of 12 fieldworkers resides within the rural study area, rather than in the station in the town.

Funding, work contracts, and improvements to the station continue to be tied to short-term project grants.

1991
Garenne is "evicted" from Niakhar following a controversy over his handling of the measles trial results. He goes on to participate in the creation of other demographic observatories in Africa.

1997–2006
Activity in Niakhar slows down; half the fieldwork team lose their jobs, while others work on short, non-consecutive contracts.

The future is uncertain.

1998
ORSTOM is renamed the Institute for Development Research (IRD).

2001
Administratively, Niakhar is turned into a "service unit" by Jean-Philippe Chippaux, introducing clearer rules and procedures for accessing the database and using Niakhar's research "platform." Several remaining fieldworkers obtain permanent contracts.

2005
Beginning of "Ecosoc" study of social and environmental change: Richard Lalou and Robert Diatte re-map tree density in Sob.

2006
A major meningitis vaccine trial is launched, rekindling hopes for Niakhar as a research site and allowing researchers to "think big" about its future.

2014
A 50th anniversary symposium is organised in Dakar by researchers who have a stake in Niakhar's future as a field site.

The event commemorates Niakhar as a model of continuous and cumulative interdisciplinary research and observation lasting beyond individual projects.

The question is asked during the event: "Should Niakhar be stopped?"

Niakhar: a field site with a history

Niakhar now

"Niakhar" is many things. Its researchers describe it as a "health and demographic surveillance system" (HDSS), a study zone, and a population, health and ecological observatory. As an "HDSS," "Niakhar" denotes simultaneously a delimited area under continuous monitoring, the population being monitored, and the resulting data being accumulated. As a "study zone," its regularly updated baseline data also makes Niakhar a space and population within which to conduct surveys and controlled trials; it is also a longitudinal "observatory" of social, biological and environmental change. "Niakhar" is also made up of researchers and a modest research station, located outside the study zone in the town of Niakhar. As a place, a population, a database, a station, Niakhar stands for the possibility of future research that builds on past investments: in other words, a research infrastructure.

"Niakhar" in the early 2010s is a set of 30 villages spread over 203 square kilometres, with its roughly 45,000 inhabitants registered in a database. Three times a year, each of these compounds is visited to update demographic and health data. Calculated portions of the monitored population are enrolled in health trials (including preventive malaria treatment, and flu and meningitis vaccines). Social science studies map social networks and validate data collection tools. Schools and wells, rainfall and trees are also counted and mapped, through surveying, tele-detection and Geographical Information Systems (GIS) software. Outside the zone, in the district town of Niakhar, is a research station: a walled compound of modest buildings serving as offices, guest-rooms and a small laboratory. Men and a few women are available locally to conduct and supervise fieldwork; some have several decades of experience. The database and station are administered by the French French State's overseas Institute for Development Research (IRD), which celebrated Niakhar's 50th anniversary in 2014.

Data histories and the observatory as memory

Routine descriptions trace the pedigree of Niakhar back through an unbroken line of regular demographic surveys to the Sine Saloum Study of 1962–1966. In this first study, Pierre Cantrelle introduced a novel demographic field method

"The first photo of Niakhar," Pierre Cantrelle in November 1962

to Africa: a census was repeated at regular intervals in a small area, with each "passage" of the survey through the zone updating the previous data set and anticipating the next. In particular, the study captured precise birth and marriage dates, which are not routinely recorded in rural Africa. Towards the end of the study, Cantrelle realised that these data series would increase in value if observation was maintained, registering the vital fates of young children, and women's reproductive histories. The origin story linking all future research to the Sine Saloum Study is above all a celebration of continuity. It depicts Niakhar as a site of science made up of pasts – pasts which are continuously carried forward by the repetition of observation. Memory – the memory that is kept, carried and updated in Niakhar's archive of demographic data – is the very fabric of a space defined as an "observatory."

This celebration of continuity incorporates Niakhar's past into the history of the IRD (called ORSTOM until 1998), glossing over the fact that the Sine Saloum Study was initially a Senegalese government initiative, overseen by Cantrelle acting as a UN technical assistant and conducted by government agents as fieldworkers. It also elides interruptions in the collection of data, as well as its shifting scales (from 65, to eight, to 30 villages) and changing rationales, and chronic uncertainty about future collection. In 1967, after funding for the Sine Saloum Study ended, the number of villages under observation was reduced to eight in order to continue collecting demographic data at lower cost. Then, in 1977, data collection was resumed after an interruption, partly to maintain data series on girls who had been born during the first study and who were now reaching child-bearing age. To continue observing was to keep this demographic memory active: updated, retrievable and extendable. To stop would rupture a suturing of recorded pasts to the population's future.

The renewal of data collection could also reconnect to more distant pasts: in 1985, the geographer André Lericollais invited colleagues to revisit villages in which they had collected reams of data on household resources, land use, and family and migration histories two decades earlier. Sob, a village within the Niakhar zone, had in 1965 been the site of an intensive and pioneering "terroir" study of land management practices on a small scale – intensively observing how social groups managed the distribution and productivity of land by counting cattle and trees, which are seen to have a crucial role in Serer control over soil fertility. In 1985, the plots of Sob were again surveyed, and reconnected to family lineages; its crop rotations, tree densities and cattle herds were re-counted and re-mapped. Old data was called up to analyse responses to drought, overpopulation and migration. After another two decades, in 2005, the counting of trees was reinitiated in Sob to launch what was intended to be routine environmental monitoring.

Trials of vaccination and other health technologies have also continued to rely on routine demographic observation for the baseline data needed to recruit infants, randomise comparison groups, and follow up effects. In 1981, Cantrelle returned to Niakhar with a student, Michel Garenne. Garenne's ambitions for Niakhar as a zone for health research led to the creation of the station and the expansion of routine monitoring to 30 villages. To set up and run a study of health interventions or determinants usually requires only a few years' worth of accumulated data: a short-term memory of the study population. But to maintain the site and its inhabitants as available for study, this data must be continuously updated. At times, fieldworkers visited each home in the study zone as often as every week.

The pasts remembered by Niakhar's data are not left dormant. Its archive is made to bear evidence of causality and change, and linked up to anticipated future research through its compounds, plots and hinterlands. Repetition dredges up old data and bears it to the surface of the present.

Ethical histories and the memory of bodies

The repetition of scientific passages through Niakhar builds up into a long history of exchange between scientists and subjects, between French and Senegalese, and between senior researchers and subordinate fieldworkers. Memories of research among these actors contain questions about the fairness of this exchange, and about the obligations and expectations arising from successive or repeated scientific practices. Research pasts sometimes intrude unbidden, in the form of memories of corporeal extractions and rumours of illicit blood economies: Garenne noted in the report of a major 1987–1989 vaccine trial that refusals to participate were highest in villages with "bad memories" of blood sampling, dating back to a nutrition study in 1968 and a hepatitis vaccination study in 1978–1979.

Yet the cumulative memory of repeated interactions is also seen as fostering trust and saving lives. The decade and a half that stretches from the beginning of a nutrition and mortality study in 1983 to the end of a pertussis vaccine trial in 1997 stands out as a period of intense field presence and embodied exchange. More than ever before in Niakhar, the rituals of census-taking mixed with practices performed on bodies: blood-drawing, vaccination, care, and emergency medical evacuations. While field-workers had previously spent only a few months each year in Niakhar, those hired or kept on for the measles and persussis trials lived within the zone continously, sometimes in the villages they were born into. They visited households weekly, watching for newborns to recruit to the studies and remaining vigilant to the vital disruptions of disease and the side-effects of experimental vaccines and treatments. They reassured local leaders and infants' mothers that injections and blood extractions were safe and fair. They often did this by affirming their own belonging to both ORSTOM/IRD and the villages, which sometimes meant enrolling their own children in trials.

Bodies are seen as bearing evidence of past commitment and abuse, and of ethical echoes rippling into the present. The capacity of the observatory to render legible tiny or incipient changes – an emerging epidemic, or the delayed effects of an experimental vaccine – is invested with ethical significance. Fieldworkers and villagers remember sick bodies, evacuated bodies and survivors as living memory of care in a time and place of research. It is said that ORSTOM/IRD made measles and persussis go away in Niakhar. Fieldworkers' physical presence is taken as material evidence of good research relations; of the labour of creating records of lives and of life, of the memories of rescue, obligation and knowledge-making of which they are custodians.

Throughout Niakhar's villages there are children and teenagers bearing the names of researchers, fieldworkers and doctors, who embody legacies of affective ties and gratitude. Yet as with stories of fieldwork friendships told as brotherhoods, they form symbolic genealogies that celebrate but also make serious demands on relations of mutual obligation formed during research. Research pasts break out into the present as antibodies, survivors, and names bestowed, bearing witness to the ethical ambiguities of repeated exchanges of blood, care, labour, and friendship in Niakhar.

Temporary fieldwork station, Niakhar or Paos-Koto District, 1971

Remains of cooperative peanut storage facility, Niakhar District, 201▮

Demographic fieldwork, Niakhar District, 2000s

Joseph Diatte and Ernest Faye checking data at Niakhar Station, Niakhar, early 2000s

"Boucarou" the meeting hut of Niakhar Research Station, Niakhar District, 201▮

Discarded perforated sheet, Dakar, 2013

Niakhar Research Station, Niakhar, 2015

In the field with car, Niakhar or Paos-Koto District, 1974

Fieldworkers at breakfast, Niakhar or Paos-Koto District, 1974

Bassirou Fall in the field, Niakhar District, 2015

Diohine dispensary (a collaborating clinic during vaccination trials),
Niakhar District, 2015

Ernest Faye (born 1940s?) is one of Niakhar's oldest living fieldworkers and among the most highly respected by French and Senegalese colleagues. He was recruited in 1966 by the ORSTOM demographer Bernard Lacombe with his cousin Michel Ndiaye. Unlike their predecessors of the Sine Saloum Study (1962–6) who were state employees and predominantly Wolof-speaking, Ndiaye and Faye were Serer and employed by ORSTOM. Soon after returning to Niakhar in 1983 after a leave of absence, Faye was appointed by Michel Garenne as fieldwork supervisor and station manager. He retired in 2000 and now lives in Mbour, a coastal city located between Niakhar and his home town of Palmarin.

Ousmane Faye (born 1958), **Abdou Diouf** (born 1951) and **Latyr Diome** (born c.1970) are part of a second wave of fieldworkers recruited for the measles and pertussis vaccine trials of 1987–97 and joined the Niakhar staff via an entrance exam in November 1986. They are originally from the area, and lived within the study zone for the duration of the trials. Diouf has three namesakes in the zone, while Diome has "one or two" and named two of his children after (Senegalese) IRD colleagues. When the fieldwork team was downsized in 1997, Faye was kept on and has now accumulated work medals for his years of service. Diouf and Diome have since then been employed by the IRD only through short, irregular contracts.

Robert Diatte (born 1980s) is the son of Joseph Diatte. He grew up among ORSTOM researchers in his father's house in Niakhar. He now lives in this house. He abandoned his plan to go to university after his father's death, and began taking short contracts with the IRD to support his family. He is particularly close to the IRD researcher Richard Lalou, with whom he has updated some of the data collected by his father in Sob. Robert is related through both parents to the founding lineage of Sob, the Dioufs.

André Lericollais/Ngor Diouf (born 1940s) conducted one of the first *terroir* studies in Sob in 1964–6 as his doctoral research. He was given the name "Ngor Diouf" by the village chief of Sob, whose daughter, Adama Diouf, married Joseph Diatte. After the Sob study, Lericollais studied the Senegal River Valley, and then went back to France. In 1985 he returned to Niakhar to launch an ambitious project to generate new data in old fieldsites and thereby identify the social and environmental effects of two decades of drought and demographic growth. Lericollais built himself a hut in Joseph Diatte's compound in Niakhar during this project, which lasted for about a decade. He then returned to France.

Joseph Diatte (1930s?–2005) was
geographer André Lericollais' longtime
fieldworker and friend. Trained as a
catechist, he worked briefly for the
French ethnologist Marguerite Dupire
in Sob before being recruited by
Lericollais for the Sob *terroir* study.
After working in various agricultural
research and development projects
around the country, Joseph returned
to Niakhar in 1985 to work again with
Lericollais. He headed a fieldwork team
that re-studied several villages, including
Sob, and built a house in Niakhar. He
joined Ernest Faye's team as a field
supervisor in 1989 until retiring in
2000. He passed away in 2005.

Pierre Cantrelle (born 1926) was
celebrated at the IRD's 50th anniversary
symposium in 2014 as the founding
father of Niakhar. He began the Sine
Saloum Study in 1962 as an UN technical
assistant to the Senegalese state
statistics agency. Hired by ORSTOM
in 1964, Cantrelle completed the study
and then continued to collect and
analyse demographic and health data
in this and two other field sites in
Senegal. Trained as a doctor, Cantrelle
is recognised for his pioneering
observations of distinctive African
patterns of fertility, infant mortality
and measles epidemiology. He left
Senegal in 1969, but kept an eye on
Niakhar as scientific secretary of the
demographic section of ORSTOM.

Michel Garenne (born 1950) can be
seen both as Cantrelle's heir and as a
competitor to the title of the founder of
Niakhar as a true longitudinal research
site. Working at ORSTOM with Cantrelle
from 1978, Garenne used data
collected in Niakhar/Ngayokhem in his
graduate research on infant mortality.
He visited Niakhar with Cantrelle in
1981, and dreamed of launching an
ambitious scientific programme using
epidemiological and demographic
observation as the basis for medical
research. He directed this programme
from 1983, until he was ousted from
Niakhar in 1991 following a controversy
over a measles vaccine trial. His
subsequent scientific career has been
successful.

Everyone can tell you –
if they're telling you the truth,
they'll tell you that it's thanks
to Abdou Diouf that all those villages
that had refused –
it's Abdou Diouf who fixed that,
all the villages of the zone!
All the villages of the zone!

Abdou Diouf, Niakhar, 16 December 2012

Custodians of the field

Ernest We listed all the children, and if there was a child we hadn't seen, one of the doctors said: "You have to be careful, when a child doesn't come you always have to go to see if there is something." And he insisted so much that I went [...] His mother wouldn't show me the child, and finally someone showed him to me, and his nose was bleeding like crazy [...] Finally I came back, and the doctor said, "We have to go and convince the family to bring him to [the hospital in] Kaolack…" I said [to the family], "Listen, we'll pay for everything…" When we got there, I'd even forgotten my blood type, and his uncle, same father same mother, didn't even want to give blood. So I gave a quarter litre, even if it wasn't the same blood type. [I said to him,] "You, aren't you ashamed? I bring you in a vehicle and you, who is the uncle of the child, you don't even want to give blood!" Well, finally he accepted, and it was the same blood type. He's a big boy now! I saw him three years ago, and he's taller than I am now.

Interview with Ernest Faye, Aïssatou and Ashley, Mbour, 24 April 2012

Ousmane Well, at the very beginning, it was a bit complicated, since it involved drawing [blood], and Serer parents wouldn't accept that. They said we took the blood to sell the blood. It was pretty complicated.

Ashley Was that the case in your village?

Ousmane Every village in the zone! Everyone! Only, in the case of a field-worker [who was known locally], these relations with the population, it could help… Here, there were only a few reluctant families. Because… if you ask me a question, I answer clearly, with dignity. So I didn't have that kind of problem.

Ashley So how did you answer, for example?

Ousmane At the very beginning, if I had a family that caused me trouble, I told them "So, me, I was born here, my daddy is there, you know him; my mum, you know her." So I'm a son of the land. I don't think I can allow myself to bring things that would go against the population. Honestly, I don't think I could put myself into anything that could hold back my village. So, whoever wants to, let's go! Whoever doesn't – too bad!

Aïssatou So to detect measles cases, it was by asking whether there was coughing…?

Ousmane Yes. You come, you introduce yourself… you say hi, you do the roll call, who's there, who's not, where did they go, what for, and so on. Then you ask: "Is there not anyone who is coughing right now?," otherwise you ask the question directly, like, "is there not a case of measles?" Because if you say it in Serer they'll understand.

Interview with Ousmane Faye, Niakhar, 12 December 2012

Abdou Everyone can tell you – if they're telling you the truth, they'll tell you that it's thanks to Abdou Diouf that all those villages that had refused – it's Abdou Diouf who fixed that, all the villages of the zone! All the villages of the zone!.

[...] Well, you know, you have to have time… To talk for a long time to convince someone… Me, I took my time.

[...] Then I started to do my meeting, talk, talk, talk. And when I finished they said: "Abdou, not one of the people from ORSTOM ever explained these things like that, never! Even that

Ousmane Faye, 2012

Aïssatou Diouf, 2012

Bassirou Fal, 2012

Diaga Loum, 2012

Ernest Faye, 2012

Moussa Sarr, 2012

Samba Diatte, 2012

Samba Diouf, 2012

Emile Ndiaye, 2012

Adiouma Faye, 2012

guy, André Lericollais; he lived over there, he never made things clear like that. Joseph Diatte, he was born here, his family is there! You see, no-one!"

Interview with Abdou Diouf, Niakhar, 16 December 2012

Latyr For example, when I got married in Poudai, village 18 [according to the surveillance system], my first wife was from Poudai. I had a child with her. Well, there was some reluctance in this population and when my child was born, there were some people who thought to themselves, "Well, let's see now if this child will be vaccinated or not." And when I made my wife vaccinate my child, there were people who thought to themselves: "Well, if really there was something bad about vaccination then Latyr wouldn't have brought his child." So there are some women who went from this observation and joined the vaccination. [...]

Ashley And at the time, were you also involved in emergency evacuations during the clinical trials, of a child or a sick person?

Latyr Oh yes, several times. Some children who had a fit, and I once had to carry a child who a fit. I carried it on my back, I tied it to my back and drove the motorcycle to get to the dispensary fast.

Aïssatou Where? Here in Toucar?

Latyr No, in Diohine, in the zone of Diohine, in Diohine Kotior. That's about seven or eight kilometres. When a child has a fit... well...

Ashley What do you mean by a "fit"?

Latyr A convulsive fit.

Ashley Epilepsy?

Latyr No, convulsions...

Ashley And the child was treated?

Latyr Yes, treated and saved.

Ashley And do you ever see this child?

Latyr I wouldn't recognise that child, but each time I come to a house as an investigator, the mother says, "Yes, that's the saviour of so-and-so..."

Interview with Latyr Diome, Niakhar, 15 December 2012

Ashley With demographic surveillance there are routine questions; with clinical trials there's experimentation. How did you perceive the change?

Émile The population asked itself the same questions I did, and maybe had the same reactions. In 1986, some sick children were brought by Garenne to the [hospital in Dakar] and it was seen as beneficial. Demographic surveillance was useless, the results weren't easy to understand, but when we got clinical trials with some healthcare, right away we realised it was good [...] We saw less and less measles in the zone. And on top of that there was a massive recruitment of young people in the zone. That was good for the place. Lots of parents saw some improvement in their lives because they had children who were making a bit of money.

Interview between Émile Ndiaye, Aïssatou, and Ashley, Niakhar, 22 April 2012

Latyr Diome, 2012

Where there used to be shelves, 2012

And here there was a door. That is, I transformed that, but from here you can see, you see, for example, the traces of shelves. So the library was just here, where he built it like this [pointing to some marks on the wall]. And now, when there were a lot of people, this is where he spent the night. You see the traces of shelves? It's like... a lot, a bit of Lericollais is with us.

But really he lived here, a real family life... It was like a station. It was the same as IRD [ie the main research station].

Guided walk with Robert Diatte, Niakhar, 18 December 2012

Where there used to be a door, 2012

Traces of a shelf

The late Joseph Diatte's family compound in Niakhar in many ways bears the imprint of his close collaboration with André Lericollais. As is common in this area, his compound ("*concession*" in the local French) encloses several one- or two-room buildings (in French "*cases*," or huts), inhabited by members of his extended family. In several visits between 2012 and 2015, we were invited on tours of this compound by Robert Diatte, Joseph's elder son.

Joseph Diatte belonged to an early generation of fieldworkers who were initially recruited as interpreters or assistants in a close association with individual European researchers. His career later took on more formal, institutionalised and clearly defined professional roles and duties as a result of changes in labour legislation in postcolonial Senegal, as well as within ORSTOM, and through the collective action of fieldworkers. Yet his initial pairing with Lericollais was the ground of enduring scientific and affective ties throughout his career and life.

Another station?

Robert Around 1983, there was IRD [ie, the station]. And my dad came back in 1985, and that's when he was recruited by IRD. There were these two rooms, there, in mudbrick...

Ashley Those were the huts they had built themselves?

Robert My dad built them, then Lericollais also had huts built. Then researchers came... Even thesis students, that's where they stayed. His interns didn't go to IRD. He built that hut there, and later those two rooms.

Ashley So it's almost like another station?

Robert Yes! Exactly! They put a garage here, with the fencing.

Ashley And the IRD vehicles... they parked here?

Robert Yes they turned like this, and parked here. If there were a lot of them, they came with tents and camp beds... [...]

Ashley But [Lericollais] had a house in Dakar too?

Robert Yes, like all the researchers. But him, he really loved fieldwork. Sometimes he comes, he spends 15 days, he leaves his students here. If his programmes were running, well, this was his base, and that's that.

Guided walk with Robert, Aïssatou, and Ashley, Niakhar, 18 December 2012

André and Robert Diatte, 2012

Where the vehicles parked, 2012

The compound is located a stone's throw away from the IRD station. The creation of the station was crucial in the transformation of Niakhar from a demographic pilot zone to a platform for medical research in the early 1980s. While never granted an official status, the home of Joseph Diatte became the centre of much scientific activity linked to Lericollais and his team at about the same time.

Lericollais and Diatte initially worked together in the mid-1960s, beginning with an intensive period of fieldwork in Sob. Diatte then worked on several projects outside the area. He came back to Niakhar in 1985, and Robert's recollections naturally focus on this period he witnessed as a child. While insisting that his father's work ethics implied a separation between work and family, he also depicts his own compound as a home for Lericollais and his family, as well as his students and colleagues. Mentioning the garage signals how the family compound could compete in terms of facilities with the nearby station, which also comprised huts used as a guest-room and living spaces, offices, meeting rooms, a garage and a car repair station.

Lericollais' library, kept by Robert, 2012

Past familiarity

Robert spoke of Lericollais not as someone who once built a hut, but rather as a long-term guest, with traces of his work and life embedded within the current home. Other, past uses of the space persist through its transformation by its current occupants: in the ghostly presence of Lericollais' shelves in a room that used to be his office but which is now devoted to the bedroom of Robert and his wife, or in what used to be the entrance to his room.

Lericollais and Diatte's friendship indeed forged family ties, and Robert's younger brother, born while Lericollais was in Senegal, was named André after him. Yet the young André himself hardly recalls his namesake, and contact and exchange of news has been very irregular since Joseph Diatte's death. What has been kept lies in the corner of the newly created room: a pile of documents, books and reports linked to Lericollais' studies and Diatte's work, of which Robert is very proud.

On keeping the books

We realised only after our first visit that we were not the first to be offered such a tour and to have a glimpse of Lericollais' documentary treasures. After his father's death in 2005, several French researchers came to consult documents, not at ORSTOM but instead in the "shrine archive" maintained by Robert.

Robert Diatte and his brother André, 2012

Robert Richard [Lalou, an IRD researcher] suggested I leave the documents at the station, but I said: "That's not safe! This is a family legacy." If I had not kept it, they wouldn't have been able to find anything.

Guided walk with Robert and Noémi, Niakhar, 11 March 2015

Why did Robert refuse to archive the documents at the station? There, they might be reinserted in an official genealogy of "Niakhar" as a place of science, dissolving the family ties that safeguard the history of Lericollais' fieldwork.

Robert's story is not that of a pious heir to his father's work who has chosen to follow his career path out of admiration and ambition. Robert has opted for a life of field science out of a combination of necessity and curiosity. While he thinks "the IRD is no longer what it used to be," he still keeps the books as something that might open up new possibilities in an uncertain present.

Where there used to be shelves, 2012

Lericollais' "hut" in the Diatte compound, 2012

Robert This is Lericollais' hut. These days my mother rests in there during the day, because it's cooler. I wanted to tear it down, but my mother refused.

Guided walk with Robert and Noémi, Niakhar, 11 March 2015

Baobab tree to show Ngor Diouf how much it has grown, 2015

Indeed, I've counted trees. When we counted them in 1965, 1985, 2005... Yes, they've diminished... In the past ten years, the rain has increased. There's more water in the soil and shoots in the fields... We will keep counting.

Richard Lalou, speaking at a public meeting, Ngayokhem, 24 February 2015

Ngor Diouf, eh? Sure, I knew Ngor Diouf. When will he come back?

Ndiafadji Diouf, speaking to Noémi, Sob, 11 March 2015

When will Ngor Diouf come back?

In Sob

Etienne, the driver, drops us off, and we enter the compound, skirting the windshield of millet stalks set in the middle of a wide opening in the fencing. We enter the first room on the right, where Robert Diatte greets a very old woman sitting on the bed. A younger but well-weathered woman (her daughter?) walks in. Robert tells her why we've come. She begins to respond in Serer directly to him, but he tells her I understand some Wolof and she turns to me, with an accusing tone: "Ngor Diouf, eh? Sure I knew Ngor Diouf..."

Ngor Diouf is the name given to the geographer André Lericollais in the mid-1960s, when he was conducting an intensive study of land use practices in Sob.

The next hut stands out from the others, circular and whitewashed, with telephone numbers scrawled in chalk on its walls. Robert introduces me to his uncle Diamene Diouf, who lives in the hut. Diamene explains that this is

called "Ngor Diouf's hut," but though it was planned by Lericollais it was built by another French researcher (who collaborated but was not affiliated with ORSTOM, and who was given the name Samba Diouf).

Diamene looks for papers. He finds an IRD newsletter that Robert gave him, containing an *hommage* to Robert's father Joseph, who was Lericollais' fieldworker and companion for many years: "Joseph Diatte: Itinerary of a man, destiny of a nation." He also finds a photo of his parents: his father Boucar Diouf (also Joseph's uncle) and his mother Die Dibor Ndong, working in the field. The photo was taken by Ngor Diouf in the 1960s.

I ask Diamene to show me around the village, especially the compound where Ngor Diouf had his hut. He tells me to take a photo of the baobab tree near the entrance of the compound, so we can show Ngor Diouf how much it has grown.

Noémi's notes, Sob, 11 March 2015

Diamene's parents, photographed by Ngor Diouf, 1960s

Diamene's documents, with Robert Diatte and a visitor, 2015

Diamene Diouf in front of his home, "Ngor Diouf's hut", 2015

IRD Homage to Joseph Diatte, kept by Diamene, 2006

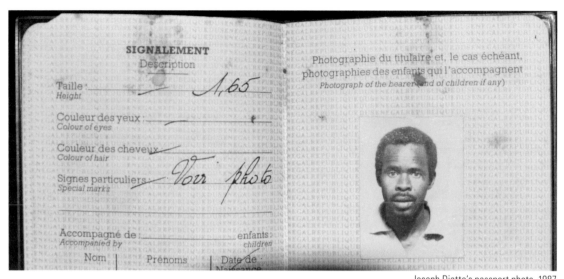

Joseph Diatte's passport photo, 1987

Robert Diatte keeps his father's land surveys, 2015

Robert Diatte

Robert is taking me over to his house to talk about his father and look for photos of him. On the way, he turns to me: "I like this project. This is a good project. Traces are important."

After showing me around, we sit in the living room. He tells me about his father's life.

"It's the village chief who gave the name of Ngor to Lericollais when he asked to be given a Serer name. Ngor Diouf is the founder of Sob. My father [Jo Diatte] is from Ngayokhem, he is from the founding family of Ngayokhem, but his uncle was in Sob.

First, he was a Catholic teacher. The priest, Père Bouvet, was a friend of Lericollais' and they talked about it and he told him he had someone, a good worker. The school had closed for the

vacation but they still owed him money. That's how he started working in the rainy seasons...

He was his right-hand man. He even became his family.

My mother was the village chief's daughter. She was 12 or 13 and Lericollais asked if she could come to do the laundry, dishes... When Jo was looking for a wife, Lericollais insisted. The next year, he insisted again. Jo finally accepted. [...]

When Richard [Lalou] wanted to do some research in Sob again, Pape [Ndiaye, an IRD fieldworker and administrator] told him, 'There are tons of documents over there [in Jo's old hut].' Pape asked me if I was working. It's Pape who told Richard: 'You have to give that family work!' I told Pape I had my baccalaureate, I showed him my diploma."

Robert showed me the documents, surveys of land and trees, which he now keeps in a box in the station's shared office. He said: "When we started the Ecosoc study [of environmental change] with Richard, we couldn't work without these forms."

We look for photos together, but there aren't very many. Robert has shared

them among the family, but also explains that Joseph was so well liked that many people have come and taken photos away. We find Joseph's passport. Robert says Joseph went everywhere with Lericollais, even to France. The visa stamps show this was in 1987.

Noémi's notes, Niakhar, 11 March 2015

Noémi I saw André Lericollais in Paris last week. He says hello.

Robert Oh, how I would like to see him again! Please tell him that my family – especially my mother – we would really like for him to come back. His namesake [Robert's younger brother] was just small when he left, he never knew him.

The first time we went to Sob with Richard [in 2005], people were coming out of their compounds... they thought Lericollais had come back!

Interview with Robert Diatte, Niakhar, 26 February 2015

Stamps in Joseph's passport, 1987

André Lericollais

Noémi You were talking about the documents you kept...

André I left a lot of things with Joseph.

Noémi Tell me a bit about the method you used in 1965.

André There were markings on the ground that were quite precise and permanent. There was an aerial photographer in Kaolack. We would lay strips of fabric around the fields. Then we did the land surveys, 700 plots. We recorded the trees... each tree has a role. They were monuments.

Noémi There are different stories about the hut you lived in then...

André There's a drawing in the publication of the hut where I lived, next to the village chief's house [round hut]. The cement house... it's [another French researcher] who had it built. Joseph worked with him too.

Noémi How did you start working with Joseph? Is it true he worked with Marguerite Dupire first?

André Joseph was still a kid when he worked with Dupire. I arranged with Père Bouvet to work with Joseph. He became my road companion. We did everything together, me and Joseph. [...]

Noémi Tell me about what you found.

André The important levels of organisation were the *mbind* [compound], the *ngak* [kitchen] and the lineage *terroir*. The village *terroir* was not dominant. The triennal [crop] rotation is at the level of the lineage, not the village. That's something important that we found... I've always been careful to distinguish between the real and the plausible.

Fieldwork gives a critical capacity, it forces one to accept complexity and diversity.

Drawing of the village chief's compound, where Ngor Diouf lived in the 1960s, 1972

People... we aren't in their place. I've enormously and passionately lived among people, but I don't know what goes on in their minds.

Noémi So then you went back to Sob in 1985?

André Joseph was delighted to come back. We built [the houses] together in Niakhar. We would go eat at the station.

We looked for people who were kids in 1965, who were 10–15 years old at the time that interested us. They had the best memory. In the 1960s, it was said that if you didn't have three full grain stores, you weren't free. Later, it became an international migrant in the family [that it was said one needed].

At first, I tried to oversee the study from Montpellier, but it was too complicated so I came back. In Sob, we recovered the framework. The state of the trees, roads, hedges... we redid all the surveys of soil use. It took about ten years to finish the study. [...]

[After that] I didn't go back. Because Joseph Diatte is not there anymore.

Interview with André Lericollais, Paris, 21 February 2015

While I was in a meeting with Maurice [Ndong, an IRD librarian] we were told: "Go see, things are being thrown out!" They were emptying that little room behind the garage [on the IRD's Hann campus in Dakar]. We kept two or three copies of each type of form. The rest we let them dispose of.

Alice's notes, Dakar, 24 April 2013

Archival fantasies

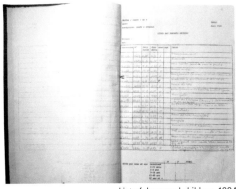

Family form from Sob, recorded in 1962, 1964 and 1965

Fiche familiale

From archival boxes put out as rubbish, a slip of paper floats free from its file. On it, moments of observation meet up on the page, and the time elapsed dissolves. 25/2/65 is gathered up with 27/1/64, next to 2/12/62; red ink respells the names of a son and a daughter; a cousin is struck out in green. On the form, coloured inks replicate passages, compress intervals, reverse past acts of recording. A population archive is written by repetition. Babies are born between passages, they age, marry, move and die. They are caught in the time of observation.

Census of a compound:
Two kinds of forms are used:
– "family form" ["*fiche familiale*"], for usual residents (cardboard 24 × 32 [cm])

– form for "passing individuals"

[…] To make the forms easier to read and to analyse, we used different coloured inks for each census:
– blue: initial census

– red: first control census

– green: second "   "
[p8, p15]

Extract from Pierre Cantrelle's 1965 report: Étude démographique dans la région du Sine-Saloum (Sénégal) – Déroulement de l'enquête

The method is completely different from that of previous demographic surveys in Africa, which were retrospective investigations during a single census-taking. […]

The repetition of observation for the same individual avoids recourse to retrospective questions, that is, the memory of the persons interrogated, except in the case of children born or deceased between two visits by the fieldworker. [p7]

Extract from Pierre Cantrelle's 1969 report: Étude démographique dans la région du Sine-Saloum (Sénégal) – État civil et observation démographique 1963–5

List of deceased children, 1984

Paper forms become disposable. They disperse, many are lost or burnt; a few are saved. Yet data survives and grows, kept as memory and added to, visit after visit, until the babies live or die, the wives give birth and the girls reach puberty. Escaped, discarded, *this* sheet of paper is no longer archival, no longer a sliver of the archive. It is not collected and stored. It is not retrievable, nor ordered in sequence. Severed from the wider gathering up of history and population, it disaggregates into the record of three visits to one family in the village of Sob.

Vaccination form, Dakar, 2013

Smoking

Abdou　Then he sent me an envelope. Because every time, if you made errors or omitted something, you got sent an envelope [containing a letter], saying, "You did this, the computer found you did this, it's not right." Well, I thought it was that, but it wasn't that. Well, sometimes the death forms... Well, I smoked tobacco, and sometimes when I didn't have any Rizla to roll the tobacco I would take the bottom of the form there where the doctor has to sign. Later, he sent me dozens of forms, and another letter, saying, "I'm really happy [with your work] [...] Use these forms for your cigarettes and leave our other forms alone!"

Interview with Aïssatou, Ashley, and Abdou Diouf, 16 December 2012

Found volumes of forms, Dakar, 2013

Le sens des archives

This [event] is an interesting exercise of memory but it is up to historians to evaluate its usefulness. I have archives in my attic. These are painful decisions.

Pierre Cantrelle, Dakar, 24 February 2014 (Presentation at Symposium for the 50th Anniversary of Niakhar)

Pierre Cantrelle, with attic archives, Montpellier, 2014

Cantrelle's attic archives "grain storage", Montpellier, 2014

Noémi What about archives?

Michel My first day with ORSTOM in 1978 – I spent it carrying boxes from INSEE [statistics institute] to Bondy [ORSTOM documentation centre] because they were going to destroy them. Cantrelle has *le sens des archives*.

Magnetic bands [analogue medium used in the past to preserve data], I tried to have them transferred, but no one was interested. When [an institute] decided they wanted them 25 years later, they were no longer usable. I don't even know where they are. Individuals took them away.

Interview with Michel Garenne, Paris, 22 October 2014

Noémi Tell me about the project to digitise African demographic archives.

Francis [...] The notion of archives has evolved a lot in our field. Paper archives are limited because they are passive archives. With microdata, archives become alive, because the researcher can sift through the information. Old archives can be re-exploited and long data series find their meaning with the new questions and techniques of today. [...]

Cantrelle had this sense of preservation very early on. He knew that one day, things would be thrown into the garbage. [...]

There is no culture of archives [in our institutions]. The statistics institute got to it recently, but things have disappeared [...] You can have magnetic bands, but they are useless without a data key.

Interview with Francis Gendreau, retired IRD demographer, Paris, 22 October 2014

Le sens des archives, a sense of the meaning of archives, is something these ageing demographers proclaim to have which institutions do not. They keep boxes in their attics and basements, and worry that fading index cards and magnetic bands might hold data hostage.

Volumes of forms, Dakar, 2013

Floppy disk kept by Emilie Ndiaye, 2013

ORSTOM perforated sheet, Dakar, 2013

Bernard to Noémi My dear, a wave of regret while awaiting remorse: I am starting to destroy archives...

Noémi to Bernard [...] I was just working out some thoughts about archives. Here's little text [a draft version of this chapter], made up of mostly raw excerpts, on the question of paper and memory in Niakhar, on safeguarding and destruction, on institutional will and private appropriation, on the relation, whether affirmed or erased, between an ethos of preservation and that of fieldwork... Might I add some of your responses and thoughts?

Bernard to Noémi Here is the commented text. Thank goodness I was not an actor after 1970!

Memory is a strange thing. I've tried to comment on what I was sure of. [...]

The "sense of the meaning of archives"??? Hum!!! I don't think so... A sense of piling things up, of abundance, of multiple approaches [...] A sense of archives as of geology that sediments rocks and bones and thus allows humans to understand the passing of time.

Email correspondence between Bernard Lacombe, former ORSTOM demographer who worked in Niakhar in the late 1960s, and Noémi, 7 February 2015

Birth form, 2013

The attic of Bel-Air

Émilie Ndiaye [IRD data entry and administrative agent] : A lot of things were burned without consulting [Charles] Becker [a social scientist who worked in Niakhar] when [the IRD administration] transferred the attic of Bel-Air [IRD campus in Dakar] to the documentation centre in Hann [another IRD campus in Dakar].

Valérie Delaunay [IRD demographer]: They didn't burn everything. Some things stayed in the attic of Bel-Air. They burned them later, I think in 2006. They brought everything down and then sent us a collective email: "Come get your things, otherwise we will burn them."

Notes from a meeting on archives, Dakar, 15 June 2012

Noémi What was kept in Bel-Air?

Michel We did genealogies, a hundred of them. But we never coded them. Some went back to the colonial period. They were destroyed with Bel-Air. During the colonial period, there was a will to keep archives.... In Bel-Air, the archives were very well organised. In metal file cabinets. Everyone had their things there... Charles [Becker] took some things [home] from Bel-Air, but not everything.

Interview with Michel Garenne, Paris 22 October 2014

Your paper evokes, through the phantasmagorias of this and that person, the big myths of the libraries of Alexandria, of Constantinople or of Mosul, destroyed by Isis. Why not add Bel-Air...?

Bernard to Noémi, 7 February 2015

Maurice Ndong and Augustin Dieme are in charge of the IRD's documentation centre. They have been with the IRD for two and three decades respectively. They are librarians, not archivists, they insist, but were asked to catalogue some things, from scales for weighing babies, to published reports, and boxes of clinical trial records from the pertussis study labelled "to be kept until March 2012." Maurice and Augustin are taking us to visit these archives, kept in a small storage room at the back of one of the office buildings of the IRD's campus in Hann, in Dakar.

Noémi's notes, Dakar, 5 April 2012

Trial archives to be kept until March 2012, Dakar, 2013

Michel We're going to a place that's not very pleasant... because there are termites and all...

Augustin We've had lots of visitors!

Maurice There were scales... All those are research objects... I think there are things here that have never been used.

Augustin We don't throw things out. I was very forceful. I told [the IRD's regional representative]: "In France, people don't throw things out. I've been to the national library in Paris. Here we are not in a hurry to throw things out. We ask the old people 'What's this for?'" Maurice asked; he wrote an email to the researchers who were responsible for units [...] for those who have libraries in their units

[...] to come and deposit [what they had] in the documentation centre... We know what is valuable here: a scientific heritage...

Maurice We created call numbers with a librarian, made a catalogue. But it's getting eaten up by termites. Soon the numbers won't correspond to anything... Someone has to be given the responsibility for that, to ensure continuity...

Ashley Are researchers aware of the importance of archives?

Maurice When it is in their interest, when they need them. Archives per se are not part of our work. For us [as experts in library systems], it's about information, documentation. The tools that served to produce [scientific knowledge] don't interest [the administration]... they just want us to disseminate the results [of scientific research].

Conversation with Augustin Dieme and Maurice Ndong, Dakar, 5 April 2012

How many rooms would Niakhar's paper fill? Family forms, concession lists, vaccination histories, forms to record migration, birth, marriage, death, records of pregnancies and weaning, verbal autopsy questionnaires, genealogies, consent forms...

The depth and value of Niakhar's history is not tied to the fate of paper or spools of magnetic band. Data is peeled off forms and entered in registers, coding forms, computers programmes, databases, disks and drives. It can be sorted, retrieved, randomised... And yet the demographers and librarians worry about what might be lost through the shedding of these meticulous inscriptions. Only paper bears the marks of the many laborious returns of fieldworkers through the households of Niakhar.

Box of pink "Ngayokheme" index cards, for disposal in Dakar, 2013

It is time for Michel Garenne to go back to Niakhar. He has come for a symposium for the 50th anniversary of Niakhar, which begins tomorrow. On the third day, a group field trip to the station is scheduled, but Garenne flies back too early and has planned his own visit. Just him, a driver and the four of us, observers of remembering and returns. It has been 23 years. This return is haunted by that departure.

Noémi's notes, Dakar, 24 February 2014

Garenne and Tofène reminiscing, Niakhar Research Station, Niakhar, 2014

Garenne's return

Eviction

Please find attached the text of my presentation for the symposium...
I hope this text will be useful, and that I will have satisfied the curiosity of the historians working on the subject.

Attached document: "Lessons from a scientific adventure: Niakhar 1981–1991," by Michel Garenne. 18,000 words.

[...] After analysing the data from Niakhar, MG [Michel Garenne] presented his first results on the excess mortality and failures of vaccination in the [measles vaccine] trial of Niakhar to the CDC [Centre for Disease Control] and the WHO, which had the effect of a cold shower.

[...] After this pilot study [on the feasibility of biological pertussis diagnosis in the field], MG wrote a preliminary protocol project to test the acellular vaccine [an experimental pertussis vaccine], but abandoned the project following his eviction from the site of Niakhar.

Email from Michel Garenne to Valérie Delaunay (cc: Noémi, Alice, Pierre Cantrelle, Ashley, and others), 15 February 2014

The document is a chronicle of exile. It sets right the science and politics of a controversy over the results of a vaccine trial that led to Garenne's "eviction" by the ORSTOM administration. But if it is about justice, it is also about an interruption: Garenne as a builder who was ousted from his construction site with the edifice half-finished. In 1991, Garenne was in the middle of things. He was banished from history unfolding.

The visit

We are entering the town of Niakhar. Garenne says, "Over there, there was nothing and we were behind... Hey, there's the station!" As we get out of the car, someone greets us, sees Garenne: "The centre is all his work!"

Tofene Ndiaye, the station manager, takes us on a tour. In the lab buildings, Garenne says, "Wow!"

"Now we do all the manipulations..." says Tofene.

"You're really well set up!"

"Even sequencing..."

"I never thought I'd see this."

Towards the back of the lot, Garenne says, "Here there was a big hole where the mason had taken some soil. We fantasised about a pool..."

Then he can't remember her name. Tofene helps: "Mame Ndao."

Garenne goes on: "Mame Ndao sold us beer. We buried them under the sink because there was no fridge... My daughter spent her time in the sink."

Near Tofene's office, Garenne wants to take a photo of the defibrillator, of the guard's weapon. "A weapon! I never would have imagined seeing that here!"

"Wow!... Super!..." As he exclaims over the lab, the kitchen, the new solar panels, the air-conditioned rooms, the fence, the doubled size of the lot... all of these things are peeled away, stripped down to 1983: two huts, an outdoor kitchen, a gas lamp, a big hole, the latrines which one scientist's wife hated, a toddler in the sink and beer bottles underneath, camp beds, four fieldworkers and the future.

Touring the station, Garenne is building it up again incrementally. Ah! He points to where the pipe came over the wall.

Garenne photographs the defibrillator, 2014

Garenne photographs Tofène at his desk, 2014

Garenne, Tofène, old solar panels and new toilets, 2014

Garenne and Tofène, with Emile Ndiaye and Anne-Marie Moulin, 2014

At first there was no running water, but Garenne got the station connected to a Chinese bore-well project.

Ah!, he exclaims: they had no electricity, but the GTZ gave them these solar panels. "We were part of an experiment; they came to record data."

Ah!, he exclaims: these were the first huts, the ones he paid a neighboring mason to build, remembering who slept in which quarter, the camp beds that always went missing.

A freezer appears to store the vaccines. The tarp-covered pickup truck, and the hats the fieldworkers wore against the dust. Garenne grabs hold of a decade, and the future towards which the trucks and freezers and huts pointed.

Tofene lays claim to some increments too. On the office manager's computer, he shows Garenne a photo of his daughter: "To tell you how far I've come since my youth!" He turns to us, and continues: "Bernard Maire was the first one who brought me to Niakhar. I came three days a week every two weeks. In December 1985, Garenne asked to borrow me and he kept me. I was a fieldworker, then I drew samples for the vaccine trial, then I administered the vaccines. A hundred and eight sessions, and I missed only two! Garenne encouraged me, 'You're doing great, keep going!'"

"And we *did* do great things!" exclaims Garenne.

Two fieldworkers, Bassirou Fall and Emile Ndiaye, emerge from a meeting and greet Garenne. The reunion is warm and awkward. Garenne takes a bill out of his pocket, sends someone to buy beer, peanuts and Coke.

Bassirou says, "Such a pleasure!"

Garenne reminisces, "When we talked ... it was around the geerte [dry roasted peanuts]... the head [researcher] learned everything [from the fieldworkers] about society, the little rumours."

Tofene tells him, "You have a name-sake here: the son of Alassane Faye, the driver..."

Garenne exclaims, "Really! Oh, how interesting! I'd love to see him!"

The beer and peanuts are on the table. They are no longer of the past.

Noémi's notes, Niakhar, 24 February 2014

After the return

I ask Garenne about the return, over lunch at the Faculty Club at the Institut Pasteur. He brushes away the strangeness of the station ageing without him, and approves: "They kept the spirit."

Noémi's notes, Paris, 22 October 2014

Ashley So the fact that the station is made like traditional huts, it's a desire to...

Michel Oh! It's a desire to be lost in the landscape [...] People going by would not take notice of us, we didn't want something durable, we didn't want something visible [...] We wanted to be melted into the landscape, eh?

Aïssatou So there was no concern for the institution to consider the station as dependent on Hann [the IRD site in Dakar], and that sort of thing?

Michel [...] Well, there was an era when I suppose it would have been accepted for the French to set up [...] and say: "There, here we are, at home," but that's not what we wanted. We wanted to do our research, be well integrated [...] We were only interested in an international reputation. The rest didn't matter to us.

Interview with Aïssatou, Ashley, and Michel Garenne, Paris, 21 June 2012

Today in Paris, Garenne makes it clearer that "melting" was not timidity, but tactical neutrality: to not take a position, to invite the administrative sub-prefect only rarely in order to avoid too much interference, to keep distance from the missionary who was "sometimes a bit colonial," to refuse invitations from the Sufi religious leaders, and to not be seen in public too much with so-and-so, the Trotskyist, though he was a good friend.

"Yes, that's what allowed it to last," he affirms, "I recognised that spirit when I returned. It's kind of the spirit of the IRD..."

Niakhar lasted, and it did so without him, as a perpetually provisional presence, by cultivating retractability as the condition for staying. Still called "huts," the station buildings are remains of remaining.

Garenne photographs the new reservoir, 2014

Garenne and Tofène touring, Noémi takes notes, 2014

Tofène points to the new solar panels, 2014

Garenne remembers the sink his child played in, 2014

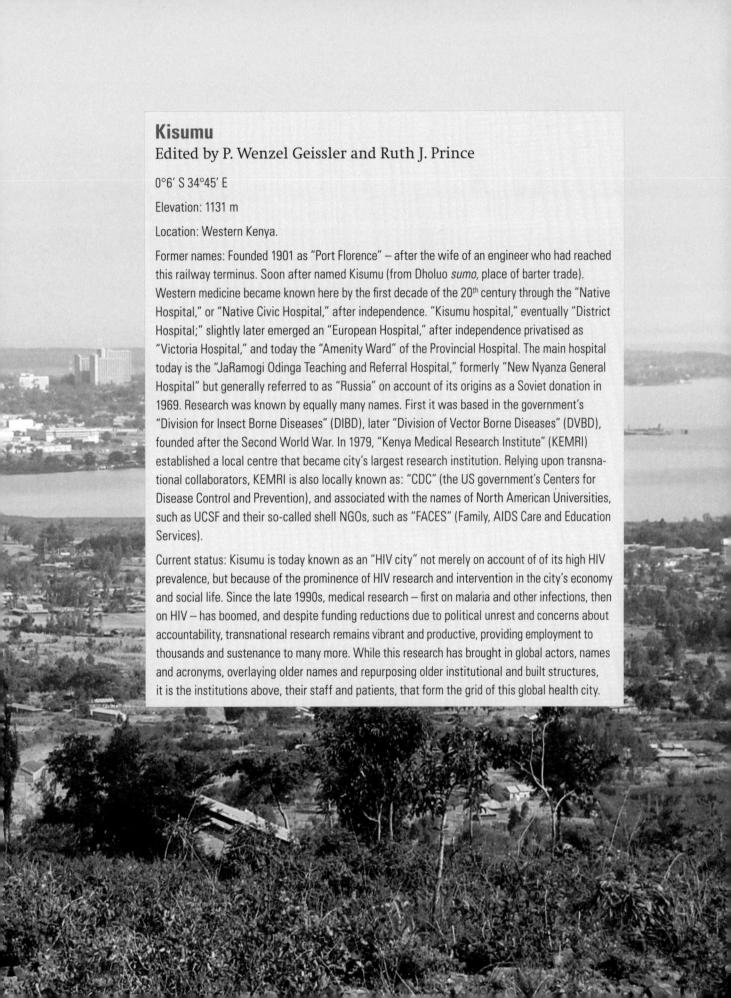

Kisumu

Edited by P. Wenzel Geissler and Ruth J. Prince

0°6' S 34°45' E

Elevation: 1131 m

Location: Western Kenya.

Former names: Founded 1901 as "Port Florence" – after the wife of an engineer who had reached this railway terminus. Soon after named Kisumu (from Dholuo *sumo*, place of barter trade). Western medicine became known here by the first decade of the 20th century through the "Native Hospital," or "Native Civic Hospital," after independence. "Kisumu hospital," eventually "District Hospital;" slightly later emerged an "European Hospital," after independence privatised as "Victoria Hospital," and today the "Amenity Ward" of the Provincial Hospital. The main hospital today is the "JaRamogi Odinga Teaching and Referral Hospital," formerly "New Nyanza General Hospital" but generally referred to as "Russia" on account of its origins as a Soviet donation in 1969. Research was known by equally many names. First it was based in the government's "Division for Insect Borne Diseases" (DIBD), later "Division of Vector Borne Diseases" (DVBD), founded after the Second World War. In 1979, "Kenya Medical Research Institute" (KEMRI) established a local centre that became city's largest research institution. Relying upon transnational collaborators, KEMRI is also locally known as: "CDC" (the US government's Centers for Disease Control and Prevention), and associated with the names of North American Universities, such as UCSF and their so-called shell NGOs, such as "FACES" (Family, AIDS Care and Education Services).

Current status: Kisumu is today known as an "HIV city" not merely on account of of its high HIV prevalence, but because of the prominence of HIV research and intervention in the city's economy and social life. Since the late 1990s, medical research – first on malaria and other infections, then on HIV – has boomed, and despite funding reductions due to political unrest and concerns about accountability, transnational research remains vibrant and productive, providing employment to thousands and sustenance to many more. While this research has brought in global actors, names and acronyms, overlaying older names and repurposing older institutional and built structures, it is the institutions above, their staff and patients, that form the grid of this global health city.

Chronology

1901

Kisumu founded as Port Florence railway terminus. Sleeping sickness epidemic.

1902

Royal Society Sleeping Sickness Commission arrives at Kisumu.

1908

Outbreak of bubonic plague; first formal hospital, by 1912 Kisumu Native Civil Hospital and European Hospital (later Victoria Hospital).

1938

"Yellow Fever Control Programme" under Department of Health, to control movements of yellow fever vectors caused by war effort. Later Division of Insect Borne Diseases (DIBD). Consolidation of scientific effort, and of ad hoc disease control.

1942

Colonial Development and Welfare Act (expanded 1946) passed; Colonial Research Committee established. Support expansion of DIBD and other colonial research institutions.

1943–54

Black fly vectors of Onchocerciasis eradicated by applying DDT to streams, after discovery of interactions between fly larvae and riverine crabs.

1948

Discovery of liver stages of malaria by P.C.C. Garnham, DIBD.

1952

Kisumu's main private Hospital, the Aga Khan hospital, opened in buildings designed by Ernst May.

1963

Kenya's independence. Native Hospital becomes Nyanza General Hospital, described as crowded and inadequately staffed, with poor facilities.

The formerly European and (since 1960) Indian Victoria Hospital remains a privileged health care facility. The DVBD station has c.50 staff, gradually "Africanised," and continues existing research and control.

1964

Visit of Soviet Trade Delegation; offer to build a new 200-bed hospital in Kisumu.

1969

26th October. New Nyanza Provincial General Hospital, a gift of the USSR, opened by President Kenyatta. Police violence at the opening.

First African Senior Entomological Field Officer (SEFO), Silas Achapa, in-charge of DIBD (d. 1996).

1968–1969

Last major outbreak of sleeping sickness. Beginning of US support for medical research. Walter Reed Army Institute of Research studies sleeping sickness outbreak with base in DVBD

1971

Last British SEFO, Barney Highton (1933–2011), leaves DIBD.

1973

Walter Reed programme permanently established, first working with DVBD, since 1979 with Kenya Medical Research Institute (KEMRI); research on malaria and leishmaniasis.

DIBD renamed Division of Vector Borne Diseases (DVBD) to include Bilharzia-related snail research.

1979

Foundation of KEMRI's Malaria and Other Protozoal Diseases Centre (MOPDC) in Kisumu District Hospital. Harrison Spencer from US Government Centers for Disease Control and Prevention (CDC) arrives in Kenya to establish malaria research with KEMRI in Kisumu area.

1980

KEMRI acquires 40 acres of land near Kisumu for MOPDC, later Center for Global Health Research.

1981

Nyanza General Hospital Research Committee Research Programme commenced as collaboration of provincial hospital and KEMRI. Research on Burkitt's Lymphoma.

1986

Construction begins for KEMRI research centre. Partial realisation of larger plan.

1989

Kenyan government introduces "cost sharing" and user fees for patients. Research becomes a source of free quality health care. Kisumu becomes one epicentre of the East African AIDS epidemic. Slow official recognition of the disease; delayed onset of scientific research.

1998

CDC and Walter Reed Programme each set up a new custom built Clinical Research Centers (for WRP including a state-of-the art paediatric ward, later Obama Ward) at New Nyanza General Hospital ("Russia").

2000

End of DVBD's last large-scale collaborative research project, Kenyan-Danish Health Research (KEDAHR, 1994–2000). Staff reduction continues to 3 in 2009. Regular running costs allowance ceases around 2006.

2004

Opening of CDC financed 3 million USD laboratory and multi-storey administration block at KEMRI center. New perimeter defined and walled.

2009

30-year anniversary of KEMRI/CDC celebrated with wide international participation.

Kisumu: global health amnesia

Kisumu, Kenya's third largest city and the western provinces' administrative and commercial hub, is a millennial "global health city." Since the last decade of the 20th century, global research agencies – including the US Centres for Disease Control and Prevention (CDC) and U.S. Army Walter Reed Programme, as well as many major North American and British universities – have conducted world-leading medical research in and around the city, in collaboration with Kenyan institutions – notably the Kenyan Medical Research Institute. They employ thousands of medical and technical professionals and involve people in clinical research and novel interventions. On the back of these research collaborations, global health interventions, funded by big charities and northern government initiatives, and implemented in government facilities and burgeoning non-governmental organisations, have multiplied since the millennium, triggered by the HIV/AIDS epidemic that ravaged the region. By 2010, Kisumu was a boomtown. Class differences were growing – between the very rich, those on wage income (often related to research or NGO employment), and the rest. "Middle-class" housing and shopping malls transformed the face of the city, its road network was overloaded, and social connections, collectives and expertise gained and lost purchase at rapid speed.

This bubbling hub – in which opportunity and innovation, best intentions and self-interest, gross deprivation and futile fantasy pushed against each other – was very different from the earlier, post-independence city. In the early 1990s, when we first came to Kisumu, it was still a quiet city. Between the 1960s and the 1990s postcolonial cold war and ethnic politics had slowed urban and architectural change, together with economic

and demographic growth. The city was shaped by downwardly mobile yet permanently employed government workers, and traders – many of Indian origin – who continued the urban life that they had become accustomed to – with slowing pace, decreasing real incomes, and decaying housing and infrastructure. By contrast, the global health city – a node on transnational circulations of knowledge, technology and capital – looks radically new, driven by innovation, promising life-saving discovery and global life-styles, and leaving the shadow of the postcolonial modern city behind. Indeed, it can appear like an amorphous conglomeration of projects that heap up in rapid turnover, externally imposed, or bestowed upon, a landscape of deficiency and need. And, by contrast to other sites in this book some of which are obsessed with their past, memory is a fragile resource in this fast-forward moving city.

Yet Kisumu has long been a site of medical research, since the Royal Society's Sleeping Sickness Commission arrived to conduct surveys in 1908, shortly after the founding of the city. The colonial urban grid is shaped by racially

Kisumu, "Mega City" shopping mall, 2009

Kisumu, Oginga Odinga Road, 2008

segregated sanitary town planning, mosquito control and public infrastructures, with medical and research institutions firmly situated in the administrative town centre. The "Native Hospital" emerged with research and control of sleeping sickness and (in 1908) bubonic plague. In 1938 the "Division of Insect Borne Diseases" (DIBD) of the Department of Health was established, focusing on yellow fever (a military and scientific concern, not a Kenyan public health issue) and malaria. For its British "officers," research and publication were an obligation, though subsidiary to public health work.

While research was originally funded by the Colonial Office and army grants, after political independence it became progressively dependent upon international collaboration, often focused on particular diseases or interventions. The new provincial hospital, built and designed by the USSR and opened in 1969, soon became a hub for ambitious, scientifically minded doctors, and established its own research programme. During the 1970s–80s research foci shifted somewhat, e.g., abandoning high-tech fields like oncology or innovative drug development, emphasising instead endemic infectious disease and large-scale interventions with basic, locally adapted or health-system independent technologies. Thus, after Bayer had discovered an efficient

drug and a molluscicide, the DIBD was renamed "Division of Vector-Borne Diseases" (DVBD), and expanded research on Bilharzia and its snail vectors. This attracted new international funders, and in the 1980s, while government medical and academic institutions decayed partly due to "structural adjustment," research collaborations allowed the DVBD and its staff to continue working, indeed thriving, for a time. Yet, it was during this age of "projects" that the ground began shifting for science in Kisumu.

After the death of Kenyatta, Kenya's first president, younger, partly US trained scientists in new disciplines like microbiology, lobbied government for a second decolonisation of science. A new national institution, the Kenya Medical Research Institute (KEMRI), was founded in 1979 as a para-statal organisation: financially independent, and mandated to collaborate. KEMRI established a centre for malaria research in Kisumu, eventually housed in a site outside the city, where decades later one of Africa's largest and most productive research laboratories was established, supported mainly by the US government's Centres for Disease Control and Prevention (CDC) and other Amerian and British institutions. Its more than 1200 staff (in 2009) included numerous former DVBD men working as microscopists and fieldworkers on secondment, or after retirement, but the weight of transnational collaboration had firmly shifted from the old ministerial Division to KEMRI/CDC.

While innovative malaria science thrived in the KEMRI centre's collaborations – with trials of insecticide-treated bednets that changed global malaria policy – Kisumu developed into an epicentre of the HIV/AIDS epidemic. Many scientific workers died. After the Kenyan government acknowledged HIV in the late 1990s, Kisumu became a leading site of HIV research, recruiting research subjects from the provincial hospital as well as rural sites. By the early 2000s, HIV research and interventions had become one of the largest employers. As a result of these new initiatives, with their dynamic, flexible institutional structures, urban change accelerated: new institutions situated themselves adjacent to older ones, older structures were rebuilt, old sites filled with new purpose. Thus, KEMRI and its North American partners developed clinical research sites with custom-built laboratory and clinical facilities within Kisumu's large but now dilapidated Provincial General Hospital, locally known as "Russia." Clinical trial patients, competing to enrol in US funded HIV research programmes that provided high-class health care, thus went to "Russia" for their trial check-ups. Similarly, the public clinic of "Lumumba," founded in the 1960s in a post-independence housing estate named after this progressive African leader, was in the early 2000s remade by the "Family. AIDS Care and Education Services" (FACES), a shell NGO of the University of California (UCSF).

The irony of such juxtapositions was lost on many global health actors on account of the urgency of their tasks and their short stays and, accordingly, memory. The contradictions remained tangible in the stark inequalities between architectures, furnishing, medical equipment, laboratory possibilities and health care practices within these composite sites, and attendant modes of exclusion and enclosure. Some local professionals, especially among the older generation, did remember and acknowledged the gap between past aspirations and present possibilities. Yet for most denizens of Kisumu, the intensity and speed of the global health boomtown left little space for remembrance, leave alone nostalgia. Health inequality, and the dominant role of international "partners" was taken for granted, if not always accepted.

By 2015, Kisumu is a clinical trials hub promising life-saving discoveries and personal opportunities, displaying global commodities and patterns of consumption; and experimenting with new forms of work. Lifelong government employment is replaced by a fragile and competitive labour market in which workers rely less on formal schooling than on informal "know-who" and "exposure" to latest concepts and opportunities, where voluntarism exploits blurred boundaries of paid and unpaid work, and where "tarmacking" between temporary jobs is part of life. Engendering a sense of possibility that exceeds that of the past, post-independence order, this entails also a fundamental insecurity, and vulnerability to economic or political crises in collaborative arrangements.

With acceleration, precarity and fictionalisation, global health sociality suffers from Paul Virilio's version of "topographical amnesia." Traces of the past – the old DVBD station in the city centre, the dreams of nationalist science at KEMRI or the socialist internationalism of "Russia" hospital – are submerged by on-going developments. It takes careful participation in residual social relations, habits and rhythms – the kinship-like bonds of older government medics, the regularities of the workdays, the circulation of correspondence and meetings between government, clinical and academic institutions – to sense older patterns. Sometimes nothing remains but toponyms: "Russia," "Moscow," "Victoria." Yet these traces, although products of defeat, continue to exercise an ambivalent force in the present.

Kisumu Oginga Odinga Road after post-election riots, 2007

Kisumu, Shauri Moyo housing estate built in 1960s, 2004

Kisumu, traffic, 2014

Kisumu, District Hospital, colonial nurse's quarters, 2005

Refreshment kiosk with funerary minivans waiting outside Provincial
Hospital, Kisumu, 2009

"Body map" painting in Kisumu HIV clinic, 2009

View from Kisumu's highest building, the provincial headquarters, half finished since the early 1990s, 2010

Kisumu municipal cemetery, alleged site of group burial of bodies that were not collected from the Provincial Hospital's mortuary, 2009

Commemorative plaque outside the US Army research clinic, now Obama paediatric ward, 2009

Kisumu, traffic, 2014

Nyanza Club, Kisumu, swimming competition of the international school, 2009

Martin Okonji (born 1938) finished school in 1944. Aged 16, he was employed by the colonial government as a Yellow Fever Inspector – a new professional category created in response to fears of war-related insect borne diseases. He continued working with the Division of Insect (later Vector) Borne Diseases contributing to research on malaria, river blindness, leishmaniasis and bilharzia, through political independence, until his retirement as a laboratory technologist, in 1982. While many of his retired colleagues found employment in one of the new overseas collaborative research sites involved in malaria and HIV research, Mr Okonji lives in his rural homestead, which is constructed in traditional Luo fashion – though consisting of modern houses – extending downward on a hill slope, with the father's solid but modest bungalow at the apex and the son's larger houses below. Below his home lies the recently opened new home of his oldest son Marx, a leading consultant psychiatrist. He enjoys his children and grandchildren, many of whom became academics, doctors and researchers, and have travelled the world.

Alfred Ilondaga Lwoba (1949–2009) or Luoba – his anglicised professional name – was born as son of what then was called a "subordinate staff" working with fly and mosquito collection at Kisumu Division of Vector Borne Diseases. He joined his father at DVBD in 1969, as a casual, temporary staff for the ongoing WHO Anopheles Control Unit. After gaining permanent employment, he was trained at Medical Training College and through "bench training" by older technicians and (then still partly European) scientists at the DVBD headquarters in Nairobi. Training also involved extensive travels around Kenya and long stays in the field – often under canvas – conducting research on insect borne parasitic diseases. Lwoba was posted to the Kenyan coast, where he married, and returned eventually home to Kisumu – 60 km from his ancestral village – where he became the in-charge. He presided over the DVBD's last period of relative bounty, marked by collaboration with Danish institutions, and conducted research for his doctorate as part of this programme. He completed his Ph.D. on the effects of earth eating among pregnant women, and its relation with parasitic infections and nutrition, within the prescribed time, publishing several articles in leading international journals. Shortly after being awarded his Ph.D. in 2005, he died from the consequences of a motorcycle accident that had been insufficiently treated, and was buried on the farm that he had bought and established in a cash cropping scheme.

John Vulule (born 1963) son of a land surveyor. His PhD in zoology, focusing on malaria vector biology, at the University of Nairobi (1996) was funded by CDC and competitive grants from WHO. Vulule is a Chief Research Officer at KEMRI. He served as director of the KEMRI Centre for Global Health Research during the time of its rapid expansion 2000–13, overseeing a labourforce of up to 1800, and over 80 research projects. At the same time (–2015), he was the principal investigator of the KEMRI/CDC collaboration and its Kenyan lead person. He participated in pioneering work on use of insecticide treated bednets for malaria control, and is co-author on over 180 international peer-reviewed publications.

Philister Adhiambo Madiega (born 1977) was born in the town of Moshi, Tanzania, is the daughter of a railway engineer and a housewife, and grew up in several East African cities, living in railway and government estates. After losing both parents due to sickness in the early 1990s, she moved in, at the age of 16, with her aunt in a village near her ancestral home. After finishing secondary school, she met a group of anthropologists including Ruth and Wenzel, and worked for several years as research assistant on a range of projects including traditional village-based ethnography, medical anthropology and health research, as well as the historical anthropological research on the DVBD, below, to which she made crucial contributions. In 2011, she completed a (distance based) Masters programme at the London School of Hygiene, funded through the collaborative project she was working on at the time, and had her first scholarly article accepted. She got employed by KEMRI, first as a Community Technologist in HIV research, later as Community Liaison Officer responsible for facilitating HIV and malaria research. She has worked with KEMRI, on annually extended contracts, from 2007 to 2016. She lives with her daughter, her sister, and her sister's son. Once the two children have completed their education, Philister hopes to continue her graduate studies in the field of public health.

Odhiambo Olel (born 1935) grew up during the late colonial era and in 1960, received a scholarship from the Soviet Union's "African-Asian Solidarity Scholarship Committee" to study medicine at Moscow State University. After returning to Kenya he served the Kenyan Ministry of Health from 1970–90, working first as an intern at Kenyatta National Hospital in Nairobi and then at various district hospitals. After government-sponsored post-graduate training in Public Health at Makerere University in 1974, he became Kisumu's Chief Medical Officer of Health. In 1990 he retired from government service for his private medical practice.

Olel was the eldest child in a polygamous Christian family. His grandfather had been a porter during the First World War and on returning to Kenya, made sure his children became literate. His father was a market clerk and his uncle a "medical dresser" for the Department of Health. Olel began primary school in 1947 in Nakuru, a town that was, as he put it, "a hotbed of settlers." He describes himself as

being "an urban rascal." After secondary school in Uganda, Makerere University College offered to send him to to the UK to qualify as a laboratory technician, but he wanted to be a doctor.

While in the USSR, Dr Olel became a student leader, participating in demonstrations against colonialism. In 1961 he and other African, Asian and Latin American students protested outside the American, Belgian and British embassies in Moscow against the assassination of Patrice Lumumba. After his return to Kenya, he continued his political activism against the one-party state, and was repeatedly arrested, jailed and, during the 1980s, placed in solitary confinement in the notorious Nyayo house. Due to his political views, opposition figures, including Jaramogi Oginga Odinga, favoured his private medical practice.

"We wait. We are bored. (He throws up his hand.) No, don't protest, we are bored to death, there's no denying it. Good. A diversion comes along and what do we do? We let it go to waste… In an instant all will vanish and we'll be alone once more, in the midst of nothingness! (He broods.)"

Samuel Beckett, *Waiting for Godot*, 1956

Staff of Kisumu Division of Vector Borne Diseases (DVBD)
in front of the laboratory, probably 1962

Staff of Kisumu DVBD, mid-1970s

Staff of Kisumu DVBD, mid-1980s

Staff of Kisumu DVBD and visiting DVBD veterans, 2005

"All I know is that the hours are long, under these conditions, and constrain us to beguile them with proceedings which – how shall I say – which may at first seem reasonable, until they become a habit. You may say it is to prevent our reason from foundering. No doubt. But has it not long been straying in the night without end of the abyssal depths? That's what I sometimes wonder. You follow my reasoning?"

Samuel Beckett, *Waiting for Godot*, 1956

Waiting

Secretariat, Kisumu DVBD, 2013

"A lot of dust"

7.00 Guards watchmen (paid for by a US programme to protect their store-rooms and cars) change over. The tired night watchman stays by gate; chats with a friend as morning traffic flows by. (The gate's hinges have broken, it now stands open permanently. The grounds are bushy; plastic rubbish has accumulated inside the fence.)

7.30 Drivers from KEMRI/CDC collect their Land Cruisers with their charac-teristic red US embassy number plates. (This parking arrangement – allowing CDC vehicles to park at the city centre protected by a watchman on govern-ment premises – is a leftover of 1980s collaboration, which was later cancelled after disagreements about mutual obligations.) F., the in-charge's secre-tary, comes in walking from the bus stop and opens doors and windows.

8.00 F. sweeps the sand near the buildings (grass seems no longer being cut since old S., the groundsman, left). Wiping the windowsills, she complains about the dust brought by all the CDC vehicles.

8.15 The Provincial Medical Officer (PMO) parks his car followed by the white Toyotas of other professionals working in nearby offices.

8.30 Three laboratory technicians

enter and gather in a sunny spot near the gate.

8.40 Mr H., the in-charge joins the technicians. The group scatters, all go on to their workplaces.

9.00 H. leaves for a meeting at PMO's. He carries the monthly report that he finalised yesterday and that F. had printed for him somewhere in town.

10.00 F. brings me a cup of tea. She gives me the funeral collection card for Mr N., the old driver who recently died. I pledge our Land Rover to transport the body (We will attend the funeral).

10.10 A young girl stands by the gate and gains F.'s attention, who then accompanies her to one of the labora-tories in the back, where the technicians sit in the shade. The girl is Mr O.'s relative who was sent from (the village) home.

10.40 A niece of F.'s comes into the admin office; she is sick and F. takes her to Mr A. in the malaria lab. He is reading some slides for a researcher from a North American University (paid by the batch). He finger-pricks the girl, makes a slide, and later writes the result on a corner of an exercise book for her to take to the pharmacist.

10.30 Two women enter and set up cooking stones and aluminium pots behind the compound (they cook lunch for the nurses and staff from the neighbouring hospital.)

10.50 Mr O. and N. set off in high spirits with a battered Renault and a megaphone. They will go for an "education drive – to tell the citizens about water treatment."

12.30 H. returns from town.

13.00 F. goes for lunchbreak, carrying a big basket.

13.00 H. goes for lunch. In passing he says, "see you tomorrow."

13.30 Joyce returns carrying a shopping bag filled with greens. In the office, she begins cutting the greens on her empty desk.

14.30 It is very hot. The watchmen and the two technicians are resting under the remaining trees. F. plays solitaire on the desktop after dusting the currently broken photocopier.

15.00 A young woman whom we got to know as HIV trial participant, who became a bookseller comes over with a bag full of Pentecostal self-help books she holds in commission.

16.00 A land cruiser from the U.S. Army Walter Reed programme stops by to deposit some specimens in the freezers (they still have their original building here, now used as freezer store).

16.30 Parked cars are collected. The technicians chat with bypassers at the gate before going home.

17.00 F. closes windows, locks the doors, secures the keys in her handbag.

18.00 The KEMRI/CDC drivers trickle back in and carefully fill the compound with their cars.

19.00 Night watchmen arrive, day watchmen change in the restrooms; darkness falls.

Activity schedule, DVBD, Kisumu,
14 November 2005

The former Head of the DVBD, Professor John Henry Ouma, in front of the Division's organisational chart in his office in the Nairobi headquarters, 2004

The Kisumu DVBD compound, 2004

How are things?
Head's office

Wenzel Good morning boss, how are things?

Head Things are bad. I had no [financial] allocation since autumn 2006. We just get by.

Wenzel How do you get by?

Head The MOH has some small funding [from the health facility revenue]: "cost sharing funds." Everybody in the DHMT [District Health Management Team] can apply. So we can also ask. But now we have no transport. The Land Rover is damaged after the hospital took it. And we have no money for fuel. We appreciate your support for fuel [in lieu of rent for our office space]; I can now visit the stations again. But we still work. Look at these reports.

[He hands over a stack of monthly reports from the district stations. Some have colourful covers, ornated with red-bellied mosquitos and local sights. One district has done over 12,000 malaria blood slides. Other stations have also done entomological surveys. How is this possible if they have no funds? They would not make up results. Ma Maybe the stations include work that staff did for external research projects? In which case, that would not allow to say much about distribution or changes, apart from that malaria still is around.]

Wenzel How do you manage to do this work?

Head We just get samples from the schools within [town]; we can't go out. We use public means. And we reuse slides.

Wenzel Why do you do this work. if you get no funding?

Head Ah, we now have performance-based contracts.

Wenzel What? [both laugh]

Head Yes, look! Since last year. Here, this is my signature; this is the PMO's stamp. Here are targets: 600-1400 blood slides for malaria, 800 to 1800 bilharzia, you see? [(He points at the signature, again.]. And if there is an evaluation, I could just be told to go.

[The secretary comes in with tea]

Secretary Sorry, no sugar today. [Smiles at visitor]

Wenzel What about the biscuits?

Secretary They are finished. You can get some.

Head You see, I keep applying for grants. I applied for one on dipstick malaria. I applied through another division, but I think they submitted an identical project and got the funding. This time I applied to WHO directly – for integrated helminth control. I applied for the whole province. I want to run it in all the stations. [Smiling at the visitor.] So when will you bring a project again?

Wenzel You know it's difficult, I have become an anthropologist; I don't do parasitology any more.

Head We can also help with anthropology, we know fieldwork, the community…

Laboratory
Wenzel Good morning. What are you doing today?

Technician 1 Nothing. There's nothing to do.

Wenzel You're reading?

Technician 1 Just to kill time. We study for our BA in laboratory science. In Eldoret. But it's expensive, especially the travel every weekend. But we share accommodation.

Technician 2 Yes, this is different from the time of KEDAHR [a Danish-Kenyan research project running from 1994 to 2000]. Then we had so much training. And people moved on to CDC, to Maseno [University]. But the last six years: nothing, no allocation, no project.

Wenzel But I can see some activity in the other lab. Who are the people working there?

Technician 1 Oh, yes, that's our laboratory, but that's another project, on schisto, but they hire their own staff. Very young men! They don't do quality control. Some of them don't even have registration.

Technician 2 I worked with them for

one month, in the beginning, but I was just doing collection and processing of stool. [They continue with the reading].

[Passing my old laboratory, I don't recognise the young technicians. The room has been repainted since I worked there. New microscopes, using smart phones for data entry, rubber gloves, concentrated work. One of the young women shows me EPICOLLEC, a web-based software – "the sponsor from the US brought it" – to which the readings are uploaded, first to the UK group, then to Atlanta. The smart-phones apparently can even read the barcodes on the slides!]

In the courtyard, meeting some staff i n a conversation

Technician 3 Good morning Wenzel, meet Mr M., he is now in charge of Bondo DVBD.

Wenzel Good morning, long time. How are you?

Visiting technician Well, I am now the biggest donor of DVBD.

Wenzel How?

Visiting technician I fund our activities out of pocket. There is no allocation. And yet, I am on performance contract. I have to be active. But that does not mean I get allocation. Like now, he [points smiling at technicial 3], he is asking me to submit my third quarterly report.

Technician 3 [laughing broadly] Yes, I will start disciplinary procedures against him.

Technician 2 Yes, they will say: you get a salary but then you don't do anything, so I have to go and do something. I must send my reports.

Technician 3 These contracts are good idea, but it does not work.

Notes and interview from visit to DVBD station Kisumu, Wenzel, 26 March 2011

Malaria Control Activities:

The department carried out routine blood slide examination on referrals from clinical areas and malariometric surveys through schools the figures below summarise the activities:

Routine:

Quarter	Age group	No. Examined	Positive for malaria parasites	% positive
1st Quarter **Jan – Mar 2007**	0 – 5 years	23	9	39.1%
	6 – 10 years	16	4	25%
	11 – 15 years	22	7	31.8%
	16 + years	196	44	22.4%
	All age groups	**257**	**64**	**24.9%**
2nd Quarter **Apr – Jun 2007**	0 – 5 years	24	7	29.2%
	6 – 10 years	28	6	21.4%
	11 – 15 years	25	1	4%
	16 + years	214	23	10.7%

Extract from 2007 Annual Report, Homa Bay DVBD station

Conclusion

This station is operating with minimal resources; a lot that should have been done were undone due to unavailability of resources. Financial allocation to the station will enable it [to] run efficiently and effectively again.

DVBD Bondo District, Monthly Reports, July August September 2009

Provincial head of DVBD, Mr Erastus Kwanya explaining the organisational structure, 2010

Stuffing (sic!)

Stations staffing level stood at three technical staff, all technologists, and one support staff.

Building
The buildings are in dire need of painting and minor repairs. The buildings have never been repainted since the first painting when they were built.

Transport
The only mode of transport at the station's disposal, motorcycle GK V829 was grounded for need of repairs for the whole year.

Constraints
lack of funds to facilitate field activities transport
Recommendation
reinstate funding to Division of Vector-borne Diseases, so that the stations can plan and systematically carry out surveillance on respective diseases as used to be.
Provide functional transport to the stations.

Division of Vector Borne and Neglected Tropical Diseases, Homa Bay Station, Annual report, 2008

Field laboratory outside Kisumu, probably late 1970s

Field laboratory Kenya-Uganda border, early 1950s

Laboratory, Kisumu DVBD, 1980s

"We are ready to work"

The DVBD station is a shady island at the centre of a rapidly changing city, sheltered from growing traffic, dust and rubbish by its numerous trees. While some of these date back to colonial times, I took part in the planting of some, in 1994, to commemorate the beginning of a Kenyan-Danish research programme – the last large project DVBD would engage in. I conducted my PhD laboratory work in parasitology in the DVBD's 1940s laboratories. My research only required a microscope, which the project had donated, and running water, then still reliable. A coat of paint was all I needed to begin my study.

Together with the DVBD men – employed since their early 20s and sharing strong institutional bonds – I enjoyed the pleasures of long days in the field, noisy drives in the 1970s Land Rovers, perched between driver and a colleague on the front bench, and weekly "member's days" in long-established roadside bars and in music venues that played the then already nostalgic mixture of traditional Luo tunes, Congolese rhythms and 1960s jazz. Until 2000 I participated in the Danish project and after converting to social anthropology, my wife Ruth and I continued to work out of the DVBD station. When our first son was born, colleagues accompanied us to hospital and the elderly secretaries advised us on our first baby shopping.

We came back to visit whenever we were in the city, to stay in touch, to pause, remember – maybe to return some day. Only in hindsight I became – and, I suspect my colleagues too – aware of the exceptional era of pleasure and bounty that we had experienced. For over six years, all staff (including subsidiary stations) had been part of one "project," which not only paid generous per-diems that multiplied staff salaries and offered technicians opportunities for Masters and PhD training, but engendered a sense of community and purpose, with its parties and workshops, field stays and challenging new encounters.

It also took time to understand the place itself. Arriving in the early 1990s, I found a dilapidated African government institution. Like the surrounding city, its familiar bureaucratic rhythms and spatial order were marked by deficiencies. My laboratory shipment from Copenhagen included microscopes and reagents, labcoats, rubber boots, even tea towels. Yet, the perception of present lack, of a stable place characterised by absences, was erroneous. It naturalised deficiencies, overlooking that incapacitation was an ongoing event. It ignored omnipresent traces of past prowess: outdated architecture, furniture and equipment that was not just not-contemporary, but referenced layers of personal and professional history, work routines and technical knowledge that had accumulated over half a century. And it was slow

Section of image-spread on Kenyan-Danish health research project,
wall of Kisumu DVBD, 1995

The author as Danish parasitologist,
Kisumu, 1995

to acknowledge the science worker's enduring personal relations. Working, and returning, I partook in a scientific kinship through which, since the 1930s, technical knowledge had been passed on through "bench training" and "field-work" – foundations of DVBD men's professional pride and of their close mutual ties.

My first impressions of DVBD also erred by taking institutional durability for granted: twenty years later, and without "projects," little remained of DVBD's seemingly reliable governmental order. By 2015, the Danish project has already become a destination of nostalgia. The faded photograph of myself in my 20s, set among all the other Danish and Kenyan staff, decorated one of the laboratories as a dusted memento. Social scientists have decried the "projectification" of stable government public health infrastructures; but projects were at least that: commitments, limited promises, if only for years at the time, and reliable everyday rhythms and positions. Fifteen years after the Danish project prematurely ended, there is no project for the three remaining staff at the station. The older colleagues have retired – often seeking more gainful employment as microscopists with the new transnational collaborative

site in town – and funerals have become the only occasions where the "spirit of the DVBD" that the old men cultivated remains alive. Research in Kisumu is thriving in the centers of US government collaborations and North American Universities, working through the para-statal KEMRI, while the DVBD "is dead," as its staff never grow tired of stating. Or not quite dead, as staff stick to routines, seek to maintain their technical competence, and wait. "We are just waiting here," they say, "we are waiting for government directives," "we are still waiting for government allocation of funds," "the vehicles are grounded at the moment" – and yet: "we are ready to work."

Signboard at the gate of Kisumu DVBD, 2007

Field team from Kisumu DVBD, 1970s

Elderly DVBD staff wearing his last uniform (received in 1983) in front of Land Rover, 2005

Waiting as present preoccupation points here both backwards and ahead. As one memorable presentation by the Kisumu station in-charge at a donor meeting concluded: "Restore the Glory of DVBD." One waits to return, for the restoration of the fifty stations, hundreds of permanent staff with their Land Rovers and vans, uniforms and equipment. But maybe this waiting makes sense also short of such miracles. It positions those who wait in relation to more modest potentials. Universal scientific promise deteriorates into local resources for near-future making: a researcher from the collaborative sites needs a fieldworker to collect specimens, or a traditional microscope reader, for a few days or weeks; an international student seeks an assistant or a small office space to rent; a staff relative needs a malaria slide or an introduction to someone in the hospital next door; a successful HIV intervention needs safe parking for their brand-new vehicles; a visiting researcher offers to sponsor a school child; during power or water shortage across the town, the hospital supplies, which DVBD is connected to, still work; and maybe, some day, Wenzel will "bring another project," though we all agree that it is not likely.

In the long meanwhile, one uses the infrequent moneys that reach the station – including the prodigal anthropologist son's office rent – to keep the buildings neat, the grounds at least periodically cleared, and the last of the 1970s Land Rovers fuelled every now and then. One opens the laboratories, goes for lunch and keeps closing time. If someone restocked sugar, one has the regular mid-morning tea, and occasionally a beer after work with the colleagues – though most of the old men's "joints" across town have disappeared, as the young NGO and collaborative science workers prefer coffeeshops in the new malls, where a cafe latte costs more than a round of beer in those roadside bars.

Title of funerary video for Dr Alfred Lwoba, retired head of Kisumu DVBD, 2007

Stills from funerary video for Dr Alfred Lwoba, 2007

Pride

Philister So are you proud of DVBD?

Edward I am proud of DVBD, because it has made me what I am, because I have worked with DVBD over these years from 1989; and out of the work that I have doing, out of the experience that I gained in DVBD, I have been able to achieve one or two things. I have been able to take care of my family, my immediate and my extended family; in terms of seeing some of my brothers and sisters through secondary school, and I have also been able to take care of my distant family in terms of fending them and I have also taken care of myself and my immediate family in terms of giving them education, shelter and food.

Interview with Edward Oloo, Philister A Madiega, 24 March 2007

Philister What is the greatest of achievement of DVBD?

Chris Well, we almost eradicated leishmaniasis, we did good work to control malaria, although it is still there, prevalent, but we could also predict using our surveys when there would be an outbreak or when the disease would go down. That prediction would help the population in terms of the drugs, bed nets and what have you, so that you would know at this particular time of the year, take care, there is going to be a lot of malaria.

Philister So what change has happened in DVBD during the time from 1987 [when you started] to now?

Chris Well, it is no longer the DVBD that it was. There is a lot of work that was done that we no longer do now. It was a big station. Now Kisumu doesn't even have a vehicle, so how can we move? How do we do those things? Funding is once in a year and if it comes it is inadequate. A lot of things have changed – in fact we no longer operate the way we used to do. The greatest change is depletion of staff. The ones who have climbed higher in terms of education have been lured to other institutions like KEMRI, the universities… because of lack of funding for the department. They are all now gone and that has contributed to a

downward trend in terms of expertise. Another problem is ever shrinking funding from government. And that they no longer train DVBD staff has caused problems.

Philister Do you think an institution like DVBD has got some future?

Chris As I said before, right now there is research saying that diseases like Leishmania, like those diseases that had been eradicated before, are coming back, which means that DVBD must be reorganized to control these diseases again, so that we eradicate them, because they are coming up again.

Philister What do you think should be done to make DVBD stronger or the way it used to be?

Chris There could be three things: one, increase the number of staff in

DVBD to cover the ever growing population in Kenya, so that they could adequately handle the situations when they arise. Two, vehicles to move in various parts of the country. Just three weeks ago there was reported an outbreak of Leishmaniasis – that gives me the indicator that it is true that these diseases are coming up again and we need to do something about them – and there must be transport to move readily. Three, funding: we need enough funds not only for the staff but also in terms of work.

Interview with Chris Nyagol, DVBD Technologist, Kisumu, Philister A.Madiega, 6 October 2006

MARTIN OKONJI ODERO
YELLOW FEVER INSPECTOR
1945

Studio portrait of yellow fever inspector Martin Okonji, 1945

Private photographs from the life of a retired DVBD technician, 1960s–80s

Mosquito collection hut, built 1940s

Dear Wenzel,

[…]

My father lived in one roomed brick walled grass thatched house on the premises of DVBD in Kisumu from 1944 to 1948. When I was born, I spent few months of my life there.

He lived in that house for convenience as he was involved in the breeding of yellow fever vector (*Aedes Aegypti*) and he had to supervise the breeding process.

Marx
Dr Marx M O Okonji, FRCPsych
CONSULTANT PSYCHIATRIST
Nairobi Hospital

E-mail from Dr Marx Okonji to Wenzel, 31 May 2016

Retired staff member Martin Okonji in front of the experimental mosquito collection hut at Kisumu DVBD, in which he lived with his family around 1945, 2005

Martin Okonji in front of the house his firstborn son, Marx, built in the family homestead outside Kisumu, 2005

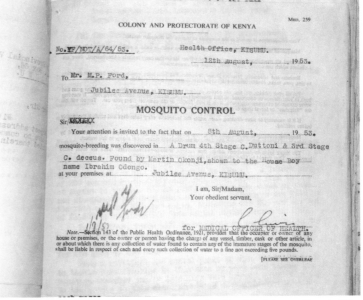

Mosquito control form filled by Martin Okonji in 1953, Kakamega Records Office

Utopias are "non-fictional, even though they are also non-existent. Utopias in fact come to us as barely audible messages from a future that may never come into being."

Frederic Jameson, The Politics of Utopia, *New Left Review*, 2004

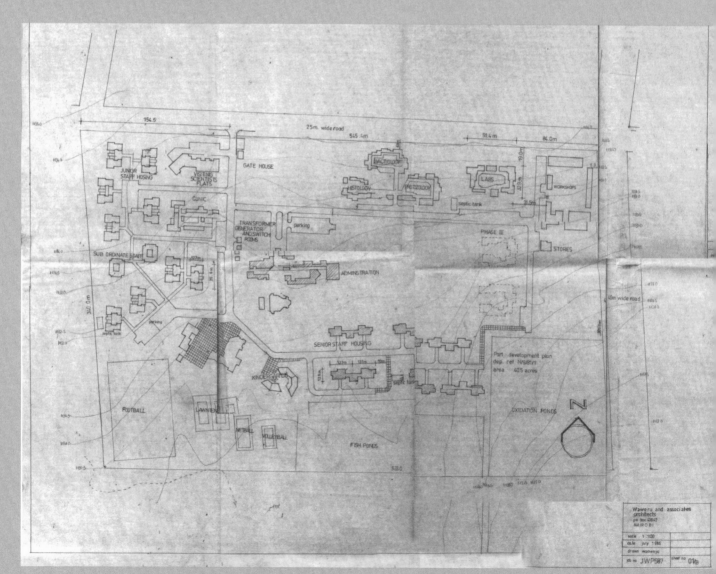

Drawing for the new KEMRI station outside Kisumu, Waweru architects, partially realised, 1986

Blueprint and building

1977–2009
Partial construction of a scientific civitas.

1977
East African Community dissolves. Kenyan scientists in research stations around Tanzania and Uganda return to Kenya (including the director of Amani, Tanzania).

1978
During interregnum around President Kenyatta's death, foundations of new national scientific infrastructure are laid, including Kenya Medical Research Institute (KEMRI).

1979
KEMRI's Malaria and Other Protozoal Diseases Research Centre (MOPDRC) housed in temporary structures in old Kisumu (formerly Native) District Hospital.

First proposals for a research station adjacent to New Nyanza General Hospital ("Russia"), opened 1969, rejected by the director who, returned from Amani hill station, prefers a rural location.

1981–3
Acquisition of 40 acre plot outside Kisumu from the local clan, facilitated by local MP and foreign minister Dr Robert Ouko, to build a malaria research centre.

Wire-mesh fencing of the entire site.

1985–6
"Phase 1" construction, administrative and one laboratory building. Stone-laying ceremony.

1986
Master plan for the development of the entire site, including civic amenities, housing, entertainment, by Kenyan architectural office Waweru. Only model senior staff houses, one multi-storey staff accommodation are built. Then construction is halted due to lack of funds.

2003–5
Completion, within KEMRI centre, of "New office headquarters and laboratory buildings for the CDC in Kisumu," designed by Nairobi office Beglin Woods. CDC funds refurbishment of old buildings, creating more homogeneous impression. Reconstruction of feeder road.

Three-metre concrete wall, only around the scientific part of the site.

Banner with KEMRI mission statement, Kisumu, 2008

1981. *Plans.*
5. Malaria and Other Protozoal Diseases Research Centre, Kisumu:
Head: Dr P. Wegesa.

Physical facilities poor, occupying small temporary structures in old Kisumu hospital. Sub-centres at Taveta and Webuye needing development.

Equipment: inadequate, partially because of lack of working space.

Scientific manpower: to be recruited, although there are excellent technologists.

Scientific programme: some research is going on mosquito vector biology, malaria transmission and plasmodium sensitivity to chemotherapy.

Collaboration established with Division of Vector Borne Diseases [....]

Dr Wegesa has been away on sick leave [...]

Land for the centre is under negotiation.

Kenya Medical Research Institute, Ministry of Health, Progress Report as on 31st March 1981 to the National Council for Science and Technology (KEMRI archive, Kisumu CGHR, MPD/RCD-TDR, no box file).

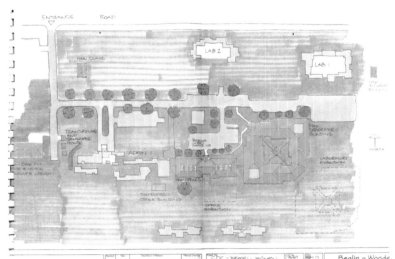

Drawing for CDC field station within KEMRI centre, Beglin Woods architects, 2000

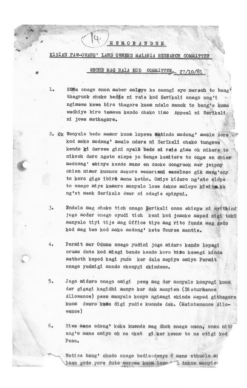

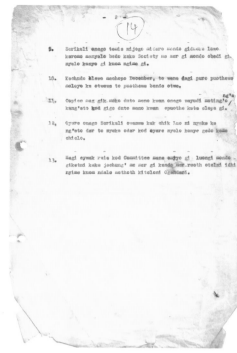

Memorandum sent by local inhabitants to the malaria research committee, KEMRI, 1981

1981. Concerns with pasts and future places.

1   What should be investigated well, since if not properly considered it will bring problems for the citizens later, is that the government should look at our livelihood. Due to resettlement, we are going to suffer a short period now, and then later on if we fail to make a living in the new places we are given, we should start to appeal [Engl.] to the government that our people are suffering.

1   We cannot be happy for our land, small pieces of land downstream and those across the road, to be taken. That the government evicts us from these pieces of land is not right, because to evict somebody from his piece of land without knowing where to take people is a huge loss. And it is against development [lit.: "growth"], because we are evicted from where we had established ourselves. Everything will go to waste. If someone is evicted from his land he should be given an alternative place to live and should not be neglected by the government.

2   When work begins, the government should ensure so much that the children of those who were relocated should get employment here. Those people who still are strong can do office work, or work as masons and carpenters, and the remaining ones can take any courses that may be there.

3   Maize permits should be obtained for those who are relocated. Their pieces of land have been finished, and their homes, and it will take them a long time before they find a home. A permit should be given to them so that it can help them during this period.

[....]

12   The government should leave for us the remains of our homes ["oyare," lit. "the soot from the smoke under the roof"], so we can carry away the rooftops in the way Luo tradition says, that if somebody resettles then he must move with the soot of the roof. The rooftops can help you build another place.

These are the grievous cries of the citizens and the committee that made us to address you as their representative.

Memorandum: Kisian Paw-Owang' Land Owners' Malaria Research Committee:

Public Issues and the Committee. 27/10/81. KEMRI Kisumu archive, free translation by Philister Madiega

Signatures and fingerprints of the original owners transferring the land for the malaria research station, KEMRI CGHR Kisumu archive, 1981

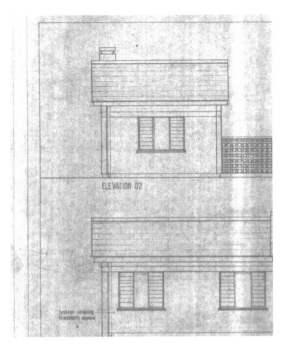

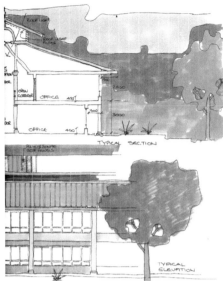

Proposed Office Building Design

far left: Drawing for senior staff housing at the new KEMRI station, Waweru architects, 1986

left: Drawing for CDC offices at KEMRI center, Beglin Woods architects, 2000

1986/2009. Blueprint

Visited Vulule, KEMRI center director, in the older administrative block, built in the 1980s before construction subsided. Seated in the deep sofas of his enormous, airy director's office, he showed me what he knew would delight me: the original 1980s architectural blueprint of the research center, drawn by Waweru architects, in Nairobi. The faded blue tracings outline a science city – set apart from the old Kisumu city itself, but, as Vulule explained, adjacent to the Kisian railway station, which then was only a 15 minute ride from Kisumu station. A civic whole with school and kindergarten, staff housing for all grades, and guest researcher accommodation, sports grounds and tennis courts, centered around extensive laboratories and administrative spaces. A dream civitas for 20th century science, a mini Gorki in the Savannah. Distant precursor (and yet the opposite of) of Africa's new IT cities. Vulule smiles at my excitement at this discovery of a dream station that never was to be built. He had, of course, known about it all along, since he trained here 25 years ago and had kept the plans in his cupboard.

But who else remembers this dream, arriving as newcomers, foreigners, to this incongruous palimpsest of old-style African officialdom, CDC's gold-plated, climatised non-place buildings, built-up, built-over and vacant overgrown spaces? Is his a wry smile acknowledging failure, apologetic that the drawing was never realised? I prefer to read it as a colluding wink – added to the satisfaction at my enthusiasm – upon revealing material evidence of a quietly retained dream. Such dreams are not mere blueprints for futures – measured, or discounted, against their concrete realisation – but reasons to exist in, and resist, the present.

Wenzel's notes, 14 October 2009

1986. Scientific life.

(2) The meeting decided:

(1) The designs should incorporate a rooftop bar/coffee facility on the flat roof side of the visiting scientists housing.

(ii) With regard to the senior staff houses' design, a third WC approximate to the living room should be included.

(iii) The plan should be amended to include a staff clinic and nursery school.

(iv) The plan and sketch designs were approved subject to these amendments.

Vector Biology and Control Research Centre, Kisumu: Proposal for Phase 2, Minutes of-Site Meeting, 10th January 1986
KEMRI CGHR Kisumu archive

Satellite image of KEMRI center outside Kisumu; original land parcel owned by KEMRI, and smaller enclosure including KEMRI/CDC facilities, 2014

incongruous against the backdrop of surrounding village and bush. After a kilometre, the road takes a 90° turn, and then a second 90° turn to a closed metal gate in a wiremesh fence. Some people say that the double right angle has something to do with the US partner's security requirements, after the drive-in bombings of Beirut, but that's probably nonsense.

Outside the gate is a small shed from reused corrugated iron, a "hotel" selling tea and snacks, with a handwritten signboard "Researchers Café," where some well-dressed young workers from the station stand and chat. From a water tap near the gate that distributes water from the centre's own well, people from surrounding settlements draw water into plastic jerrycans.

After some time, an elderly watchman arrives – the same who worked here when I first came 15 years ago. He asks the driver to fill in some details about the car – familiar procedure in Kenyan government institutions – and slowly opens the gate. Somebody explain to me that this is the gate of the original KEMRI compound; the 40 acres acquired in the 80s. Inside, the road follows a high concrete wall up to a second gate, again at a right angle, marked with the bright signboards of an international security company. Along the concrete wall are tidy flowerbeds, on the opposite side of the road, away from the inner enclosure, the land is less tidy. A storeyed concrete house from the 80s stands

2009. Ground view.

Google images' portrait of the scientific enclave tell one story of global health enclosure and exclusion, maybe, but they are also as De Certeau had it, a visual simulacrum. If we enter the enclave as "Wandersmänner," we first travel along the seriously potholed highway from Kisumu to the Ugandan border, full of minibuses, lorries and fuel tankers. Probably one of the most heavily trafficked and least maintained highways in Kenya. Opposite the now abandoned railway stop, we reach the large and well maintained signboard indicating the KEMRI Center for Global

Health Research (erected at the same time, and in the same material quality, as the new access road was constructed), which for some time was defaced by election slogans.

We turn onto the exceptionally neat feeder road, constructed from concrete flag stones, with neatly marked pavements, painted speed bumps with warning signs, and regular, functioning streetlights. Some well-dressed young staff, who must have missed the CDC shuttle from the city and come to work by public means – which do not service this road – look somewhat

far left: Wall and gate of the inner enclosure, KEMRI center Kisumu, 2009

left: Staff housing from the original architectural plan, outside the concrete wall of the present day research station, 2009

slightly unmotivated against a back-drop of irregular fields and bush land, inside the wire mesh enclosure. Apparently, these ageing houses in the no man's land have recently become very attractive to KEMRI staff, on account of low rents and proximity to work.

The second gate is manned by a group of well-trained guards of the international security provider, who operates from Congo to Iraq, who in this location wear Stars & Stripes on their sleeves. They examine the vehicle with mirrors, walking around it and looking into the boot, sometimes they ask you to open the car – standard procedures executed with polite professionality. Irrespective of one's discernible origin, they check staff badges, and in the case of outside visitors, contact the host inside the enclosure.

Once the gate is opened, the car is temporarily trapped between gate and a turnstile, which is opened after the gate has been closed. Ahead of the visitor lies a shady campus of well painted buildings, clearly demarcated parking places, cropped lawns and well-watered plants, which contrasts starkly to the irregular bushland out-side. As one drives towards the main parking place, one leaves to one side a row of lower, early postcolonial style bungalows, in front of which flies the Kenyan flag, the administrative offices of the KEMRI centre. However, most visitors would be inclined to drive on towards the largest building ahead, a newly built, broad two-storey building striking, not least on account of its reflex windowpanes. In front of this building, funded by CDC and housing the KEMRI CDC collaborative pro-gramme, the lawns are interspersed with airy pavilions for group meetings, as well as a clean and attractive looking staff canteen.

Wenzel's notes, remembering the site after return, 14 October 2009

Video stills from commemorative video produced by the CDC field station on the occasion of the KEMRI/CDC collaboration's 30-year anniversary, 2009

2009. On my own

Wenzel Here [on the 2004 architects' drawings for the CDC buildings] there are two Directors' offices beside each other. It says, 'Director KEMRI' to the left and, 'Director CDC' to the right. The office where there is [the US embassy chief administrator] now, it is here designated to you! Why are you not there in the big building but out here?

Vulule You see, the CDC is only a project among others. There is nothing called CDC in Kenya. This place is all KEMRI, and they have a project here. And I am not CDC. … Also, I prefer to be here [in the 1984 bungalow offices near the entrance], on my own.

Interview with Center Director in his office, KEMRI CGHR, Kisumu, 12 February 2009

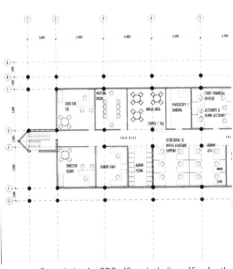

Ground plan for CDC offices including office for the KEMRI director, Beglin Wood architects, 2000

"The provision of the new hospital in Kisumu is a matter that exercises the minds of the local population to a very large degree."

Letter from Regional Medical Officer, Nyanza, to Permanent Secretary, Ministry of Works, Communication and Power, Nairobi, 24 October 1963.

Jaramogi Oginga Odinga Teaching and Referral Hospital, also known as "Russia", March 2014

"Russia", stairway to the operating theaters, 2014

"I feel that the hospital will be a show piece in Kenya and as it will be the most modern and up to date, it is essential that it should run smoothly from the beginning."

Letter from Provincial Medical Officer (PMO) to Permanent Secretary, Ministry of Health and Housing, Nairobi, 16 January 1967 (Kakamega Provincial Record Center (KPRC), "Medical," shelf 462, ND/2/4, "New Russian-Aided Hospital," BG/4A/4 and BG/5A/67/110)

"Russia"

"I have read newspaper reports that one of the items to be discussed by the Russian Trade Mission in Kenya is a proposed hospital as part of the Russian Government's offer of assistance to Kenya. The purpose of this letter is to forward once more the views of the council on the need for a new hospital to serve the Nyanza region, and to replace the present ugly and unsatisfactory hospital buildings."

Letter from Town Clerk, Kisumu, to Permanent Secretary (PS), Ministry of Health and Housing, 23 July 1964

"The specialists of the State Project institute GIPROZDRAV, of the Ministry of Health, USSR, […], have submitted a general layout and drawing of a 200-bed hospital to be constructed in Kisumu Kenya as a gift from the USSR to the people of Kenya […]. The representatives of the Kenyan government and Municipality in Kisumu, […] have considered the general layout and drawings of the proposed hospital jointly with the Soviet specialists."

Minutes of meeting at Regional Medical Headquarters, Kisumu, 1 September 1964: "USSR Hospital Project, Kisumu: Recommendations for the Design and Building of the USSR 200-bed hospital in Kisumu, Kenya."

"The Russian engineer Mr Ousenko estimates the building will be completed May 1967. And the first Russian staff should be arriving March 1967."

Report sent by the PMO to the PS, Ministry of Health and Housing, and to the Director of Medical Services

"There will be 8 wards of 25 beds […], 2 operating theatres, an outpatient department with X-ray facilities and waiting space and clinic rooms. The ground floor of the main block will have a well-supplied laboratory with departments of bacteriology, haematology, biochemistry and histology. There will 3 X-ray departments within the main block. The Russians will provide 3 new X-ray machines; the present machine in Nyanza hospital being rather old. There will be a large pharmacy. It will be an extremely modern well equipped pharmacy dealing with the latest drugs."

Report by PMO on "The new Russian-aided Hospital," 29 April 1966, PMO HQ, Kisumu

"The Russians will completely equip the hospital from operating theatre lights to normal items of hardware etc."

Letter from Town Clerk to Medical Storekeeper, Nairobi. 29 April 66

"Russia", view from covered walkway, 2014

"The USSR will send fifteen Russian specialists for a three year period and ten Russian specialists for a two year period. The latter will be paid for by the Government of Kenya. The Russian experts will be entitled to GOK housing."

Letter from the PS, Ministry of Health and Housing to PMO, 9 Feb 1967

(KPRC, BG/4A, "Medical," shelf 462,ND/2/4,"New Russian-Aided Hospital," documents BG/4A/64/20, BG/5/64/2, BG/5A/65/8, BG/5A/66/32A, BG/5A/66/29 and 38/128/Vol II/58)

"Russia", view from balcony, 2014

"Russia", courtyard, 2014

Historic photograph of violence at the hospital's 1969 opening, reproduced in *The Daily Nation*, 23 October 2009,
"The incident that turned Kenya into a One Party State"

"Marred by tragedy"

In 2013, Kenya celebrated its 50th years of nation-hood. During the year the media focused on some "key events" that, it claimed, had defined the new nation. On 29 October 2013, the Standard newspaper reported on the opening ceremony of the new Russian-built hospital in Kisumu, in October 1969, under the heading "Witness recalls the 1969 Kisumu massacre that marked Jomo Kenyatta's visit." On this day, the hospital, the site of so much expectation and hope, became, in the words of witnesses, "a bloodbath," when the presidential guard opened fire on the crowd.

On 26 October 1969, President Kenyatta travelled to Kisumu to conduct the official opening ceremony of the hospital amid rising tensions with politician (Jaramogi) Oginga Odinga, whose close ties with the USSR had resulted in the hospital's construction. Just months earlier, Odinga had left the government to set up a new political party and the assassination of politician Tom Mboya had led to riots in Kisumu amidst rumours of the state's involvement. Crowds lined the

streets to see Kenyatta's motorcade but Kisumu was tense. In the hospital grounds, people shouted opposition slogans and asked, "Where is Mboya?" In the chaos that ensued, Kenyatta's security forces opened fire on the crowds. Between ten and thirty people died and hundreds were injured. The hospital's wards were overrun while the mortuary was full. According to an eye-witness I interviewed in March 2014, "the hospital was baptized that day in blood." Kenyatta left Kisumu immediately. Three days later, Odinga was placed under detention and his party banned. This was Kenyatta's last visit to Kisumu during his increasingly authoritarian rule (1963–78). Fifty years later, on 23 October 2009, the Kenyan Daily Nation, which reproduced a photograph of crowds fleeing gunfire, suggested that this event was a "pivotal moment" marking the consolidation of state-supported violence and the oppression of political opposition.

From its beginnings, then, the hospital was associated not only with hopes in medical modernity and national development but also

October 26, 1969, President Mzee Jomo Kenyatta opens the New Nyanza Provincial General Hospital – Kisumu, built and equiped with Russian Aid.

Historic photograph of 1969 hospital opening by President Kenyatta, reproduced in self-presentation of New Nyanza Provincial General Hospital, 2009

with an event that revealed their bitter betrayal, the growth of state violence and authoritarianism, the suppression of opposition, and rising ethnic tensions. The opening ceremony anticipated a long period during which western Kenyan, regarded as the hotbed of support for the political opposition, was marginalized and, according to its inhabitants, excluded from the fruits of development.

"I attended this function as a nine-year-old. I had to run for my life and luckily we lived in the hospital grounds and the run for dear life was thus shorter for me than for most. We revered Kenyatta, but now as a grown up I can look at his record with better lenses. I find little positive that this man contributed to the well being of the nation he purported to have created; tribalism, nepotism, corruption, dictatorship, and theft are just but a few of the ills he bequeathed to the rest of us."

Comments made online in 2012 in response to the Youtube screening of President Kenyatta's speech during the hospital's opening ceremony in 1969 (https://www.youtube.com/watch?v=WmWx3eB4oqg)

"I would like to express my thanks to all members of staff for the tremendous effort they made to ensure that the hospital was clean and in good order for the Presidential visit. The hospital looked spotless; the patients looked comfortable and well cared for and many people remarked on this to me. We are all very sad that this occasion was marred by tragedy. I would like to thank all those who rendered assistance to the injured. In particular, I would like to commend the sisters, staff nurses, Enrolled nurses and Pupil nurses (on day and night duty) who remained in the Hospital and cared for the patients until the early hours of the morning. I was immensely impressed by the way you all acted in this crisis and I wish you to accept these few lines as a token of appreciation."

Letter from Provincial Matron to staff at the New Nyanza General Hospital, 31 October 1969

(KPRC, BG/10 "Medical," shelf 462, ND/2/8, "Opening of the New Nyanza General Hospital, Kisumu")

"Although we had to learn Russian, science was universal"

Dr Olel The British were very economical with education for Africans. They did not give us a chance for a professional education. [...] They regarded Africans as third-rate persons [...] We were hot-headed then, as students and young people! We felt that the British had mistreated us, and we wanted a change [...] And we had not invited the British here, so we felt that they should not stay. [...]

I arrived in the USSR in 1960 [on a scholarship from the Soviet Afro-Asian Solidarity Committee], and first we had to learn Russian. We had to learn the language, just like we had to learn your British language. I did well in the preparatory course for medicine. I did not sleep, it was very tough and I worked hard. The stipend was good. We got enough for accommodation, even for clothes. [...] But although we had to learn Russian, science was universal. [...]

You know, we were ambitious. We were activists. We wanted to be a good example. We did not want to fail. That was the time of the Cold War, of ideology. We were siding with the USSR. We felt they were on our side to fight the British, in the British colonies [...] In the USSR I was President of the Kenya members of the African Students Union. We were so hot-headed! We demonstrated in 1961 when Lumumba was killed. Not only the African students. We were joined by the Latin Americans, the Asians. We smashed the windows of the British and American and Belgian embassies in Moscow. We burnt things, we burnt their vehicles...

Ruth You demonstrated against colonial rule?

Dr Olel Yes. And in the Soviet Union, they also supported us. So they named the university [after Patrice] Lumumba. It was significant. In their sympathy and their recognition of, you know, what was done.

Ruth That was a time of friendship between Soviet Union and African countries. Did you experience that on a personal level?

Dr Olel Russians were very keen on friendship; they were very friendly. It was a new experience, also for them. But that was because they had a revolution [when they] overthrew the tsar, the king. So they were liberated and they felt that they had been, you know, under domination. The Communist ideology brought them up to be very patriotic. And so when they learnt that people in Africa and Asia were still under colonialism, they became more friendly.

Interviews with Dr Odhiambo Olel, retired Chief Medical Officer of Health in Kisumu, who was trained in the USSR, 24 September 2013 & 12 November 2014

HEALTH

Jaramogi Oginga Odinga Teaching and Referral Hospital in Kisumu. [PHOTO: FILE/STANDARD]

Crisis engulfs Jaramogi Oginga Odinga Hospital

By STANDARD TEAM

A health crisis looms in Nyanza and Western regions after Kenya Medical Research Institute (Kemri) and Centre for Disease Control (CDC) shut down a major public health research project in Kisumu town.

The decision is likely to affect operations at the Jaramogi Oginga Odinga Teaching and Referral Hospital, which serves more than 100 district and sub-district hospitals in more than 10 counties in the region. The development is as a result of a cash scandal at Kemri involving the loss of more than Sh7.2 billion in research funds. The gravity of the situation was captured by Health Executive Elizabeth Ogaja.

"We are faced with a dire situation in healthcare provision. We have relied on Kemri for our research work and operational support. We may not be able to bridge the financial gap left by their withdrawal," she said.

The Standard, 18 June 2015

"Russia," 1969/2015

In 2012 the New Nyanza Provincial General Hospital in Kisumu was renamed the Jaramogi Oginga Odinga Teaching and Referral Hospital, in honour of the late opposition politician. It is still, however, known to most Kenyans by its nickname, "Russia." Calling the hospital "Russia" is not, however, an act of remembering its origins, the excitement that permeated its beginnings as a gift from the Soviet Union, or its ambivalent symbolic role in Soviet friendship and cold war politics as they played out in Kenya. Indeed this past – present in the solid tropical modernist architecture as well as in toponyms such the modernist housing estate built in the 1970s and known locally as "Moscow" – appears absent in people's memories.

During the 1960s and 70s the hospital embodied the country's hopes for medical modernity, egalitarian public health care and postcolonial nationhood. In the 21st century, however, the overriding association of the hospital is as a hospital for the poor. During the 1980s and 1990s, the hospital experienced repeated crises in the supply of drugs, the breakdown of equipment and the supply of staff. There were no funds for repairs, maintenance or cleaning, and patients and staff remember the hospital at that time as being dirty and rundown. Only those who had no other options used its services, while middle class and salaried citizens preferred private medical facilities. Despite recent infrastructural additions, such as the new maternity wing built by the Norwegian government in 2012 and more recent agreements with multinational companies to lease new medical equipment, experiences of sub-optimal care remain acute. Meanwhile the hospital has become an important site of medical research conducted by global health organizations such as the US Centre for Disease Control and US and European universities, which partner with KEMRI. This research is not conducted on the city's middle classes but on its poor.

Today, Kisumu's residents express little pride in the modernist building that once stood for the new nation. Instead, there is excitement about the new private hospitals that emerge across the city, such as "Avenue," completed in 2012, which is part of a chain of private facilities offering "state-of-the-art technology" to the middle classes. Like the new shopping malls that have appeared since 2010 with Starbucks-style coffee bars, Avenue hospital is built in an almost temporary fashion with poor quality concrete. Yet for many residents these buildings, with their reflex windowpanes and token post-modern ornament, offer material connections between Kisumu and the rest of the world. They make Kisumu like Nairobi and like other places. For the middle classes Avenue hospital is a demonstration of how far Kisumu has developed. It is no longer being "left behind." Even those excluded from such costly medical care appreciate this vision of development. The future – patients' hopes for medical treatment or medical professionals' ambitions – no longer lies with the public, government hospital but with private hospitals, private medicine, NGOs and transnational research.

This excitement about global futures alongside the acceptance of expanding local inequality as

New private hospital in Kisumu, 2015

Victoria Hospital, originally the European hospital in Kisumu,
now the private "amenity ward" of the provincial hospital, 2015

The Standard, 20 September 2015

a fact of life is revealing of the contemporary
moment, in which utopic visions about collective
futures have been replaced by concerns, fears
and anxieties about securing individual livelihoods. Only occasionally does a breakdown or
failure of medical care in government hospitals
lead to eruptions of indignation and debate,
seen in newspaper headlines drawing attention
to the "abandonment" of citizens by the government or to the "shocking state" of the country's
public hospitals.

The story of "Russia," then, is not a story about
nostalgia for the lost 20th century social collective of public health. Rather, it is a story about
amnesia and the neoliberal moment – the
breathless "moving ahead" that Kisumu's residents
variously take pride in and complain about, and
the attempt to keep up with the curve, to learn
the new language of global health and development, and gain access to it. This amnesia about
Russia's past (and about the futures that the
hospital stood for at the time) is all the more
interesting because Kisumu is a future-orientated
city. Yet the hope in the future that was embodied
in the idea and realization of the new, modern,
public hospital during the 1960s is very different
from the future-orientations that saturate 21st
century Kisumu as a city of "global health."

"Russia," like the city it forms part of, emerges
as a palimpsest, a site of hope, of violence,
bitterness and anticipation. The role it played in
the political and developmental futures of the city
remains submerged in the flurry of partnerships
and projects, plans for new buildings and new
research. But then these pasts surface in toponyms
that recall colonialism or point to independence
with its promises and cold war rivalries, or, like
the modernist housing estates named after
assassinated political figures ("Lumumba estates,"
"Tom Mboya road," "Robert Ouko flats"), evoke
the violent history of the new nation and the
struggle for political freedom amidst western
imperialism and government repression.

**"The government is not treating
us well"**

Dr M I am also looking for other jobs,
making applications to NGOs, to
research. We feel the government is
not treating us well. People are still
waiting for their salaries to be paid.
It's been three months.

Interview with Dr M, recently qualified
medical Intern, Kisumu, 17 March 2015

From medical internship in 'Russia' …

Ruth What is it like working as an intern in the hospital?

Dr A With some donors coming in, with funds here and there, the working environment is quite good. Like the [children's] ward is better funded (than other wards) because there is research being conducted there and these studies have the funds to cover certain things. It's just that the numbers of doctors, although it has increased in recent years, is not enough. So your workload is too much.

But working in the hospital can be frustrating! The pay, the government, the numbers of patients… And the stress. Sometimes the gloves are not there. Or you have the sterile gloves but you lack the sterile liquid, or you have those, but lack something else. …You use whatever you have. If you don't have it, what can you do, you have to assist the patient. It's also stressful, handling patients. Find the problem, diagnosing… You look at a child, you send a blood sample for a lab test, but it takes long, you are losing your patient! 'Oh my god!', you think – you feel responsible for the death!

In fact, socio-economic conditions mean that you lose patients. And this makes you feel bad. You wish you could have done something.…And many patients cannot buy the drugs. Sometimes you just take your money and pay for the drug. Or you give the patient the [transport] fare [to get to a private laboratory] to get the test, because it's faster. You can't just look at a patient and see he's not being treated!

…. But I also get angry about it. I get angry with the government. After all, we are being taxed too. Such things should be given to the patients for free with the taxes we are paying. But we pay taxes and then we also have to help the patients buy medication. It is stressful.…because you, as a doctor, you are there to help, to intervene,

with your knowledge, but you also have to attend to the patient's social situation, you have to consider that too!

Interview with Dr A, former medical intern at "Russia," 1 April 2014

…to a career in medical research

Ruth It must have been difficult to get the research job at [the international research organization].

Dr A I was surprised because other people who were interviewed had master's degrees. I was lucky to get it. When I started I did not know much about research.

Ruth It must be very different from working on the hospital ward?

Dr A In research, you are just focusing on one thing. You don't get patients coming to you with so many conditions, so many diseases. If there are adverse

effects, you monitor them closely. And the study participants are followed-up – there are resources to do that.

Ruth What kind of contract do they offer you?

Dr A They [the research organization] give you one-year renewable contracts. But your employment is not tied to a specific project. And the good thing is that you get exposure. You go to conferences. You get exposure to science. In research, you are encouraged to think about what you are interested in, what you want to do.

Ruth Doesn't the government sometimes sponsor doctors to study further and specialise?

Dr A That was for the older generation. Those opportunities are now long gone.

Interview with Dr A, 13 March 2015

Hospital plans to request upgrade funds from Russia

KISUMU COUNTY

By HEZRON OCHIEL

Jaramogi Oginga Odinga Teaching and Referral Hospital (JOOTRH) is lobbying for financial support from the Russian government.

The hospital wants Russia to help it modernise. The facility constructed in the 1960s with support from the Russian government is currently grappling with ageing infrastructure and equipment.

In an effort to ease congestion and modernise its services, the hospital has been putting in place a master plan to present to different organisations for funding.

Under the new plan, the facility will pull down its old buildings to pave way for construction of a modern unit in the 22-hectare piece.

The hospital wants to double its bed capacity from the current 200, expand the laboratory services as well as construct a psychiatric unit under one roof.

Speaking during Hospital Master Plan Stakeholders Forum yesterday, the referral's officials said the original master plan was outdated and scattered services, making it hard for sick patients and persons with disabilities to effectively get medication.

"The new plan is going to bring services together. We want the facility to become a one-stop shop to serve the local population of about half a million and those from neighbouring counties," said Medical Superintendent Juliana Otieno.

Dr Otieno added: "With the coming of partners such as medical training schools, there has been growing need to have a proper plan to attract more investment."

Dr Juliana said many investors who had shown interest in putting up a modern facility were asking for a proper master plan to enable them know which areas to invest in.

Jaramogi Oginga Odinga Teaching and Referral Hospital Medical Superintendent Juliana Otieno addresses the Press yesterday. The hospital is lobbying the Russian government to help raise Sh100 billion. [PHOTO: HEZRON OCHIEL/STANDARD]

Chairman of the master plan Mark Odawa said once the plan is ready, it will be presented to the Russian Embassy for funding consideration.

"We want to have a plan before approaching them (Russian government). The hospital had an operational lift, which no longer works making it hard for pregnant women to access services," he said.

Nyanza region has one of the worst cases of maternal deaths. The recent withdrawal of research funding by Kenya Medical Research Institute (Kemri) and Centre for Disease Control (CDC) has seen most operations grounded.

The Standard, 18 September 2015

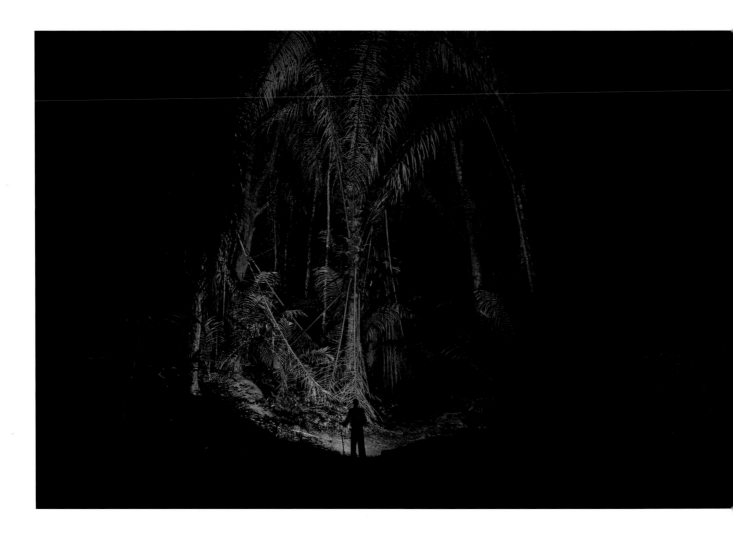

Iruka Okeke

Epilogue: reflections on projects "brought"

The colonial explorations that marked the debut of Western biomedical science in Africa were followed by an optimistic post-independence period with the inception of Africa-led research. Science soon met a crushing wave of structural adjustment that prompted mass migration of African scientists to Europe and North America. Today, African biomedical science departments in institutions from Makerere to Ibadan are in recovery mode, re-growing from cut shoots. During the lean times, not all were crushed: the Niakhar HDSS continued, and research from internationally renowned institutions in Fajara, in Legon, and in Kisumu, featured in *The Lancet* even in "hard times" after other institutions dropped from fame. Kisumu has experienced growth and Ayos was reborn to lesser fame. At the other extreme, Amani and Uzuakoli were submerged and did not resurrect. Collectively, whilst having no cause to collaborate with one another, the institutions presented in this volume represented a critical conglomerate of scientific centres that was key to the progress of knowledge in tropical biology and medicine in the early to mid- twentieth century. Patients were cared for, health professionals were trained, and biomedical knowledge of leprosy, trypano-somiasis, malaria, and other diseases has been advanced. During the heyday of now diminished Ayos, Amani, and Uzuakoli, African bioscience was not just relevant; it was pivotal. Where and why do biomedical research institutes fight and thrive, or give up and die? It is fashionable, almost required, to give lip service to capacity building in contemporary global health initiatives, but how is capacity maintained? My read of the previous chapters is that whenever science ended, it is not just facilities, laboratory rooms, or equipment that died, but also dreams, ideas, and potential.

Each of the institutions examined in this volume made sufficient impact to be selected for this research and in every case, a poignant history was revealed. Is the most valuable impact of research facilities those discoveries that made their way into indexed biomedical research papers? Then Uzuakoli continues to live in *The Lancet* archives and in the lives of patients and clinicians that have experienced the wonder of antileprosy chemotherapy with dapsone. We could argue that Uzuakoli has lived out a useful life by shrinking the global leprosy endemic focus, or even that, with the *International Journal of Leprosy* no longer in press, the institution's work is dated and done. But why would a world-class residential *Mycobacterium leprae* clinical and research facility precede inadequate capacity to treat tuberculosis, tubercular diseases of AIDS, or even to suitably rehabilitate patients with leprosy, which is the situation in eastern Nigeria today? If we accept that the lasting impact need not be biomedical, is it then in the generations of patients and staff whose lives within these communities were tied together by purpose and disease rather than genetic or societal relationships? Then Kisumu's DVBD, Amani, and Ayos live on through the lives of their savvy and resourceful descendants whose voices decorate the ethnographies, but whose statements suggest that their quality of life is far lower than that of their ancestors or predecessors.

Uncertainty about the most important legacies of these institutions is complicated by the mythology surrounding credit for achievements. Records may have been lost, and residents departed, but gravestones, monuments, and colonial documentary footage endure, telling of scientific breakthroughs and life-saving health care delivery that happened or was believed to have happened. Of the real marks, some foot-prints are shallower than others because the weight that pressed onto the feet that made them was light. Colonially knighted doctors, or those recognised by the so honoured, leave deeper prints than anonymous nurses, technicians, and patients. Other footmarks, once printed by a heavier press, have since been eroded. The German legacies of Ayos, and to a lesser extent Amani, for example, had been carefully scrubbed away, and at all the institutions, contributions from Africans that qualify as anything but menial service are, for the most part, difficult to discern. Even local successors of the British and the French were complicit in de-emphasising African contributions and attributing founda-tional credit to their most recent colonists. The oral histories collected for this volume uncover supplementary institutional biographies. Deep prints are not always along the expected path and therefore are at risk of being overlooked. It is the revelation of off-the-road footfalls that make this volume so valuable and also hint that we will not find some marks that were, or could have been made. We must accept that some raised feet were never put down or took so long to make a step that the first foot fell on hardened ground.

Aside from missing histories, too many other numbers do not add up. The records, or what remains of them, focused predominantly on the architects and managers of biomedical activities. Who else lived in these places, where did they go, who did they tend, where were they buried, and by whom? What about knowledge and experimentation? We cannot be sure what was planned in the era before competitive grant proposals and Institutional Review Boards. A little of what was done is captured in a handful of highly significant research papers, but we know far less about those experiments that were incomplete, inconclusive, or could potentially even be re-probed. In biology, ideas can be

resurrected a century later so that when the right technologies became available, ancient hypotheses can be tested. Similarly, a recent genomic revolution has allowed new questions to be tested on old material. Archived microbial strains, slides, or other specimen material, appropriately logged, can be really useful for retrospective inquiry but, with the possible exception of Kisumu, that kind of material was rarely reported from the sites. Just as documen-tary evidence to support oral statements was often lost, biology is presented with little more than crumble and dust.

Perhaps one thing to learn from this volume's examples is that dreams and potential are hard to excavate. Thus, as much as we wonder whether all has been captured from Niakhar's earlier records, or yearn for the documents of Uzuakoli, we also must ask how to capture and preserve African scientific knowledge and ideas. What would present-day Kenyan scientists work on if they were not beholden to others for much of Kisumu's resourcing? Among the most startling revelations from the disused research sites is that indigenous intellectual contributions were rarely openly solicited or recorded. Expatriate scientists brought their research problems along with their flora and furniture. They left records of their research foci on site, in memories, and in the biomedical literature. African scientific work is mostly recorded as a faithful following of repetitive protocols: essential for the tasks at hand but largely devoid of intellectual input. Otherwise, the records only document Africans as providing community and household services. Altogether, if they existed at all, African dreams were harder to decipher retrospectively. Even after the foreigners had departed from some sites, leaving a vacuum that may have offered possibilities, admittedly with few resources, the residents of those sites still eagerly ask which projects new visitors had *brought*.[1]

We scientists and our laboratories are composed of inorganics and organics that respectively harden or rot. Each biomedical group, field, institute, or school is defined by those who question, what they ask, and how they can answer. A question cannot be photographed but the presence of absence of "live" questions is reflected in photo-documented Ayos, Uzuakoli, and Amani. As an Amani ethnographer has asked, "How does one reenact this: not the past script, but the essence of the work it entailed?" Without the framework of a question, science is not knowledge generation, merely technical application. As in modern Kisumu, technical prowess can be bought and sold but does not necessarily address the questions of those executing tasks. Tasks can be outsourced, questions are typically not. When all else folds, questions can be passed on. When questioning ends, a science becomes extinct. *Traces* reveal that science based on imported but unincorporated questions meets a similar fate.

For those who would like to press forward, myself included, to new African biomedical discoveries and syntheses, what are the lessons from these *Traces*? Amani Hill Station, Kisumu's DVBD, and Uzuakoli's Leprosy colony par excellence are more or less gone – at least to biomedical science – but what is the potential of those institutions that survived, were reborn, or built more recently? Today there is a growing and diverse mix of scientific activity at African universities, hospitals, and research institutes but much of the most visible biomedical research continues to occur on projects conceived elsewhere. These are undisputedly needed and useful projects that will address Africa's modern health concerns, including AIDS, malaria, and tuberculosis. As Kisumu illustrates, they can even be the foundation of a research community as vibrant as anywhere else in the world. And then what: will the institutional homes (or hotels) of projects evolve with the disease landscape? Or will they meet the fate of facilities that were built upon leishmaniosis, leprosy, and sleeping sickness, dying even while the diseases fade away elsewhere but continue to plague Africans?[1]

What of the African scientist, in the true sense of the word? While much of Kisumu and Niakhar's work is expatriate-led, both institutions are home to African principal investigators. Why then does the work of hustling African technologists hopping from project to project, or the struggles of government departments without funding appear more visible in Kisumu? Why does Jamot's departed legacy override more recent work on *Mycobacterium ulcerans* in Ayos even within Cameroon? Are Africa-led initiatives just too new or will the future be one in which the newer scientists' prints are also washed away? Is there any chance that homegrown projects will achieve the prominence that imported ones seem to hold?

Perhaps the best lesson is from non-scientific activity at a depreciated health institution. Music composer Ikoli Harcourt Whyte worked towards the goal of his institution's proprietors and his own. There are imported and domestic influences on his work. He created and disseminated something recognisable that did not exist before his affiliation with Uzuakoli. His work offered the colony's residents more than they or the institution could have expected. And the intertwined legacy of Harcourt Whyte and Uzuakoli lives on, continuing to impact individuals beyond the site, its operators, and its disease. Why this type of emergent outcome did not occur in science or the health profession is a worthy question to ponder.

1 See *Amani*, this volume.

Author biographies

Evgenia Arbugaeva is a Russian-born freelance photographer known in particular for her work in the Russian arctic.

Alice Desclaux is a medical anthropologist, and Director of Research at the Institut de recherche pour le développement/TransVIHMI.

P. Wenzel Geissler is Professor of Social Anthropology at the University of Oslo (and, part-time, Director of Research at the University of Cambridge).

René Gerrets is Assistant Professor of Anthropology at the University of Amsterdam.

Nancy Rose Hunt is Professor in History and African Studies at the University of Florida, Gainesville (and Professor Emeritus of History, University of Michigan).

Ann H. Kelly is Senior Lecturer of Global Health in the Department of Social Science, Health and Medicine at King's College, London.

Guillaume Lachenal is Associate Professor in History of Science at the Université Paris Diderot and Junior Fellow at the Institut universitaire de France.

Peter Ernest Mangesho is a social anthropologist and Principal Research Scientist with the Tanzanian National Institute for Medical Research, and currently a postdoctoral fellow with the Southern African Centre for Infectious Diseases Surveillance at Sokoine University.

Philister Adhiambo Madiega is Community Liaison Officer with the Kenya Medical Research Institute, responsible for social aspects of HIV and malaria research.

John Manton is Assistant Professor in History at the London School of Hygiene and Tropical Medicine.

Aïssatou Mbodj-Pouye is an anthropologist and CNRS Research Fellow, based at the Institut des mondes africains, Paris.

Anne-Marie Moulin is a historian and a medical doctor, and is Emeritus Director of Research at the CNRS.

Mariele Neudecker is a visual artist and Professor at Bath School of Art and Design, examining notions of the Contemporary Sublime.

Joseph Owona Ntsama is a historian, Researcher at the Fondation Paul Ango Ela pour la Géopolitique en Afrique Centrale (FPAE), Yaoundé, Cameroon.

Iruka N. Oreke is Professor of Pharmaceutical Microbiology at the University of Ibadan, Nigeria.

Ashley Ouvrier is an anthropologist, Post-doctoral Fellow at the CERMES Researcher at Lassa (Laboratoire de sciences sociales appliquées) in Marseille, and teaches at the Université d'Aix-Marseille.

Ruth J. Prince is Associate Professor in Medical Anthropology at the University of Oslo.

Noémi Tousignant is Affiliate Member of the Department of Social Studies of Medicine at McGill, and Guest Researcher in History at the Université de Montréal.

Acknowledgements

Research in Uzuakoli was carried out as part of two separate projects, one of which preceded the common research programme at the heart of this publication. These projects depended on the logistical support of the German Leprosy Relief Association, especially Joseph Chukwu, Ute Velten, Matthias Mmah, Tivi Bojeghre, and Klaus Gilgen, and the assistance of the Methodist Church, Nigeria, Diocese of Umuahia. The initial research, funded by the Wellcome Trust, relied greatly on the cooperation of the Leprosy Mission International, through Bassey and Jannine Ebenso, and Lawrence Muyiwa and family, and the Medical Missionaries of Mary, especially Isabelle Smyth, and Anastasia Taggart (RIP). The second project could not have come to fruition without the kindness, tireless advocacy, and hospitality of Achinivu Kanu Achinivu, of Arochukwu and University of Port Harcourt, the memories, archives, and songs of Ndubueze Obioma, Aba and the memories of Godwin Dagogo Harcourt Whyte and the Harcourt Whyte family, Port Harcourt and of Isaac Onoh, Arochukwu and Rosalind Colwill, Umuahia. In addition to the collective debts recognised below, invaluable assistance, encouragement, and intellectual support was provided by Gérard Chouin and Martin Mbella, IFRA-Nigeria; the priests and brothers at Mount Carmel Prayer House, Enugu; Ed B. Attah, Uyo; Chidi Ugwu, C. Krydz Ikwuemesi, and Peter Sylvanus, Nsukka; Irene Brightmer, Martin Gorsky, Jo Robertson, Kay Yamaguchi, Nao Hoshino, Juliette Kristensen, Jen Clarke, and Pedro Rebelo.

Research in Ayos was conducted in collaboration with the *Fondation Paul Ango Ela pour la Géopolitique en Afrique Centrale* (FPAE). We thank its director Kalliopi Ango Ela and its administrative coordinator Jean-Claude Edjo'o. We benefited from the logistical and scientific support of the *Institut de Recherche pour le Développement* (IRD) and its representative in Yaoundé, Bruno Bordage. For their invaluable help we thank Dr Amougou, former director of the Annex Regional Hospital of Ayos, Dr Alphonse Um Boock, Susanna Hausmann-Muela, Jean-Marie Milleliri, Dominique Baudon, Francis Louis, Jean-Luc Portal, Joseph Funtim, Guy Vernet, Daniel Claude Wang Sonné, Elise Wang Sonné, Muriel Same Ekobo, Jean-Lucien Ewangue, Sinata Koulla Shiro, Dora Mbanya, Albert Same Ekobo, Richard Njouom, Soeur Danuta, Soeur Tatiana and Valentin Angoni. In Ayos, we would like to thank the Mayor of Ayos, Francis N. Zibi Samba, and the Sous-Préfet Ndimbeu Diefe, the current director of the hospital, Dr Nomo Eteme Martial, the "économe" Eric Eyengue, Simone Eyengue, Ze Mvodo Jean Jacques, and the Surveillant Général Philomène Etong Mvé for facilitating our research. For sharing with us their memories, archives and images of the medical history of Ayos, we thank Amba Mbida Benjamin, Nama Jean Bosco, Kombang Ekodogo, Ze Bekolo Daniel, Mveng Akamba David, Mempocka Mimpo Jean-Claude, Zangbwala, Minyono Gervais, Mengue Bekala Mariette, Meyanga Samba David, Messanga Didier Luc, Zang Akono Marie Paule, Mvolo Venant Zachée, Bekala Blaise, Ondoua Markus, the late Ateba Mvodo André, Ateba née Ngono Emilienne, Samba Marie Ngono, Désiré Tchipane, Michel Samba, the late Jacques Emmanuel Bekala.

Research in Amani was conducted in cooperation with the National Institute for Medical Research (NIMR) of the United Republic of Tanzania. Many thanks to the Director of NIMR-Amani Medical Research Center at Ubwari, Dr William Kisinza, Amani Hill Station Head, Dr Robert Malima, and Dr Leonard Mboera, who throughout offered their advice and support, and to NIMR and Commission for Science and Technology (COSTECH) for research clearance and permission to publish. On-site, we were guided by Aloyce Mkongewa, third-generation research assistant and resident of Amani Hill Station, by Bunzigwa Salum Bofu, and by Dr John Raybould. Archival research was supported by Japhet Kimbesa, Amani Hill Station librarian, and Patrick C. Hege, Tanzanian National Archive. We are indebted to the Tanzanian and European veterans of research in Amani, who came together for reunions in Amani and Cambridge in 2013 and 2015, welcomed us to their homes, introduced us to their families, and shared documents and images. We were generously received and cared for by the workers of Amani Hill Station – notably the welcoming Amani Hill rest house staff Lilian, Matiba, Juma, and January, and Mwanaidi Kijazi and staff at Amani Nature Reserve. Current and retired staff of Amani Hill Research Station and their families and other inhabitants of the area gave us their time, memories and mementos, and hospitality. In addition to the scholars and artists who contributed to this book, our fieldwork was enriched by visitors: Professor Steve Feierman took it upon himself to travel with us back to Usambara to explore intergenerational perspectives on historical change; Branwyn Poleykett came formally as research assistant but contributed much more; Astrid Ghyselen systematically explored Amani's architecture and provoked unexpected insights; Steve Joyce's iceberg brought the art into the project.

Research in Niakhar was conducted in collaboration with the IRD and Université Cheikh Anta Diop. The nature of this research has made our intellectual debts inseparable from those incurred for the generous provision of time, information, hospitality, reflection, facilitation, as well as moral and logistical support. In Niakhar, Dakar, Paris and Montpellier, we are grateful to (in alphabetical order): Charles Becker, Pierre Cantrelle, Jean-Philippe Chippaux, Rene Collignon, Valérie Delaunay, Michel Garenne, Francis Gendreau, Aldiouma Diallo, Samba Diallo, André Diatte, Robert Diatte, Augustin Dieme,

Latyr Diome, Abdou Diouf, Aissatou Diouf, Diamene Diouf, Samba Diouf, Bassirou Fall, Adiouma Faye, Alassane Faye, Ernest Faye, Ousmane Faye, Bernard Lacombe, Richard Lalou, André Lericollais, Diaga Loum, Nathalie Mondain, Emile Ndiaye, Emilie Ndiaye, Michel Ndiaye, Tofène Ndiaye, Pape Ndiaye, Maurice Ndong, Georges de Noni, Gilles Pison, Branwyn Poleykett, Ndeye Aïssatou Pouye, Moussa Sarr, Fulgence Seck, Ngor Sine, Cheikh Sokhna, Laurent Vidal, and Paul Whitney. We especially thank inhabitants of the area who have given so much of themselves to science over the years, especially those who shared memories and opinions with us, and the audience and participants of a workshop held at the IRD in Dakar in December 2012, of a fiftieth anniversary symposium for Niakhar held at the Université Cheikh Anta Diop in 2014, and of three fiftieth anniversary village meetings held in Toucar, Ngayokheme, and Diohine in 2015.

Research in Kisumu evolved over a long time, and precedes the larger pro- ject this book arose from. Throughout, we were hosted by the Division of Vector-Borne Diseases (DVBD), and during one earlier project by the Kenya Medical Research Institute (KEMRI). In regard to this earlier research, we are most grateful to Professor John Henry Ouma, former director of DVBD, and co-supervisor of Geissler's biology PhD, and to Dr John Vulule, former center director, KEMRI-CGHR, as well as to the many DVBD and KEMRI colleagues, and their collaborators, notably from the Centers for Disease Control and Prevention (CDC), who have supported our research in the past. Particular debts gave been incurred to the late Dr Alfred I. Lwoba, former head DVBD Kisumu, Mr Erastus Kwanya, former DVBD Nyanza Province, Mr Christoffer Nyagol, DVBD Nyanza Province, and Mr Martin Okonji, former DVBD staff, who together with numerous other elderly colleagues welcomed us to his home and shared his life's memories with us, as well as to Biddy Odindo, research assistant, and to Dr Philgona Otieno, KEMRI-CRC, and Dr Benson Mulemi, Catholic University, Nairobi. Fieldwork would not have been the same without Father Alois and the Mill Hill Fathers who offered us hospitality through the decades.

This collaborative research endeavour would have been impossible without an extended group of people who held together ideas and work. We list them alphabetically, doing little justice to their diverse and vital contributions: Gemma Aellah, Linda Amarfio, Andrew Barry, Uli Beisel, Filip de Boeck, Virginia Berridge, Hannah Brown, Brigitte Bruun, Tracey Chantler, Gail Davies, Rijk van Dijk, Jean-Pierre Dozon, Damien Droney, James Fairhead, Steve Feierman, Sjaak van der Geest, Peter Geschiere, Tamara Giles-Vernick, Dan Hicks, Nancy Rose Hunt, Lauren Hutchinson, John Iliffe, Freya Jephcott, Ferdinand de Jong, Helge Jordheim, Patricia Kingori, Johan Lagae, Hannah Landecker, Murray Last, Melissa Leach, Javier Lezaun, Marianne E. Lien, Julie Livingston, Tim Livsey, Christos Lynte- ris, Sloan Mahone, Doreen Massey, Lotte Meinert, Marissa Mika, Anne- marie Mol, Henrietta Moore, Vinh-Kim Nguyen, Morten Nielsen, Iruka Okeke, Ferdinand M. Okwaro, Mike Pearson, Kris Peterson, David Pratten, Francesca Raphaëly, Peter Redfield, François Richard, Richard Rottenburg, Arnd Schneider, Simon Schaffer, Bob Simpson, Nikolai Ssorin-Chaikow, Alice Street, Megan Vaughan, Claire Wendland, Susan Reynolds Whyte.

Our research project 'Memorials and remains of Medical Science in Africa' was funded under the Open Research Areas in Europe scheme, by the Economic and Social Research Council (ESRC) of the UK (grant RES-360-25- 0032), by the French Agence Nationale de la Recherche (ANR)(grant ANR- AA-ORA-032), and by the Netherlands Organisation for Scientific Research (NWO)(grant 464-10-021). The publi- cation of this book was generously supported by ESRC and ANR, and the Department of Social Anthropology at the University of Oslo. Geissler's Leverhulme Trust Research Leadership Award (F02 116D) provided vital funding for the British collaboration. The Wellcome Trust funded reunions of former Amani-based staff in Tanzania and in the UK (GR 102603/Z/13/Z and 107011/Z/15/Z). Additional funding was provided by the Institut Universitaire de France, the British Academy and the British Institute in East Africa. Parts of the book were inspired by research funded by the Norwegian Research Council, and earlier projects funded by the Wellcome Trust (GR 074772 and 092699/Z/10/Z).

Credits

Traces of the Future

An Archaeology of Medical Science in Africa

Edited by Paul Wenzel Geissler, Guillaume Lachenal,
John Manton and Noémi Tousignant

Designed by Herman Lelie and Stefania Bonelli

Copy-editing by Francesca Raphaely
Produced by fandg.co.uk
Printed in Italy by EBS

ISBN: 9 781783 207251

Frontispiece: Amani Research Station, crossroads below "Lion Hill,"
dubbed "Piccadilly Circus," c.1970

First published in the UK in 2016 by
Intellect
The Mill
Parnall Road
Fishponds
Bristol BS16 3JG,UK
+44 (0)117 9589910   www.intellectbooks.com

First published in the USA in 2016 by
Intellect
The University of Chicago Press
1427 E. 60th Street, Chicago
IL 60637, USA

The publication and most research was funded by

The authors gratefully acknowledge additional financial assistance from